Self-Translation

BLOOMSBURY STUDIES IN TRANSLATION

Series Editor: Jeremy Munday, Centre for Translation Studies, University of Leeds.

Published in association with the International Association for Translation and Intercultural Studies (IATIS), Bloomsbury Studies in Translation aims to present a series of books focused around central issues in translation and interpreting. Using case studies drawn from a wide range of different countries and languages, each book presents a comprehensive examination of current areas of research within translation studies written by academics at the forefront of the field. The thought-provoking books in this series are aimed at advanced students and researchers of translation studies.

BLOOMSBURY STUDIES IN TRANSLATION

Self-Translation

Brokering Originality in Hybrid Culture

Edited by

ANTHONY CORDINGLEY

B L O O M S B U R Y

LONDON · NEW DELHI · NEW YORK · SYDNEY

Bloomsbury Academic

An imprint of Bloomsbury Publishing Plc

50 Bedford Square	1385 Broadway
London	New York
WC1B 3DP	NY 10018
UK	USA

www.bloomsbury.com

Bloomsbury is a registered trade mark of Bloomsbury Publishing Plc

First published 2013
Reprinted 2013

© Anthony Cordingley and Contributors, 2013

British Library Cataloguing-in-Publication Data
A catalogue record for this book is available from the British Library.

ISBN: HB:	978-1-4411-2541-5
PB:	978-1-4411-4289-4
EPDF:	978-1-4411-4729-5
EPUB:	978-1-4411-7575-5

Library of Congress Cataloging-in-Publication Data
A catalog record for this book is available from the Library of Congress.

Typeset by Newgen Imaging Systems Pvt Ltd, Chennai, India
Printed and bound in Great Britain

CONTENTS

GENERAL EDITOR'S COMMENT

The International Association for Translation and Intercultural Studies (IATIS) provides a global forum for scholars and researchers concerned with translation and other forms of intercultural communication.

The Association facilitates the exchange of knowledge and resources among scholars in different parts of the world, stimulates interaction between researchers from diverse traditions and encourages scholars across the globe to explore issues of mutual concern and intellectual interest.

Among the Association's activities are the organization of conferences and workshops, the creation of web- based resources, and the publication of newsletters and scholarly books and journals.

The Translation Series published by Bloomsbury Academic in conjunction with IATIS is a key publication for the Association. It addresses the scholarly community at large, as well as the Association's members. Each volume presents a thematically coherent collection of essays, under the co-ordination of a prominent guest editor. The series thus seeks to be a prime instrument for the promotion and dissemination of innovative research, sound scholarship and critical thought in all areas that fall within the Association's purview.

Jeremy Munday
University of Leeds, UK

CONTRIBUTOR DETAILS

Susan Bassnett is a scholar of comparative literature. Author of over 20 books, her *Translation Studies,* which first appeared in 1980, has remained in print ever since and has become an important international textbook in this field. Her *Comparative Literature* (1993) has also become internationally renowned and has been translated into several languages. In 1996 she co-edited *Constructing Cultures: Essays on Literary Translation* with André Lefevere, and together with Harish Trivedi she is the editor of *Post-colonial Translation: Theory and Practice* (1998). *The Translator as Writer* (2006) was co-edited with Peter Bush. Her most recent books are *Translation in Global News* (2008) with Esperanca Bielsa and *Reflections on Translation* (2011). In addition to her scholarly works, Bassnett writes poetry.

Anthony Cordingley is Lecturer in Translation and English at the Université Paris VIII – Vincennes-Saint-Denis. He has published widely on Beckett, bilingualism and philosophy in specialist and general journals, is co-editor of the electronic genetic edition of Beckett's *Comment c'est/How It Is* and is currently working on a study of Beckett's education in languages, philosophy and psychoanalysis.

Elin-Maria Evangelista was recently awarded a PhD in Creative Writing from Monash University, Melbourne. 'Views from Above', a chapter of the creative component of her thesis, is to appear in the upcoming Monash/ Warwick anthology, *The Voyage: New Journeys.* Elin-Maria has been an editor for *ABES* Routledge and a chief editor of *Verge,* the Monash anthology of short fiction. She has been a 'Living Book' at the *Emerging Writers Festival* in Melbourne and has also done many public readings of her prize-winning short stories. Elin-Maria is Swedish and has a background as an actor and translator. She is currently teaching fiction writing at Monash.

Mark Gibeau is a Lecturer in Japanese language, literature and culture at the School of Culture, History & Languages, College of Asia and the Pacific at the Australian National University. In addition to Okinawan literature and literary translation his research interests include novelists Abe Kôbô, Murakami Haruki and the theme of the unreal in modern and contemporary Japanese literature.

Rainier Grutman is Professor of French and Translation Studies at the University of Ottawa. He was trained at Namur, Leuven, and Madrid universities before going to Montreal to obtain his PhD. He has published widely on both bilingual writers and multilingual texts. His work in translation studies has appeared in journals such as *Target*, *TTR*, *Quaderns*, *Ellipse*, *Texte*, *Atelier de traduction* and *Linguistica Antverpiensia* (of which he co-edited an issue with Dirk Delabastita in 2005), as well as several collective volumes, the most notable of which is Mona Baker's *Encyclopedia* (1998, 2009).

Rainer Guldin is Lecturer for German Language and Culture at the Faculties of Communication and Economic Sciences at the Università della Svizzera Italiana (USI) in Lugano (Switzerland). He studied English and German Literature in Zurich and Birmingham (England). His PhD thesis focused on the work of the German writer Hubert Fichte. Recent publications include: '"I believe that my two tongues love each other cela ne m'étonnerait pas": Self-Translation and the Construction of Sexual identity', in: *TTR* 20.1 (2007), 193–214; 'Metaphor as a Metaphor for Translation', in *Thinking through Translation with Metaphors*, edited by J. St. André, Manchester 2010, pp. 161–91.

Jan Hokenson is Emeritus Professor of French and Comparative Literature, Florida Atlantic University, where she created the graduate programme in Translation Studies. Currently residing in Vermont, she is co-author of *The Bilingual Text: History and Theory of Literary Self-Translation* (2007), and author of *Japan, France and East-West Aesthetics: French Literature 1865–2000* (2004) and *The Idea of Comedy: History, Theory, Critique* (2006).

Aurelia Klimkiewicz is Associate Professor in the School of Translation at York University in Toronto. Her research interests include Western and Bakthinian hermeneutics, the ethics of translation and the trialogical model of communication. Her recent work has focused on translation in multilingual contexts, particularly on the identity and mobility of the translator, and the author-(self)translator relationship.

Susanne Klinger has recently completed a PhD in Literary Translation at the University of East Anglia, focusing on hybrid language in Anglophone Nigerian writing, particularly its role in conveying the world-view of characters and narrators, and related translation issues. Her research was funded by the Arts and Humanities Research Council, and she is now working on a book based on this research for St. Jerome. She has worked for many years as a translator, editor and subtitler, and has taught at Middlesex University, London Metropolitan University and the University of Surrey.

Corinna Krause is a freelance translator and researcher with an MSc in Translation Studies and a doctorate from Edinburgh University. For her PhD thesis she researched the phenomenon of self-translation in the context of contemporary Scottish Gaelic poetry. As a translator she works from Scottish Gaelic and English into German. Her literary translation work includes prose translations in *Der Schädel von Damien Hirst* and poetry translations for the anthologies *Intime Weiten* and *Beredter Norden*. She lives and works in North Uist, Outer Hebrides, Scotland.

Will Noonan is Lecturer in Translation and English at the Université de Bourgogne. He completed his PhD thesis on the interactions between humour and reflexivity in French and English literature at the University of Sydney in 2011 and his current research focuses on multilingual and crosscultural aspects of humour.

Julio-César Santoyo is Full Professor of Translation Studies at the University of León, Spain, where he has been Dean (1981–2), Vice-rector (1984–6) and Rector (1990–2000). His publications include: *Sobre la traducción: Textos clásicos y medievales* (2011); *La traducción medieval en la Península Ibérica* (2009); *Historia de la traducción: Viejos y nuevos apuntes* (2008); *Historia de la Traducción: Quince apuntes* (1999); *Bibliografía española de la traducción* (1996); *Teoría y crítica de la traducción: Antología* (1987); *El delito de traducir* (1985); *La cultura traducida* (1983), etc. He has directed some 28 doctoral dissertations, and is a translator into Spanish of Christopher Marlowe, Tolkien, Stevenson, Oscar Wilde, Poe, Kipling, Flannery O'Connor, Willa Cather, Washington Irving, Jack London, etc.

Introduction:

Self-translation, going global

Anthony Cordingley

The self-translator has been a relatively neglected species within the menagerie of translators – this is the first book with a collection of articles in English devoted to the art of self-translation and its practitioners. The volume's subtitle, 'Brokering Originality in Hybrid Culture', suggests, if not a little too much ambition on the part of its editor, the centrality of negotiation in the self-translator's work. Writing at the nexus of at least two languages, two cultures and for at least two different reading publics, the self-translator is a particular kind of crosscultural interlocutor. Like a language broker, the self-translator is an intermediary who facilitates communication between two different linguistic or cultural parties. Yet the self-translator is the intermediary of and for an 'original' text and, in some interpretations of the term, also for his or her own 'self'. The contributions in this volume probe into the fact that our thinking about the 'original' is presently bound up with questions of 'originality', and notions of the 'self' are difficult to extract from thinking about 'self-translation'. Yet these facts are less obvious when one uses the 'synonym' for self-translation, auto-translation. In English the connotations and echoes generated by this term – whose equivalent in Romance and some other European languages is the habitual term for self-translation – are entirely different from those of the self in self-translation. In English, the 'auto' of auto-translation may even suggest the very opposite process – the negation of the self – as if a text was on autopilot, performing automatic or machine translation, transporting itself into another language code. Using the term 'self-translation' concentrates attention on the presence of the translator, and, as many contributions to this volume demonstrate, on the various

morphing of the self which occurs not only in the act of translation but
during the composition of its 'original'. Yet, how does the 'originality' – a
term that the development of translation theory has increasingly called into
question – of this author change when s/he shifts between languages? Does
the process of translation change this 'originality'? To what extent can a
singular 'original' be said to have been 'translated'? What distinguishes
self-translated literature from migrant literature? What affinities can be
found between different self-translators?

Research to date has shown that self-translators bestow upon themselves
liberties of which regular translators would never dream; self-translation
typically produces another 'version' or a new 'original' of a text. What is
being negotiated is therefore not only an 'original' text, and perhaps the self
which wrote it, but the vexatious notion of 'originality' itself. Most scholars
of translation are aware of Lawrence Venuti's persuasive demonstration
that historically valuing and requiring the translator's invisibility from
the text sustained pressure upon the translator to suppress his or her
originality. Indeed, this fetishizing of the 'original' maintained the myth of
the translator's invisibility, or lack of originality. It follows, thus, that the
special status accorded to, and assumed by, the translator who is also the
author of the original means that the self-translator is unique in not being
sanctioned for overtly exercising creativity in translation.

Yet the ideological demand that the translator assume the authority
of the original in becoming equal to its author is a Modern affair. In the
Middle Ages and in Early-Modern Europe translation was habitually
performed in pairs or in teams, with individuals specialized in different
languages taking on separate roles in the process of interpreting a text in
one language and transposing it into another. However, demands for unity
within institutions and discourses of Early-Modern Europe – such as the
standardizing of language and the consolidating of faith, household, state,
monarchy and Church under their respective singular patriarchs – were
coupled with demands for poetic unity in action, time, place and style.
These pressures are felt in Renaissance theorizations of translation, which
elided the existence of collaborative translation by conceptualizing it in
the singular. Devolving upon the individual the task which was often
performed by the many allowed them to imagine the translator to be a text's
surrogate author, thus giving the translator the daunting task of equalling
the comprehension of the author in the author's tongue and matching
that author's skill and style in another. Belén Bistué (139–64) has recently
argued that the prominent discourse of translation's infamous 'difficulty',
even its 'impossibility', is the direct inheritance of the way in which
Renaissance theorizations of translation give priority to this individualist
model at the expense of competing ones, such as collaborative translation.
No other figure embodies this ideological trajectory in thinking about
translation as much as the self-translator. Indeed, one could even consider
the self-translator to be the ideal *telos* of modern translation theory, with

its teleological reading of translation as the quest to attain oneness with the original and its author.

Unfortunately, textual and biographical evidence points to anything but such a convenient panacea: the 'difficulties' of translation persist, and in many cases intensify. Be that as it may, the aim of this book is to move beyond thinking self-translation through a binary logic of source–target/text–reader and its attendant notion of fidelity to the original. Rather, perspectives from other disciplines are brought to bear upon the act of self-translation, as are new theoretical approaches within Translation Studies itself. Self-translators from 'minor' languages who previously passed under the critical radar allow us to rethink the question of self-translation, while the most distinguished self-translators may here be compared from different points of view – various chapters discuss the better-known examples of Samuel Beckett (Bassnett, Cordingley, Grutman, Hokenson, Noonan, Santoyo), Nancy Huston (Bassnett, Cordingley, Grutman, Klimkiewicz), Milan Kundera (Bassnett, Klimkiewicz), Vladimir Nabokov (Bassnett, Cordingley, Grutman, Hokenson, Klimkiewicz, Santoyo) and Rabindranath Tagore (Bassnett, Grutman, Santoyo).

But just as the translator was never really devoid of 'originality', cultures are inevitably, and in the age of globalization, increasingly, hybrid. The fact is most evident to the author who self-translates, who is inevitably conscious of both the hybridity of the culture(s) s/he is writing within and of her or his own writing. Equipped with expert competence in more than one language, moving freely between cultures, or having been forced into exile, the self-translator's stereolinguistic optics puts any one of her or his languages/cultures into relief with respect to the other. Consequently, self-translators share with many other writers from the margins the tendency to subvert the possibility that their writing affirms a singular national culture or literature. Indeed, the subject of the self-translated text is very often hybridity itself. Typical literary scenarios include: wanderers and their confrontations with the limits of language(s), characters who are faced with their doubles, identities which morph with the use of different languages, the mystery and frustration of the untranslatable or that which falls between the cracks when two cultures meet. Hybridity characterizes not only many self-translators' external and textual environments, but the internal bilingual and bicultural space out of which their creativity emerges.

This book is divided into four broad sections: 'Self-translation and Literary History', 'Interdisciplinary Perspectives', 'Post-Colonial Perspectives' and 'Cosmopolitan Identities/texts'. Opening the section, 'Self-translation and Literary History', Susan Bassnett's 'The Self-translator as Rewriter' sets the tone of this book with a challenge to our notion of self-translation itself. She evokes Jorge Luis Borges' view that all narratives spring not from the individual genius of their authors but from the continual process of reading, writing and rewriting existing narratives. For Borges, these narratives are always shifting from one language to another and thus to designate any point of origin in this process of reading and writing is absurd. Bassnett argues that within our current frame of source–target thinking there is indeed no such thing as 'self-translation'. Rather than undermine the very raison d'être of this book, her critique zooms in on the limitations of our vocabulary when it equates this act of rewriting with translation. In a similarly Borgesian fashion, in 'On Mirrors, Dynamics and Self-translations', J. C. Santoyo sets out the paradoxes within the recurrent metaphor of the 'mirror' of self-translation. He shows how self-translation can invert the source–target logic of translation by confusing and confounding its order of primacy and secondariness. Focussing on various situations where an 'original' is overshadowed or even supplanted by its translation, Santoyo investigates the historically common and currently widespread phenomenon of translations of a text into a third language being made not from the original but from the second version, the self-translation. Linguistic and cultural politics are at the heart of this dynamic, and Santoyo observes how retranslations are typically made from an author's self-translation into a major language such as English, French or Spanish, rather than a minor language 'original'.

The 'cultural turn' in Translation Studies has encouraged researchers to expand their field of investigation beyond the movement of texts from one language to another, and to chart and analyse the movement of cultural products, ideas, bodies and selves between different linguistic communities. If the English term 'self-translation' invites this 'cultural' interpretation of translatorial action, this has not dampened the need for sustained research into its textual dimensions, for this kind of translation/rewriting has been conspicuously underresearched. If one excludes works devoted to the stars of self-translation, Samuel Beckett and Vladimir Nabokov, one discovers only a handful of books which explore this phenomenon in any depth. Jan Hokenson and Marcella Munson's *The Bilingual Text* is a pioneering work in the field and is to date its only attempt to provide a comprehensive history of its subject. Keeping step with Hokenson and Munson as they comment upon their vast fresco of self-translators from the Middle Ages to the present, one becomes aware of how the fruits of this historical approach to self-translation are born also in a richer understanding of our globalized world, where every day millions of individuals, either out of choice or necessity, 'translate' themselves into different cultures and languages. Indeed, the steady increase of journal articles and conferences devoted to self-translation since the turn of the millennium suggests something of its *Zeitgeist* potential, if only in academia. Yet maintaining a historical perspective upon self-translation helps to protect us from deploying the term in a facile manner, as if it were another empty buzzword, and to focus our attention upon the potential for a genealogy of self-translation to deepen our understanding of the factors impacting upon today's language brokers. In her contribution to this volume, Hokenson turns her thinking once more to this form of authorship, probing her evidence for traces of common 'historical forces' or 'private motivations' which might compel one to self-translate. She writes: 'Motive is not a common rubric in translation studies. [. . .] Yet it is a loss, eliding an important constituent of translation history. If common or mutual drives to self-translate are identified, then a taxonomy of self-translators will be the richer for it'. Transhistorical in its vision, her chapter, 'History and Self-translation' approaches a definition of our theme by identifying commonalities within different self-translators throughout the ages.

The next section, 'Interdisciplinary Perspectives', offers three examples of how the definition of self-translation and the self-translator shifts when such writers are considered within different disciplinary perspectives. The critical lens pans back, from agent to society, when Rainier Grutman observes the great disparity between the attention which has been devoted to Samuel Beckett when compared with that given to other self-translators. In 'A Sociological Glance at Self-translation and Self-translators', Grutman examines the longer-than-expected list of twentieth-century Nobel Prize winning self-translators. Using Pierre Bourdieu's field theory, he identifies four possible categories of self-translators by facing off two kinds of language couplings: exogenous versus endogenous bilingualism and symmetrical versus asymmetrical language pairings. The results of this study are surprising: viewed from this sociological perspective, Beckett's practice turns out to be the exception rather than the rule. Grutman concludes that if we continue to view Beckett as the self-translator *par excellence* we will necessarily blinker our perception to the breadth of activity conducted in the field of self-translation.

Boring, frustrating, painful. Such is self-translation, if we are to believe the testimonies of many who contract their labour out to it. My contribution to this volume, 'The Passion of Self-translation: A Masocritical Perspective' enquires into the displeasure which some self-translators inflict upon themselves. Using psychoanalytic diagnoses of the masochist from Freud through to Theodor Reik and Gilles Deleuze, I focus upon one strand of self-translators: the suffering cosmopolitan. My subject self-translates out of his or her own freewill, submitting voluntarily to the 'torture' and tedium of self-translation. Noting the self-critical aspect of self-translation, and thus the close proximity between self-translation and literary criticism, and using certain insights from Paul Mann's Freudian study of the desire for servitude in literary scholarship, 'Masocriticism', I attempt to go beyond the complaints of the self-translator to see what compels one to submit to an enterprise one finds so distasteful.

Authors are, on the other hand, often compelled to self-translate when political events displace them from their own cultures. The Czech-Brazilian writer and philosopher Vilém Flusser is especially interesting because he developed a multilingual poetics to further his philosophical thinking, after he was forced to flee from Europe when he lost his entire family during the Holocaust. In 'Translating Philosophy: Vilém Flusser's Practice of Multiple Self-translation' Rainer Guilden discusses this extremely rare case of a philosopher self-translator who deployed up to four languages (Portuguese, German, English and French), systematically translating and retranslating all of his texts. Guilden argues that Flusser's 'interest is primarily a philosophical and less a literary one'. That is, Flusser used self-translation as a formal technique to distance himself from an earlier text or intellectual process. In this way, argues Guilden, Flusser tried to view his earlier texts through the lens of another language with a view to 'verify their inner coherence', while also 'systematically expanding and deepening the original thought that prompted his writing impulse'. Guilden offers a beguiling demonstration of this theory when he develops a hypothesis of the order of one of Flusser's unpublished texts as it evolves through Portuguese, English and German versions.

The next three articles consider the act of self-translation from a post-colonial or minor language perspective. By juxtaposing three different language contexts – Anglophone Africa, Okinawan/Ryūkyūan Japan and Gaelic Scotland – they offer a snapshot of how different states of political struggle and dominance influence the roles of the self-translator and the effects of the self-translated text. In 'Translated Otherness, Self-translated In-betweenness: Hybridity as Medium versus Hybridity as Object in Anglophone African Writing' Susanne Klinger crosses narratological with post-colonial literary reading techniques to show how self-translation is not just the medium of production – translation and creation are habitually evoked as simultaneous processes for the post-colonial author – but often the object within the narrative, when fictional characters code-switch inside a text. She shows how in African contexts the practice of code-switching between different forms of English and pidgin may or may not be political, depending on which characters are doing the switching and when.

On the other hand, in "Why Bother with the Original?': Self-translation and Scottish Gaelic Poetry' Corinna Krause argues that the publication of bilingual editions of Scots Gaelic poetry in English paradoxically reinforces the invisibility of the Gaelic text and language, 'denying it a development towards a habitual medium for cultural communication'. The historical context for the disparity between major and minor languages in the English-Scots Gaelic situation leads Krause to argue that the bilingual text in fact allows the reader conveniently to elide the Gaelic text or read it as if it were a translation from English. Conversely, the contemporary situation in Okinawan/Ryūkyūan language and literature compels Mark Gibeau to advocate the opposite point of view in 'Indigenization and Opacity: Self-translation in the Okinawan/Ryūkyūan Writings of Takara Ben and Medoruma Shun;' that is, bilingual editions which include Okinawan/Ryūkyūan-Japanese literature increase the visibility of its language. The difference between these two analyses of self-translation might well correspond with the different states of self-determination with respect to the colonizer in Okinawan/Ryūkyūan and Scots communities, as well as the level of self-critique operating within the colonizer's culture, for Gibeau argues that the very appearance of the Okinawan language in a bilingual text provokes in the mainland Japanese reader the highly unusual experience of feeling their own potential otherness within 'Japanese' culture. When Gibeau reads Takara Ben's poem, 'Cape Kyan', a poem about the horrors inflicted on the local population during the Battle of Okinawa, he notes that the Ryūkyūan text is in fact a version of the Japanese 'original', yet its position on the page would suggest otherwise. The reasons for the mere presence of the Ryūkyūan language on the page relate less, Gibeau suggests, to a reality of trying to foster a community of readers of Ryūkyūan language literature than to the self-translator's desire to erect a barrier to make the 'Japanese' reader aware of his or her delimited access to the poem. Following Gibeau, self-translation would appear to reveal to readers the repressed narratives of their own history, of the buried or silenced traumas within their 'Japanese' selves. Here, one may even interpret the 'self' of self-translation nationally: as the national self inscribes itself within the plurality of its languages, self-translation challenges the myth of the nation's monolithic culture – the very myth which justifies the expendability and domination of its minority cultures.

Indeed, the historical proximity between the self-translated text and certain horrors perpetrated by the colonizer is a determining factor here: if, as Gibeau suggests, 'Reflected in an Okinawan mirror, the mainland reader cannot help but feel somewhat uneasy', the same cannot be said today for contemporary English readers of bilingual Scots Gaelic-English texts. Such differences illustrate the site specificity of self-translation, and if space allowed, this volume would have permitted such confrontations to be compared with those between Catalan and Spanish, Indian versus standard English, Ukrainian and Russian, and many others. While numerous volumes could, and indeed should, be devoted to the different ways in which self-translation embodies the negotiations and clashes between 'major' and 'minor' languages, the purpose of the current volume is to illustrate the diversity of research currently being undertaken into this literary phenomenon.

The third group of articles, listed under the rubric 'Cosmopolitan Identities/Texts', emphasizes not so much the political confrontation of languages and borders by self-translators as these writers' development of bi- or multilingual poetics to embrace, or reach out to, the foreign. Cosmopolitanism has a long history of advocates and detractors from ancient to contemporary moral, political and economic philosophy. Marx and Engels, for instance, equated cosmopolitanism with the bourgeois ideology which justified capitalist globalization. Yet their own objective, the creation of a global classless proletariat, shares many features of 'world citizenship' and equality of rights which are central to cosmopolitanism. Be that as it may, in this volume the term is used with reference to the 'cultural cosmopolitanism' of certain self-translators. The distinction is imperfect because political circumstances may well have affected these authors' literary practice – one thinks immediately of Nabokov's relationship to his Russian homeland and its language. However this grouping is designed more from the perspective of the researcher than the practice of the author(s) studied, which can always be read in political terms.

What would a volume on self-translation be without an article on Samuel Beckett? In 'Self-translation, Self-reflection, Self-derision: Samuel Beckett's Bilingual Humour', Will Noonan turns to this model of the cosmopolitan self-translator to analyse how Beckett's bilingualism has been interpreted by his critics. Noonan thus gives a clear overview of the major trends in criticism of Beckett's self-translation before moving on to argue that 'Beckett's presence as a self-translator is evident not only in comparisons between French and English versions of his works but also within individual texts irrespective of the language or order of composition'. As such, Noonan reads Beckett's creativity as essentially bilingual and Beckett's writing to be in a permanent state of comic relief from itself. The pertinence of studying such irony in the context of chapter in this volume becomes apparent as Noonan demonstrates how, in a bilingual work such as *Mercier et/and Camier*, Beckett can create a narrator who situates himself within the monolingual and monocultural universe of his narrative despite the fact that his language betrays himself to be multilingual. Noonan shows how Beckett's exploitation of such a disjunction tends towards the self-effacement of his narrators and characters. However, Beckett's humour is the vital element which repels just such an effacement and it resists the critic's ability to transfer it upon Beckett.

Just as humour in Beckett forms a barrier against reducing his self-effacing tendencies to a discourse which would have his self 'lost' in translation, the final two contributions by Elin-Maria Evangelista and Aurelia Klimkiewicz turn to this question of 'loss' and rupture in the self-translator. They move away from the strictly textual definition of self-translation: rather than presuppose the existence of an original text and its translation, they draw self-translation into the realms of phenomenology and identity politics. Both authors concentrate on the self-fashioning which can be an integral, even motivating, factor in self-translation. Focusing on writers in exile, these two articles are in many respects representative of two tendencies in research in this domain. In 'Between Languages: Metalinguistic Elements in Fiction and Multilingual Self-dialogue' Klimkiewicz discusses Vladimir Nabokov, Milan Kundera and Nancy Huston, taking it as given that self-translation follows a period of loss and grieving. This division of the self is precipitated by the severance of self from the contexts of its mother tongue before self-translation then offers the possibility for a positive reconstitution of identity. Evangelista, on the other hand, questions the discourse of loss and suffering in 'Writing in Translation: A New Self in a Second Language', arguing instead that with different circumstances – in cases of voluntary exile – second language writing as 'self-translation' can be a means to further the positive development of self without needing to bridge a rupture. It must be stressed that in these two articles, the authors do not use 'self-translation' simply as a metaphor for processes of relocation or cultural transfer and negotiation precipitated by exile, migration or travel. Rather, they are grappling principally with the dialogues that occur within the self, the intangible process of linguistic translation that accompanies such events, the effects which these events have on the 'self' and the self's active, potentially positive, role in these events. Klimkiewicz, moreover, offers an impassioned call for the study of self-translation because it can 'forge new genres, new spaces of enunciation that allow one to articulate the experience of displacement' and because it 'increases the visibility of the translation process and challenges a binary logic of translation'. The study of self-translation may also serve a pedagogical function in translator training by demonstrating how the playful and transgressive stratagems of multilingual writers can offer useful insights and models for translators generally.

To conclude, the aim of this book is to move beyond the kind of analysis which points to individual differences in source and target texts so as to support the established claim that self-translation produces another 'original'. Rather, its purpose is to probe into this little-understood art and ask, what kind of 'originality' are we dealing with – a question which for a number of contributors has implied another: what kind of self, or translator, are we dealing with? This volume is published in collaboration with the International Association of Translation and Intercultural Studies (IATIS) for 2012; it offers an overview of current research into this question without prejudicing any one perspective or group of authors. All of the articles have undergone a rigorous process of peer review and about a third have been developed out of contributions to the three sessions on self-translation which I organized at the IATIS conference at Monash University in Melbourne, in July 2009. Finally, and inevitably, this collection testifies to the fact that there is no model self-translator, only trends and exceptions. The heterogeneity of this global practice renders each encounter site-specific, dependent upon myriad personal, political, linguistic and historical factors. Rather than offer a definition of 'self-translation', this book testifies to the fact that the hybridity of self-translators presented here reflects the hybridity which gives birth to self-translation itself.

The self-translator is a node where critical trends intersect and bend, a point where one can read changes in successive waves of Translation Studies research: the attention devoted to this translator has shifted from offering textual readings which stress his or her creativity, to the location of his or her place in history or the sociological field, to his or her agency within cultural transfers. Finally, by concentrating on this node, this individual translator, the present volume is perhaps symptomatic of a renewed interest in the author, an interest which, hopefully, has learnt the lessons of poststructuralism but which remains vigilant in its inquiry into how individual motivations and choices resist and are shaped by wider historical forces and events.

Works cited

Bistué, Belén. 'The Task(s) of the Translator(s): Multiplicity as Problem in Renaissance European Thought'. *Comparative Literature Studies* 48.2 (2011): 139–64. Print.
Venuti, Lawrence. *The Translator's Invisibility: A History of Translation.* London and New York: Routledge, 1995. Print.

PART ONE
Self-translation and literary history

CHAPTER ONE

The self-translator as rewriter

Susan Bassnett

Abstract: This chapter considers the multilingual work of a range of writers – including Nancy Huston, Rabindranath Tagore, Ngugi wa Thiong'o, Amalia Rosselli and Samuel Beckett – and argues that the concept of self-translation is misleading and unnecessary. All these writers negotiate between languages in different ways, and for different reasons. Borges' witty dismissal of originality serves as a framework concept, along with Andre Lefevere's redefinition of all translation as rewriting.

Research across the landscape of Translation Studies over the last decades has diversified to the point where we could say that there are now a number of clearly discernible pathways. One such pathway, that has been one of the most significant approaches to translation, is polysystems theory, which evolved through the 1970s and 1980s, and has led in particular to a great deal of valuable research into the history of the transmission of translations over time. Ever since Itamar Even-Zohar first suggested that variations in translation activity in different cultures were not only apparent but could also be mapped, scholars have investigated the role played by translated texts in literary systems with surprising results, and such investigations continue to proliferate. One clear manifestation of this line of approach has been research into changing norms of translation, along with a re-evaluation of translation as a literary activity, and of the role played by translation as a shaping force in the history of different literatures.

The dominance of polysystems theory and Descriptive Translation Studies in the 1980s gave way to the cultural turn of the 1990s. When

Andre Lefevere and I edited the collection of essays, *Translation, History and Culture* in 1990, we argued that the object of study had been redefined and that what had come to be studied 'is the text embedded within its network of both source and target cultural signs' (12). Translation Studies, following the cultural turn, should employ tools not only from linguistics and literary studies but also from cultural history and cultural studies. What was needed was greater understanding of the complexities of the translation process in toto, of the agency of the translator, of the socioeconomic factors that determine the selection and publication of translations, of the diffusion of translations in the target culture and of the ways in which translation serves to construct an image of an author, a literature or even of a whole society for a target readership.

The cultural turn has led to a vast amount of important work into the sociocultural aspects of translation. Emily Apter, Bella Brodzki, Michael Cronin, Edwin Gentzler, Harish Trivedi, Sherry Simon, Maria Tymoczko, Lawrence Venuti and many others have written important books that take thinking about translation into new, exciting realms. Venuti's theorizing about the invisible translator in particular has been highly influential. In his book that first appeared in 1995, *The Translator's Invisibility*, Venuti explored the history of translation in the Anglo-American tradition and concluded that the emphasis placed in that tradition on creating an illusion of fluency, by which he means creating the impression that a text has not been translated at all, both marginalizes translation as a literary activity and serves to make the translator seem invisible. Post-colonial translation scholars developed the idea of the translator's invisibility to highlight ways in which an uneven balance of power between languages and literatures had been exploited in translation.[1] It is important to remember that translation plays a vital role in determining how a society receives work produced at another time and in another culture, and far from being an invisible filter through which a text passes, the role of the translator is fundamental. Lefevere's call for translation to be re-labelled 'rewriting' strikes a powerful chord; rewriters, he argues are 'responsible for the general reception and survival of works of literature among non-professional readers, who constitute the great majority of readers in our global culture, to at least the same, if not a greater extent than the writers themselves' (1).

The cultural turn in Translation Studies opened the way to a proliferation of research into the politics and economics of translation, into the inequitable power relationships between languages and literatures, into ethical issues and into the agency of translators. At the same time, we have witnessed a growing number of leading international literary figures such as Seamus Heaney, Ted Hughes, Eva Hoffman or Milan Kundera both engaging in translation themselves and writing about translation, which doubtless reflects the reality of today's globalized world where millions of people have, through choice or necessity, become bi- or multilingual.

Translation has therefore assumed a global significance that it did not have in previous generations. Hence Bella Brodzki can argue that translation is as significant as gender in that it underwrites 'all cultural transactions from the most benign to the most venal' (2). At this juncture we can see translation studies and the study of comparative and world literature starting to come together in their investigations of the translator/rewriter. What is just beginning to develop, as greater attention focuses on the translator as rewriter, is a more profound investigation into individuals who write in more than one language, writers who may (or may not) be categorized as 'self-translators'.

The term 'self-translation' is problematic in several respects, but principally because it compels us to consider the problem of the existence of an original. The very definition of translation presupposes an original somewhere else, so when we talk about self-translation, the assumption is that there will be another previously composed text from which the second text can claim its origin. Yet many writers consider themselves as bilinguals and shift between languages, hence the binary notion of original–translation appears simplistic and unhelpful. Nancy Huston, the Canadian author who writes versions of her novels in French and in English (just to note: her first language was English) deliberately rejects such facile labelling. In a public interview at the University of Toronto, Victoria College, on 24 February 2003, she dismissed attempts to persuade her to adhere to the original–translation dichotomy:

> Do I take the same liberties with the French language as I do English? No idea. Don't want to know. . . .

In that same interview she professes herself to be uncomfortable with the shift between languages, wishing that she could make a definitive choice, but instead has to accept that she is 'Handicapped in both, not happy, not satisfied', adding that 'because if you've got two languages, you haven't really "got" any at all'.

Significantly, when her *Cantique des plains* won a major award for Canadian French language fiction, there were protests because it was held by some to be not an original work but rather a translation of her *Plainsong*, which speaks volumes about the differentiation in status between what is seen as 'original' and what is seen as 'translation'. In Huston's case, the choice of languages appears to be an impulse driven by issues of identity, as she wrestles with a sense of discomfort in both her languages. Her work implies that there is neither an original nor a translation, rather there are two versions of a piece of writing in two languages, each with its own set of significations.

Huston has drawn an intriguing and powerful parallel between the self-translator struggling to exist in two distinct languages and a child caught up in her parent's divorce, running back and forth between father and mother:

> trying to explain mummy to daddy and daddy to mummy, listen you guys, it may not sound like it but in fact you're saying exactly the same thing, listen listen, you're compatible, stay together, don't break up, don't fly apart, don't destroy us all by destroying your marriage, (. . .) why such a deep rift between anglophones and francophones, the important things are the same in all our lives, aren't they? (personal communication)

Yet by the end of the process, Huston acknowledges that she feels a sense of satisfaction at being able to tell the same stories in two languages: 'as if that somehow proved that I'm not a schizophrenic, not crazy. Because ultimately the same person in both languages' (personal communication). To Nancy Huston, self-translation is difficult and painful because it appears at first to expose gaps between languages, to raise the spectre of a divided mind and of a divided world, but when the translation is completed, the gaps are closed, the process has become a healing one and the self-translator is no longer caught between languages but able to exist fully in both. Huston acknowledges that, somehow, the split between her two language selves has been healed through translation.

Borges saw shifting between languages simply as part of a creative process that drew upon a variety of sources. He declared that he always rewrote, that he repeated himself, even going so far as to accuse himself, ironically, of plagiarism:

> I have read so much and I have heard so much. I admit it: I repeat myself. I confirm it: I plagiarize. We are all the heirs of millions of scribes who have already written down all that is essential a long time before us. We are all copyists . . . there are no longer any original ideas. (Borges in Kristal 135)

For Borges, creativity in writing practice was indissolubly linked to reading; texts are endlessly being transmitted and retransmitted so that any notion of a point of origin, of an original, becomes absurd. Borges would have loved the Internet, I think, for here too notions of originality dissolve. We have only to look at multilingual advertising to become aware that what is going on here is not so much translation of a single original, but rather target-focussed versions of a template intended to market a particular product. Reading the instructions of a globally marketed product in a range of languages shows subtle (and not-so-subtle differences) in the presentation of that product for different consumers, suggesting that rather than there having been a single source text from which translations have been made, there has been a product template which is then modified in accordance with the expectations and conventions of the target audience.

In her book on the Brazilian writer and self-translator, Joao Ubaldo Ribeiro, Maria Alice Gonçalves Antunes stresses the importance of the differences between different language readers. If writers write with a particular readership in mind, then once their work is translated, a whole new set of readers need to be identified. Her book, which is yet to appear in English, is one of the few volumes that tackles the question of self-translation and endeavours to provide an overview of some of the issues. She draws attention, for example, to the practice of writers such as Mario Vargas Llosa whose knowledge of the target language is good enough to enable them to work closely with their translators, a practice that may be said to border on self-translation, and through close analysis of some of Joao Ubaldo Ribeiro's work, she examines the degrees of modification that have taken place between his Portuguese and English versions. Her conclusion is that understanding self-translation is highly complex: on the one hand, there is the question of the role played by a different readership, while on the other hand there are other factors linked to an individual writer's own creativity. She suggests that some of the changes introduced by Ribeiro derive from his wish to conform to the expectations of his English-language readership, while ensuring that specifically Brazilian cultural signs are not lost. Yet she also concedes that 'a certain number of changes can be attributed to the author's desire to rewrite his own original' (253).

The urge to rewrite in other languages is by no means a recent phenomenon. Long before the Internet, some writers were consciously experimenting with languages in an endeavour to find an authentic voice. We can see such a process at work in the writing of Amalia Rosselli, the poet who composed in English, French and Italian before finally settling down to write in Italian, publishing *Serie ospedaliera* in 1963. In the following brief extract from her 'Diario in tre lingue', written in 1955–6, we can trace how her reading in all three languages failed at that stage in her life to help her determine which linguistic path to follow in her own work:

dal francese si passa al surrealismo
nell'italiano predomina il concreto, verso greco-latino inconscio, anche
     stornello
Montale-Proust
italian stornello popolare
greek-latin prose
Joyce, frantumazione
surrealismo (french)
classici
argots
Chinois
strutture lingue straniere
eliot-religious
nous voulons nous rapprocher du contenu

(de ses droigts humides)
'per dir la verita non son contenta di nessuna di queste'. (76)

Rosselli referred to her early writings as poetic exercises during the process of deciding which language to write in; English she saw as primarily a language in which to write about religion, while French offered her surrealism and Italian was the language of 'concrete rhythms'. In some of her poems she switches languages, while her sequence *October Elizabethans* is a kind of pastiche, composed in an artificial mock-Elizabethan English. For Rosselli, moving around linguistically was a means of finding her poetic voice and establishing her own poetic identity.

For other writers, the decision to change languages may be linked to a desire to speak to a wider readership, as in the case of Milan Kundera who shifted from Czech to French, though another factor here may well be the flight from a language and a culture that has painful associations. Vladimir Nabokov is another famous example of a writer shifting from his native tongue, constrained by circumstances to become creative in a learned language. Nabokov, however, had a very low opinion of translation, and in his 'On translating *Eugene Onegin*' compared translation to 'A parrot's screech, a monkey's chatter', even going so far as to declare it 'a profanation of the dead' (1). In compensation, Nabokov wanted mountainous footnotes, paratexts that would compensate for all that was lost in the shift from one language to another. If Nabokov felt that translation was profanation of the dead, we may imagine how gravely he viewed translation of the living.

Not all writers are driven by circumstances to write in a globally significant language. The case of a writer like Ngugi Wa Thiongo reveals a shift of language as a means of asserting the status of a minority language. Ngugi chose to make a political statement by rejecting English, the global language, preferring to write in Gikuyo, despite the obvious implications of turning his back on the Anglophone market. In an autobiographical essay, he explains the reasons for this decision. It seemed natural, he declares, to have started writing in English while a student at university in Kampala in the 1960s, because the writers he was reading and studying wrote in English, and the new wave of African and Caribbean writers in whom he found inspiration were also writing in English. It was not until he came to work with a radical community theatre group in 1977 that he began to write in Gikuyo, and following a spell in prison as a political activist, he wrote his first novel in that language.

Ngugi's account of his movement between languages highlights the significance of translation. 'Looking back', he declares, 'I realized that I have always lived in translation' (18). Gikuyu was his first language, English became the language of education, writing in English 'became a literary act of mental translation' (18). Ngugi asserts that writing in a language that is not one's mother tongue becomes an act of mental translation, and raises the important question of how much of one's own language is then retained in that mentally translated text. The decision to break with English was for him a liberation, in that he no longer felt constrained by having to signal through the medium of English that his characters were speaking in an African language. He explains how his decision to switch back to his mother tongue was life-enhancing for him and resolved an identity crisis with which he had lived for decades:

> One of the saddest results of writing in English was that, through mental translation of my creative process, I had lost what would have been the 'original text' in Gikuyu. It was lost in the mind. It did not exist. Writing in Gikuyu directly now ensured the existence of the original text. Its life was not dependent on translation. (19)

He then endeavoured to translate his Gikuyu novel into English, but was not satisfied with the result, for by endeavouring to make his new readers aware of the African language of the original, through 'bending' the target language so as to try and suggest some of the original rhythms and structures, he ended up with an unintentional result, that of making the wise and complex African characters appear simple and childlike in English. His next novel was translated by someone else who avoided the pitfalls of mental translation, but in 2006 he published his own translation of another of his Giukuyu novels, *Wizard of the Crow*. Here, Ngugi points out that his strategy was different: he was determined not to make the source language intrude into the target language, and instead engaged in what he calls constant dialogue with both languages:

> Quite often I found myself having to translate a draft I had thought was complete, only to find, in the process of translation, that there the original was inadequate. The muse would possess me again and I would go to the Gikuyu original, write more drafts, which I later subjected to yet another translation into English. (20)

What Ngugi sketches in this brief essay is a gradual recognition that self-translation involves far more than working from a source text and rendering it into another language; rather, it involves rewriting across and between languages, with the notion of an original as a fluid rather than a fixed concept.

The question as to whether writers such as Ngugi wa Thion'go or Nancy Huston may be termed 'self-translators' is a tricky one, though referring to them as 'bilingual writers' presents another set of problems. There may be many reasons why a writer changes language, in some cases without ever returning to the first language, in other cases moving around between languages, perhaps across genres or text types. Whether such writers can be termed 'self-translators', however, is a moot point. Translating one's own writing seems to involve more than interlingual transfer, it involves reconstructing, perhaps, as Ngugi puts it, being possessed once again by the Muse and starting off along another creative path. What is clear is that the concept of the original in self-translation is far more fluid than in other kinds of translation, and indeed raises doubts as to whether an original can be said to exist at all.

Rabindranath Tagore is an interesting case of a writer who decided to translate his own poetry, from Bengali into English and, for a time at least, acquired great fame as a result. W. B. Yeats wrote an introduction to Tagore's collection of poems, *Gitanjali* or *Song Offering*, in 1913 which led to the latter being awarded the Nobel Prize. Before going to England in 1912, Tagore had seen some of his poetry translated into English and had not been very happy with the result. Yet at that time, despite fluent English as a product of the Indian colonial educational system, he did not consider himself capable of translating his own poetry, even though he did check over the drafts with his translator. In his book, *Translation as Recovery*, Sujit Mukherjee demonstrates that soon after his arrival in England, Tagore took on the task of translating his own work and appeared reluctant to allow anyone else to do so. Mukherjee notes the huge divergences between the Bengali and English versions, and cites a letter of 13 March 1913 in which Tagore declares his intentions: 'to carry the essential substance of my poetry in the English translation, and this means a wide divergence from the original' (119). This phrase, 'essential substance', is highly significant. Tagore does not explain what he means by it, but it is reminiscent of Ezra Pound's thinking about translation. In the midst of an essay on Cavalcanti, Pound comments that it is not that one language cannot be made to do what another has done, but that it is not always expeditious to approach the same goal by the same alley. Translation is rewriting, in that a text is composed again in a second language. Tagore was quite clear that such rewriting would mean that the 'original' and the 'translation' were vastly different.

Mukherjee comments that the last three English volumes of Tagore's six volumes of verse do not even mention that they are translations. He also notes that Tagore, in his later correspondence, acknowledged the inadequacy of his translations of his own poetry. In a letter to Amiya Chakravorty he writes:

> You probably know that when a calf dies, the mother-cow stops producing milk. At that time, the calf-skin is stuffed with straw to make an artificial creature, on seeing whom and smelling the resemblance, the cow's udders begin filling with milk again. Translation is like that figure of the dead calf – it deceives but cannot allure. (Mukherjee 120)

Mahasweta Sengupta is more critical of Tagore's decision to translate his own poetry. In an essay entitled 'Rabindranath Tagore in Two Worlds', she points out that Tagore's awareness of English poetry was conditioned by the Romantic and Victorian aesthetic, hence the conservatism of his English versions, which are in stark contrast to his innovative writing in Bengali. Moreover, she considers the way in which he selected poems for translation, highlighting mysticism and innocent 'Eastern wisdom' which matched Western stereotypes of the Orient. As a consequence of appealing to the vogue for Eastern mysticism, Sengupta argues that Tagore transformed his writerly identity and 'became a representative of the alluring "Other" to the Western world' (62). She also explains why Tagore should have so abruptly fallen from favour after three decades of being almost a cult figure: once the vogue for mysticism passed, and the Second World War and its aftermath changed Western aesthetical ideology, Tagore's poetry in English ceased to have any significance. Yet he continues to be seen as a major figure in Bengali literature and in Indian literatures more generally, an innovator and an outspoken social critic. Self-translation in Tagore's case, according to Sengupta, can be viewed as a kind of self-delusion.

William Radice, however, who translated a selection of Tagore's poems for Penguin in 1985, takes a different view. In a speech given at the Commonwealth Club in London in 2006, Radice explains how he started out by believing that Tagore had done his own writing an injustice when he produced his English translations of his Bengali poetry. Radice even goes so far as to suggest that he started to learn Bengali himself *despite* the off-putting nature of what he had read of Tagore in English. But Radice argues that there has been a reassessment of Tagore's contribution to world literature in the last two decades, and that attitudes to Tagore as self-translator have also shifted. His argument is that there are several factors lying behind this shift of perception: a wealth of scholarly editions of Tagore's work and commentaries produced since the 1980s; a new wave of translations of Tagore's writing; and, perhaps most significant of all, an aesthetic reassessment of Tagore's English poetry. Explaining the meteoric rise to fame of the Bengali writer in 1913, Radice argues that when Tagore came along, 'he seemed to embody the Indian ideal' that people were seeking:

> With the huge success of *Gitanjali*, it became apparent that many readers in Britain were tired of the cynicism of Oscar Wilde, embarrassed by the imperialism of Kipling, baffled by the experiments of early modernism: they wanted a different sort of writer, and judging by the response of the Nobel prize Committee and the explosion in sales of secondary translations of *Gitanjali* across the world, it seems that many readers in other countries, in the frightening and disillusioning context of the First World War and its aftermath, wanted a new, sincere, beautiful, spiritual sort of writer too.

What Tagore did, according to Radice's convincing hypothesis, was to create a kind of prose-poetry with Biblical overtones that was very easily translateable into other languages, because it was not bound to any specific poetic form. These lines from *Gitanjali* illustrate just how easily readable Tagore's English poem could be, despite the use of archaisms and the somewhat stilted language. His sentences are short and clearly structured, the imagery is strong and the theme, that of a man struggling to find a way of expressing the glory of God's creation, has universal appeal:

> I know not how thou singest, my master! I ever listen in silent amazement.
>
> The light of thy music illumines the world. The life breath of thy music runs from sky to sky. The holy stream of thy music breaks through all stony obstacles and rushes on.
>
> My heart begs to join in thy song, but vainly struggles for a voice. I would speak, but speech breaks not into song, and I cry out baffled. Ah, thou hast made my heart captive in the endless meshes of thy music, my master! (14)

Radice argues that Tagore's English translations need to be seen today as a significant part of his oeuvre, read as poems written not in Bengali, but 'as durable and authentic as his writings in Bengali' nevertheless. *Gitanjali* stunned W. B. Yeats, and acquired international success through the ease with which it could be translated from English. Rather than dismissing Tagore's English translations as a diminishing of his creative artistry because he chose to write in a rather antiquated poetic mode, the antithesis of the modernist experiments of his contemporaries, it would be more productive to see that writing as an interlingual experiment that not only fed back into his Bengali work but also gave him access to the world stage.

Possibly the most often-cited case of self-translation is that of Samuel Beckett, well-known as a writer who produced works in both French and English. His *Waiting for Godot* first appeared in French, then in English, while his novel *Murphy* came out first in English and then in French. Although his poetry is far less well-known than his plays and his prose writing, a small volume that appeared in 1961 entitled simply *Poems in English by Samuel Beckett* offers intriguing examples of Beckett's swings between the two languages and raises interesting questions about rewriting. Most of the collection is indeed in English, but Section IV, entitled '*Quatre Poemes*' consists of four short poems, in French on the left hand page and in English on the right hand page. A note under the last poem declares 'translated from French by the author'. These poems are remarkable in shedding light on the complexity of reshaping that necessarily happens during translation, in this case by the same person. For something more than restructuring is taking place in these poems – the English is overtly different in places from the French and not for any obvious reasons determined by syntactical rules or any absence of vocabulary. If we take the first poem, 'Dieppe', we see that the first two lines are rendered straightforwardly, taking into account the rules governing the positioning of the adjective in English: 'encore le dernier reflux / le galet mort' becomes 'again the last ebb / the dead shingle'. Then the two poems start to diverge: 'le demi-tour puis les pas' becomes 'the turning then the steps', altering the image of the half-turn, while 'vers les vieilles lumières' becomes 'towards the lighted town'. The idea of 'old' lights disappears; instead we have the final word 'town' that serves as a contrast with the emptiness of the beach and the receding tide. The effect of these small changes is that the English poem ends on a slightly more hopeful note, with the speaker turning away from the deadness and turning, not half-turning, towards the lighted town that promises life. In the French version the melancholy tone is maintained throughout.

Similar shifts can be seen in the fourth, untitled poem. The opening lines again are very closely rendered: 'je voudrais que mon amour meure / qu'il pleuve sur le cimetière' becomes 'I would like my love to die / and the rain to be falling on the graveyard'. The third line is also close, though with a shift of register, the English being more colloquial: 'et les ruelles ou je vais' becomes 'and on me walking the streets'. The last line, however, is completely different. The French is 'pleurant celle qui crut m'aimer', which translated literally would be 'weeping for the woman who believed she loved me'. Instead Beckett's English version has 'mourning the first and last to love me', which introduces a whole new line of thought. In short, although there are discernible elements that might be considered as 'translations', that is to say there are correspondences between the two versions in terms of semantics, syntax and meaning, there are also divergences that lead the reader in other directions.

Umberto Eco, who has become increasingly fascinated by translation, has explored the complex semiotic processes involved when texts move across linguistic and cultural boundaries. Eco acknowledges that sometimes he has acted as a co-translator, working closely with someone translating his work, and he recognizes the inevitability of changes made that become evident when a text is adjusted to fit into a new universe of discourse. Eco's thoughts about translation as rewriting shed light on the apparent unfaithfulness of self-translators such as those discussed in this chapter, where neither Beckett nor Tagore, for example, appeared constrained by any concept of a fixed 'original'. In an essay entitled 'Translating and being Translated', he declares himself forced to use the terminology of rewriting:

> There are cases in which the loss involved in adhering strictly to the text is quite irreparable. In such cases, if we wish to obtain the same effect that the text was designed to provide, we have to *rewrite*. (57)

Where then is the boundary between self-translating and rewriting? Lefevere sees such a boundary as non-existent, for all translation involves rewriting in a more or less overt manner. All the self-translators discussed in this chapter have effectively rewritten their work, in some cases operating in a kind of dialogic way with something that might be termed an original, in other cases acknowledging an identity shift as they rework what they have written and so create another original. There is, of course, always some kind of relationship between the two texts, but, as we have seen when reading the Beckett poems side by side, that relationship is surely one of creative reworking, an example of a writer choosing to rewrite for a new readership.

Michael Riffaterre states bluntly that 'whereas units of meaning may be words or phrases or sentences, *the unit of significance is the text*' (6). When we compare 'originals' with 'translations' all too often the focus is on individual units of meaning: scholars rummage around, pointing out something lost here, something added there, something distorted, something overlooked. But if we think in terms of the text being the unit of significance, then we are better placed to accept the idea of translation as rewriting, albeit recognizable as rewriting because of the move across languages. If we consider the translation/rewriting in a Borgesian manner, as one of many drafts or readings of a text, then we can dispense with the terminology of self-translation altogether and look more holistically at a writer's work.

Note

1 For further details of postcolonial thinking about translation see: Tejaswini Niranjana, *Siting Translation: History, Post-structuralism, and the Colonial Context*; Anuradha Dingwaney and Carol Maier, eds, *Between Languages and Cultures. Translation and Cross-Cultural Texts*; Susan Bassnett and Harish Trivedi, eds, *Post-colonial Translation. Theory and Practice*; Maria Tymoczko and Edwin Gentzler, eds, *Translation and Power*.

Works cited

Bassnett, Susan and Andre Lefevere, eds. *Translation, History and Culture*. London: Pinter, 1990. Print.

Bassnett, Susan and Harish Trivedi, eds. *Post-colonial Translation: Theory and Practice*. London: Routledge. 1999. Print.

Beckett, Samuel. *Poems in English*. New York: Grove, 1961. Print.

Brodzki, Bella. *Can These Bones Live: Translation, Survival and Cultural Memory*. Stanford: Stanford UP, 2007. Print.

Dingwaney, Anuradha and Carol Maier, eds. *Between Languages and Cultures: Translation and Cross-Cultural Texts*. Pittsburgh: U of Pittsburgh P, 1995. Print.

Eco, Umberto. *Experiences in Translation*. Trans. Alastair McEwen. Toronto: U of Toronto P, 2001. Print.

Gonçalves Antunes, Maria Alice. *O respeito pelo original: João Ubaldo Ribeiro e a autotradução*. San Paolo: Annablume, 2009. Print.

Huston, Nancy. Personal Communication. 2011. Print.

—. Untitled. University of Toronto, Victoria College. 24 Feb. 2003. Public Interview.

Kristal, Efrain. *Invisible Work: Borges and Translation*. Nashville: Vanderbilt UP, 2002. Print.

Lefevere, Andre. *Translation, Rewriting and the Manipulation of Literary Fame*. London: Routledge, 1992. Print.

Mukherjee, Sujit. *Translation as Recovery*. Delhi: Pencraft International, 2004. Print.

Nabokov, Vladimir. 'On translating *Eugene Onegin*'. *Eugene Onegin: A Novel in Verse*. Aleksandr Sergeevich Pushkin. Trans. Vladimir Nabokov. Princeton: Princeton UP, 1991. Print.

Ngugi wa Thiong'o. 'My life In-Between languages'. *Translation Studies* 2.1 (2009): 17–21. Print.

Niranjana, Tejaswini. *Siting Translation: History, Post-structuralism, and the Colonial Context*. Berkeley: U of California P, 1992. Print.

Pound, Ezra. '*Cavalcanti*'. *Literary Essays*. London: Faber, 1934. 149–200. Print.

Pushkin, Aleksandr Sergeevich. *Eugene Onegin: A Novel in Verse*. Trans. Vladimir Nabokov. Princeton: Princeton UP, 1991. Print.

Radice, William. 'Tagore the World Over: English as the Vehicle'. *Tagore's Gifts to English*. Commonwealth Club, London, 22 Mar. 2006. Web. www.williamradice.com/Recent%20Events/Tagore_the_world_over.htm

Riffaterre, Michael. *Semiotics of Poetry*. Bloomington and London: Indiana UP, 1978. Print.

Rosselli, Amalia. *Primi scritti 1952–1963*. Milan: Guanda, 1980. Print.

Sengupta, Mahasweta. 'Translation, Colonialism and Poetics: Rabindranath Tagore in Two Worlds'. *Translation, History and Culture*. S. Bassnett and A. Lefevere, 1990. London: Pinter Publishers, 1990. 56–63. Print.

Tagore, Rabindranath. *Gitanjali (Song Offerings)*. Intro. William Butler Yeats. Boston: International Pocket Library, 2000.

Tymoczko, Maria and Edwin Gentzler, eds. *Translation and Power*. Amherst: U of Massachussetts P, 2002. Print.

Venuti, Lawrence. *The Translator's Invisibility: A History of Translation*. London: Routledge, 1995. Print.

CHAPTER TWO

On mirrors, dynamics and self-translations

Julio-César Santoyo

Abstract: *Mirrors, glasses, reflections, images. . ., old metaphors that conceptualize the process of translating. And of self-translating. However, as with self-translations, both original and translated text are brought forth by the same hand, and the hoped-for faithful, specular image may become as deformed as the author fancies, because the author is, de facto, the 'mirror' in which the original looks at itself. That is why, from the point of view of the auctor-itas, the self-translated text is a second original, rendered into a second language with all the liberty an author enjoys. It is that authorial liberty alone which makes the translated text a second original, creating a very particular play of mirrors, and, most importantly, establishing a dynamic relationship between the original and its specular image. The process may even end up incorporating the mirrored image into the original, thus forming a unique text in which original and translation are both complementary, intimately bound together, intertwined in one textual entity, as in the case of intra-textual self-translations.*

In 1974 Reuben A. Brower published in Harvard a well-known and frequently quoted book, *Mirror on Mirror*, whose very subtitle shatters and falls in three different directions: 'Translation, Imitation, Parody'. Brower's title did not introduce any new metaphor: it simply joined a rather long tradition of *specular* allegories on the nature and purpose of translation. Suffice it to remember Antoine Crappier, in the dedication of his translation of the short treatise *De la calomnie* (1551): '*Vous aurez cette présente mienne traduction comme un miroir* [. . .]'; or the anonymous critic who in 1793 published in volume 24 of *The European Magazine and London Review* a review of Alexander F. Tytler's *Essay on the Principles of Translation*: 'The sober sense of criticism [. . .] bids a translator to be the faithful mirror of his original' (188); or, one more among the many, Félix Bouchot in 1847, in the preface to his French translation of Polybius's *Histoire Générale*: '*Un auteur n'est traduit que si la traduction, comme un miroir fidèle, reproduit exactement tous les traits de l'original, beaux ou laids*' (xxiii; An author is not translated unless the translation, like a faithful mirror, recreates exactly the features of the original, beautiful or ugly).

Mirrors, glasses, reflections, images . . ., such metaphors capture visually and conceptualize the process of translating . . .; and there are refractions too, because 'a translation, like an image in a mirror, is a reflection of the original, but the 'glass' of the 'mirror' not only reflects but also refracts or distorts' (Orzech 60). Such metaphors presuppose in every case the existence of two different, individual, separate texts: *one* (the translation) derived from the *other* (the original), the *former* being, or trying to be, the image and reflection of the *latter*.

A self-translation, just like any translation, is also *another* text, derived from a former original and, consequently, its reflected image (my apologies for such an obvious statement). But the self-translated text is not something alien to the original from which it derives, nor does it come from the hand of another author we call the *translator*: in self-translations both original and translated text are brought forth by one and the same hand, and therefore the hoped-for faithful, specular image may appear as deformed and distorted as the author may fancy. Only the author retains the right to change, alter, deform or distort the reflected image of the original, and we could not in any way accuse the author of mistakes or inaccuracies, because the 'mirror' is not something foreign to him or her: the author is, *de facto*, the 'mirror' in which the original looks at itself.

Miguel Sáenz has observed:

> In the best of cases (and the best of cases is called Samuel Beckett) the result [of a self-translation] is a new work, different from the original, a translation which no independent translator would have ever dared to make, wherewith occurs the phenomenon of a work which, in fact, has not been translated, but which has two versions – in the case of Beckett, in French and in English – without anyone being sometimes able to tell which is the original. (113)

It is therefore more than evident that, from the point of view of the *auctoritas* (auctor-itas), the self-translated text *is* a second original, rendered into a second language with all the liberty an author always enjoys (but never a translator); an original that has the benefit of *authorial intentionality*, according to Brian T. Fitch, something denied to versions made by other translators (125). 'What is wonderful about self-translation', Robert Wechsler observes, 'is that it allows the translator to take any liberties he feels like taking' (24); or, as the Turkish self-translator Talât Sait Halman admits:

> With one's own poems, there is also the splendid advantage of doing new and quite different versions; after all, one is not constrained by the duty of remaining faithful to the original composed by someone else; translating your own work provides the best kind of freedom; taking liberties functions as a creative prerogative that you can enjoy to your heart's content. (qtd. in Pultar 48)

The self-translator often makes good use of such *creative prerogative* to recast *ad libitum* his/her text into the codes, norms and reading habits of the target polysystem, modifying in consequence the initial focalization of the text. In the translation into Spanish of Carme Riera's *Contra l'amor en companyia i altres relats*, for example:

> names and characters of the Catalan world are often transmuted into their (more or less) equivalents in the Castilian culture. Perhaps one of the most successful are the adaptations taking place in the short story 'La novel.la experimental', where the references to the world of the Catalan literature are neatly transplanted into the world of the Castilian literature. Thus, the main character does not refer in the Spanish version to [the Catalan poet] Espriu but to Cervantes, the 'premi Prudenci Bertrana' gets transformed into the prize Planeta . . ., and 'el germà de la cunyada d'en Rocard Massó' becomes 'the brother of the sister-in-law of Lara's wife', etc. (Cotoner 165)

This is but one of the many examples of what André Lefevere named '*refractions*', and defined as 'the adaptation of a work of literature to a different audience, with the intention of influencing the way in which that audience reads the work' (234–5).

It is precisely that authorial liberty which puts its stamp on the translated text, making it a second original, creating a very particular play of mirrors (reminiscent at times of fun-fair mirrors), and, most importantly, establishing a dynamic relationship between the original and its specular image. Because the relationship between a self-translation and its original, or vice versa, is not static, as in other types of translation, quite frequently there is a dynamic relationship, one specific to self-translations, that makes an original look at itself in the mirror of its self-translation and adopt or incorporate the textual changes the author may have brought into the translated text.

The self-translated text 'bounces' back onto the original as rarely, if ever, as any other translated text, or any other type of rewriting. Rewritings do not 'bounce' back onto their originals. No rewriting of Umberto Eco's *Il nome della rosa* (and there have been many: translations into dozens of languages, quotations in books, articles, doctoral dissertations, etc.) has had any influence on, or has changed one comma of, the Italian original. No translation, and there are many, of Gabriel García Márquez's *Crónica de una muerte anunciada* has ever modified the first text of that novel. On the other hand, self-translations do, at times, end up modifying their original. If the act of translating is a creative one, there is little doubt that self-translation is its most creative expression, because the second, self-translated text may even revert to the first text, and in its 'rebounding from one language to another', in its 'schizophrenic ping-pong game' (Monzó 44) it may finish up creating a second original, different from the first. In a short article published on 18 September 1999 in the newspaper *El Mundo*, the Galician novelist Suso de Toro commented briefly on his personal experience in this respect:

> Self-translation appears as a sort of wasting your time instead of writing something new [. . .]. But translating oneself is also a new opportunity to recast and remake one's work. When I translated [into Spanish] my novel *La sombra cazadora*, I added some twenty pages that afterwards I also included in the fourth edition of the original in Galician. In my novel *Calzados Lola* I added several pages, a couple of them qualifying the last pages of the book, which I also added to the new Galician edition. And the same in *Ambulancia*, I rewrote, I expanded [. . .], and even brought back to life one of the characters, Inspector Maquieira [. . .]. It seemed to me that a guy as vile and despicable as that wretch didn't deserve to die; it made me sad to have bumped off someone as wicked and disgusting as him. The translation gave me the opportunity to give him a new life [. . .]. (2, my translation)

Josep Miquel Ramis has lately studied the case of the novel *Terres de l'Ebre*, by the Catalan writer Sebastià Juan Arbó, self-translated into Spanish as *Tierras del Ebro*: 'The 1940 self-translation into Spanish derives from the 1932 original in Catalan; however, the 1947 Catalan edition derives rather from the 1940 self-translation than from the 1932 original, and so on' (24–5), and so forth, in the later Catalan and Spanish (Castilian) editions of 1948, 1955, 1956, 1966, 1971, 1980 and 1992.

This dynamic relationship is born especially when original and self-translation face each other during the writing process, and both become witnesses and protagonists of their common development, recreating and influencing each other as the author writes one text in parallel with the other. This process of writing and rewriting, wherein both texts, original and translation, get involved in a sort of creative, parallel and simultaneous dialogue is exemplified, Luisa Cotoner observes, by the Catalan novelist Carme Riera in the epistolary novel *Qüestió d'amor propi / Cuestión de amor propio*:

> In *Qüestió d'amor propi*, the original and its translation alternated with each other, so that a sort of dialectics was established between both texts, with the result that the translated text often led the author to modify and even rewrite the original, as she herself explained in the 5th Seminar on Translation in Catalonia: 'I was writing and translating it at the same time; that offered me a different point of view to observe how it all worked in the other language and correct whatever I thought pertinent, because in that way I was turned into a critical reader of my own text, much more distanced from it than when, after writing, I read in my own language to correct the text'. (165)

This dynamic relationship creates a sort of complementarity between the original and its translation, a reciprocity whereby one text supplements and/or depends on the other as both texts become, de facto, the head and tail of the same coin. The process ends up incorporating and integrating the mirrored image into the original, thus forming a unique text in which original and translation are both complementary and appear intimately bound together, face-to-face and back-to-back, constantly intertwined in one textual entity. The reader, who is necessarily bilingual, is immersed in a simultaneous, complementary play of two mirrors, a vision that enables him/her to estimate the quality of the reflected image (whichever of the two it may be, or both). Such a complementarity reaches its height in what I have called 'intra-textual' self-translation ('La autotraducción'), a textual singularity in which the poetic discourse unfolds in two languages, one translated from the other, as in Alastair Reid's poem 'What Gets Lost / *Lo que se pierde*':

> I keep translating *traduzco continuamente*
> *entre palabras* words *que no son las mías*
> into other words which are mine *de palabras a mis palabras.*
> *Y, finalmente, de quién es el texto?*
> Who do words belong to?
> *Del escritor o del traductor* writer, translator
> *o de los idiomas* or to language itself?
> *Traductores, somos fantasmas que viven*
> *entre aquel mundo y el nuestro*
> translators are ghosts who live
> in a limbo between two worlds.
> *Pero poco a poco me ocurre*
> *que el problema* the problem *no es cuestión*
> *de lo que se pierde en traducción*

is not a question
of what gets lost in translation
sino but rather *lo que se pierde*
what gets lost
entre la ocurrencia –sea de amor o de agonía
between the happening of love or pain–
y el hecho de que llega
a existir en palabras
and their coming into words.
Para nosotros todos, amantes, habladores
for lovers or users of words
el problema es éste this is the difficulty -
Lo que se pierde what gets lost
no es lo que se pierde en traducción sino
is not what gets lost in translation but rather
what gets lost in language itself *lo que se pierde*
en el hecho, en la lengua,
en la palabra misma. (221)

Or, again, as in the poem 'Third-World Theme', by the Chicano poet Ángela de Hoyos:

with savoring eyes
con los ojos saboreando
and trembling fingers
y trémulos los dedos
partimos el pan
we broke the bread
y no alcanzó para todos
– not enough to go around –

de esta manera alguien
se acostará con hambre
from this table tonight
someone will go hungry

señor presidente
President Paleface
¿qué nos aconseja . . .?
what shall we do
for tomorrow . . .? (qtd. in Villanueva 303)

Poems such as 'The Deadlier of the Species', also by Ángela de Hoyos; 'Translation for Mamá', by Richard Blanco; 'All of Us', by AmaLuna; 'L'invasion / Invasion', by Mari E. Zeleznik or 'Reloj = Clock', by Ada M. Álvarez Conde are all samples of this specular, intra-textual sort of self-translation (Santoyo, 'La autotraducción intratextual').

There are even cases, though certainly not many, in which the play-of-mirrors dynamic is reversed, and the specular reflection may chronologically precede the original it claims to reflect; or, in other words, cases in which the self-translation (pseudo self-translation, in fact) antedates the text from which it pretends to derive. More than a play of mirrors, it looks like a play on words, but it is not. Actually, this is what happened in the complex case of the novel by the Basque writer Jean-Baptiste Dasconaguerre, *Les échos du Pas de Roland*, published in Paris in 1867, whose title contains the comment, 'traduit du basque'. That same year, 1867, a translation into Spanish was also published in Bayonne, *Ecos del Paso de Roldán*, by J.-B. Dasconaguerre, the title page of which also stated that it had been 'traducido del vascuence' (translated from Basque). A year later, in 1868, a second edition of the novel appeared in French, with the same title and an identical statement on the title page: 'Traduit du basque'. Therefore, two translations into French and into Spanish, *traduit du basque / traducido del vascuence*, are allegedly mere reflections of an earlier original in Basque. But no one has found this original, and there is no report, evidence or record whatsoever of its existence, because, in fact, the French 'translation' was no translation at all, and it did not derive from any original in Basque. It was just one more of the many pseudo translations that throughout history have mimicked an original, be it Horace Walpole's *The Castle of Otranto*, from Italian, or Robin Chapman's *The Duchess's Diary*, from Spanish. And as readers looked for the Basque 'original', which did not materialize, Dasconaguerre had to 'invent' it. With the help of two colleagues, Julian Vinson and Edmund Guibert, he recreated in Basque an until-then imaginary original, which, two years later, in 1870, was finally published in Bayonne under the title of *Atheka-gaitzeko: Oihartzunak*. An 'original' which was nothing but a self-translation from the French! In spite of this, the first original in French continued to be accepted as a translation (reflection) of a previous text in Basque. In 1872 a new translation into Spanish was published in Madrid, also from the French: *Un drama en la frontera . . ., traducido al castellano*. In his short preface ('Two Words to the Reader'), Vicente de Manterola makes it clear that the 'translation' device had worked quite well, and that, in fact, he himself believed in the existence of a Basque original:

That is the history of the book Mr. Dasconaguerre published in the very old Basque language under the title of *Ecos del Paso de Roldán* [. . .] In France, newspapers and periodicals of every sort and condition have celebrated, and enthusiastically praised, the publication of a book that has come to reveal to the world the many charms and beauties hidden in the little-known Basque literature [. . .] Translated by its author into French, it was shortly after translated again into English and into some other languages [. . .]. (vi)

Eight years later this belief was still shared by the distinguished critic and historian of the Basque language, Arturo Campión: 'Ecos del paso de Rolan [sic] was first written in Basque under the title of Atheka-Gaitzeko Oihartzunak [. . .], being soon after translated into French by the author himself [. . .]' (331).

Bearing all this in mind, it is no wonder then that quite often originals of self-translations end up being overshadowed by their translations, even supplanted by them, for the image reflected in the mirror often becomes the 'real' text, not its mere copy. It is this very factor that determines that translations into a third language are made, quite frequently, not from the original but from the new text translated by the author. The phenomenon is all the more prevalent because authors often self-translate from 'minor' or non-western languages into major European languages (typically English, Spanish or French). So it happens that the original stays confined to its own language and culture, while its self-translation becomes almost the only source from which versions into third languages are made. Most French, German, Italian or Spanish editions of Rabindranath Tagore were made from the English texts translated by the author from Bengali in 1911–12. His versions were an immediate success all over Europe and America, and in 1913 they won him the Nobel Prize for Literature, awarded, according to the Swedish Academy, 'because of his profoundly sensitive, fresh and beautiful verse, by which, with consummate skill, he has made his poetic thought, expressed in his own English words, a part of the literature of the West' (Levinovitz and Ringertz 154). And as a result, and from then on, Tagore's English self-translations, not the originals in Bengali, were the source of further renderings into who knows how many languages all over the world.

From his own English texts Tagore was translated into Spanish by Victoria Ocampo in Argentina; into Russian by two poets who in their turn became Nobel-Prize winners, Ivan Bunin and Boris Pasternak; into Portuguese by the Brazilian poetess Cecilia Meireles; into French by another Nobel-Prize winner, André Gide; and also into Spanish by the 1956 Nobel-Prize winner Juan Ramón Jiménez and his wife Zenobia Camprubí. For nine years, from 1914 to 1922, Juan Ramón and Zenobia translated from English into Spanish 22 titles by Tagore. The reception those Spanish versions met was amazing; edition after edition, thousands of copies were sold every year. Nowadays, almost a hundred years later, they are still being printed and published over and over again. As Howard Young points out, 'it was galling for Juan Ramón to accept the fact that his books collected dust on the shelves while Tagore's sold in the thousands' (43), a testimony also confirmed years before by the poet, Gerardo Diego, who recalled that in those years 'all books by Tagore sold out, whereas those by the poet of Moguer sold but slowly' (qtd. in Young 43). Translating Tagore as they did, Juan Ramón and Zenobia turned him, in Young's opinion, into a great poet, 'greater than many other Spanish poets; for decades, the Jiménez version of Tagore was Tagore for the vast Spanish-speaking world, functioning as the original, even though the original in this case was an English rewrite of Bengali [. . .]' (44–5).

Be that as it may, it is solely thanks to his self-translations from Bengali into English that Tagore remains what he has always been in the West. While in his last days Tagore regretted having made his self-translations, they are the only reason why there are today two different Tagores; or rather, two very different perceptions of this author: one, what Tagore means for Bengali literature and culture in particular, and Indian in general; the other, what Tagore has been thought of in the West throughout the last 100 years. One has little to do with the other. As Somjit Dutt has written: 'Tagore's image in the West [. . .] is not entirely an authentic one, when compared with his true identity as expressed through his Bengali compositions [. . .], which are necessarily inaccessible to the West in the original'.

This same point is valid of the novelist Chingiz Aitmatov, who has almost always been translated into foreign languages from his own Russian translations, not from the originals in the Kirghiz language. It can almost be said for Wassil Bykau, as well, who self-translated works into Russian from his Belarusian originals, and then from Russian re-translated into German, French and English: *The Schlinge*, '*aus dem Russischen von Thomas Reschke;*' *Sotnikov*, '*traduit du russe par Benadette du Crest;*' *Les morts n'ont plus mal*, '*traduit du russe par Frédérique Longueville-Pujol;*' *His Battallion & Live until Dawn*, also 'translated from the Russian' by Jennifer and Robert Woodhouse.

The case of the Basque writer Bernardo Atxaga, self-translator and co-translator of much of his own work, is identical: '*qui a déjà été tradui[t] en espagnol et partant de cette langue en portugais, en catalan, en français, en italien, en allemand, en grec, en anglais, en hollandais, en norvégien, en polonais, en roumain, en albanais et en serbe*' (Zabaleta 45; who has already been translated into Spanish and from that language into Portuguese, Catalan, French, Italian, German, Greek, English, Dutch, Norwegian, Polish, Romanian, Albanian, and Serbian).

Nabokov wrote one of his first novels, *Camera Obscura*, in Russian. Dissatisfied with a previous translation into English by another hand, he 'brought out a new English version, this time his own' (Grayson 5), publishing it in 1938 in New York under a different title, *Laughter in the Dark*. The subsequent translation into Spanish by Javier Calzada, *Risa en la oscuridad*, was made, as expected, from the English text, not from the Russian original.

The Kenyan writer Ngûgî wa Thiong'o wrote one of his novels, *Caitaani mūtharaba-Inī*, in Gikuyu, his mother tongue, and it was published in that language by Heinemann in 1980. Two years later the same publishing house brought out the English translation of the book, *Devil on the Cross*, with the following note on the title page: 'Translated from Gikuyu by the author'. A few years later it was translated from English into Spanish by Alfonso Ormaetxea: *El diablo en la cruz*.

And so on and so forth. . . . In all these cases, and in many more, the self-translated text has ended up superseding the original, which stays 'isolated' in its first language as in a sort of greenhouse, its diffusion in other languages and cultures taking place only through the text translated by its author into a second tongue.

This has one immediate consequence: when an author translates his or her work into another language, he or she is at the same time killing the likelihood of different translations into that language by other hands. In January 1611 John Donne published in Latin his satire against the Jesuits, *Conclave Ignatii*.

> Donne [. . .] almost at once set to work to turn it into English. Another translator, who has remained anonymous, was also attracted by the pamphlet, and he must barely have completed his English version when Donne's own translation, entered in the Stationer's Register on 18 May 1611, came off the press. The anonymous version has accordingly lain unnoticed among the Harleian manuscripts [Ms. Harleian 1019] for two hundred years under the title *Ignatius His Closet* [. . .]. (Le Comte 228)

Except for his own *Il burbero di buon cuore. . .*, *traduzione fatta dall'autore medesimo*, there are no *other* translations into Italian of Goldoni's French original, *Le bourru bienfaisant* (1789). Again, except for her own *It Does Not Die*, there are no *other* translations into English of Maitreyi Devi's biographical narrative *Na Hanyate*, originally published in Bengali in 1974.

No doubt, professor Snell-Hornby was *not* thinking of self-translations when she wrote:

> Only rarely however does the literary translation attain the stability of an original work [. . .]; it is hardly ever handed down from one generation to another as a work of art in itself, more often it becomes ossified as merely a dated text. In other words, it loses its communicative function as a work of literature within a continually shifting cultural system. This explains why the need so often arises to create new translations of literary works [. . .]. (114)

Evidently, self-translations do not fit well into such sweeping generalizations, perhaps because self-translations and their authors frequently operate at the limits of, and sometimes with no regard for, the theoretical presumptions and assumptions of the discipline we know as Translation Studies.

Works cited

Anonymous. 'Review of Alexander F. Tytler, *Essay on the Principles of Translation*'. *The European Magazine and London Review* 24 (1793): 186–9, 278–82. Print.

Brower, Reuben A. *Mirror on Mirror: Translation, Imitation, Parody.* Cambridge, MA: Harvard UP, 1974. Print.

Campión, Arturo. 'Escritores euskaros contemporáneos: J. B. Dasconaguerre'. *Revista Euskara* 3 (1880): 329–36. Print.

Cotoner, Luisa. 'Ética y estética de la autotraducción: Una cala en las versiones al castellano de Josep Pla, Joan Perucho y Carme Riera'. *Panorama actual de la investigación en traducción e interpretación.* Ed. Emilio Ortega Arjonilla. Granada: Atrio, 2004. Vol. III. 2004. 159–67. 2nd edn. CD-Rom.

Dasconaguerre, Jean-Baptiste. *Les échos du Pas de Roland . . ., traduit du basque.* Paris: Rouges Frères, 1867. 2ª edn.: Paris: Firmin Marchand Libraire-Éditeur, 1868. Print.

—. *Ecos del Paso de Roldán . . ., traducido del vascuence.* Bayona: Viuda de Lamaignère, 1867. Print.

—. *Atheka-Gaitzeko: Oihartzunak.* Bayonan: Lamaignère Alhargunaren Imprimerian, 1870. Print.

—.*Un drama en la frontera . . ., traducido al castellano bajo la dirección de D. Vicente de Manterola.* Madrid: D. Guio, 1872. Print.

De Toro, Suso. 'La traducción: Todo un milagro'. *El Mundo* [Madrid] 2 (18 Sep. 1999). Print.

Dutt, Somjit. 'A Foreign Shine and Assumed Gestures: The Ersatz Tagore of the West'. *Parabbas: Special Rabindranath Tagore Section.* Web.

Fitch, Brian T. *Beckett and Babel: An Investigation into the Status of the Bilingual Work.* Toronto: U of Toronto P, 1988. Print.

Grayson, Jane. *Nabokov Translated: A Comparison of Nabokov's Russian and English Prose.* Oxford: Oxford UP, 1979. Print.

Le Comte, Edward. *Grace to a Witty Sinner: A Life of John Donne.* London: Victor Gollancz and New York: Walker, 1965. Print.

Lefevere, André. 'Mother Courage's Cucumbers: Text, System and Refraction in a Theory of Literature'. *The Translation Studies Reader.* Ed. Lawrence Venuti. London and New York: Routledge, 2000. 233–49. Print.

Levinovitz, Agneta Wallin and Nils Ringertz, eds. *The Nobel Prize: The First 100 Years.* London: Imperial College P, 2001. Print.

Monzó, Quim. 'Me apasiona el cuento porque está a un paso del poema'. *ABC* [Madrid], 44 (22 Feb. 2002). Print.

Ngũgĩ wa Thiong'o. *Caitaani mũtharaba-Inĩ.* Nairobi: Heinemann, 1980. Print.

—. *Devil on the Cross.* London: Heinemann, 1982. Print.

—. *El Diablo en la cruz.* Tafalla: Txalaparta, 1994. Print.

Orzech, Charles D. 'Metaphor, Translation, and the Construction if Kingship in *The Scripture for Human Kings* and the *Mâhâmâyûrî vidyârâjnî sutra*'. *Cahiers d'Extrème-Asie* 13 (2002–3): 55–83. Print.

Polybius. *Histoire Générale: Traduction nouvelle [. . .] par Félix Bouchot.* Paris: Charpentier, 1847. Print.

Pultar, Gönül. 'The Mad Nomad: Interview with Talât Sait Halman'. *JAST: Journal of American Studies of Turkey* 5 (1997): 43–58. Print.

Ramis, Josep Miquel. *Sebastià Juan Arbó, autotraductor: De* Terres de l'Ebre *(1932) a* Tierras del Ebro *(1940).* PhD Diss., U Pompeu Fabra, 2008. Print.

Reid, Alastair. 'What Gets Lost / Lo que se pierde'. *Delos: A Journal on & of Translation* [Austin, Texas] 1 (1968.): 5. Reprinted in: *An Alastair Reid Reader: Selected Prose and Poetry.* Hanover, NH: U P of New England, 1994. 221. Print.

Sáenz, Miguel. 'Autor y traductor'. *Senez* 14 (1993): 103–18. Print.

Santoyo, J. C. 'Rabindranath Tagore: Memorias de un autotraductor arrepentido'. *A World of English, A World of Translation: Estudios Interdisciplinares sobre Traducción y Lengua Inglesa.* Eds. F. J. Díaz Pérez and A. M. Ortega Cebreros. Jaén: Universidad de Jaén, 2004. 155–91. Print.

—. 'La autotraducción intratextual'. *Aproximaciones a la autotraducción.* Xosé Manuel Dasilva and Helena Tanqueiro, eds. Vigo: Editorial Academia del Hispanismo, 2011. Print.

Snell-Hornby, Mary. *Translation Studies: An Integrated Approach.* Amsterdam and Philadelphia: John Benjamins, 1988. Print.

Tytler, Alexander F. *Essay on the Principles of Translation.* Edinburgh: T. Cadell and W. Creech, 1791. Print.

Villanueva, Tino, ed. *Chicanos: Antología histórica y literaria.* Mexico: Fondo de Cultura Económica, 1980. Print.

Wechsler, Robert. *Performing without a Stage: The Art of Literary Translation.* North Haven, CT: Catbird Press, 1998. 213–16. Print.

Young, Howard T. 'The Invention of the Andalusian Tagore'. *Comparative Literature* 47.1 (1995): 42–52. Print.

Zabaleta, Josu. 'La fonction de la traduction en langue basque'. *Translatio: Nouvelles de la FIT* XIII.1–2 (1994): 45. Print.

CHAPTER THREE

History and the self-translator

Jan Hokenson

Abstract: Are there common historical drives that have impelled writers into self-translation through the centuries? Historical pressures and forces seem to arise not only from the macro-level, social realm that often produces standard translators and second-language writers, insofar as self-translators are certainly driven into the second language by similar (often political) circumstances. Historical drives originate also, indeed chiefly from common micro-level, private and especially literary ambitions of a uniquely dual nature, in a perceived juncture of certain cultural or canonical conditions that enable the self-translator to innovate in the mimetic traditions in both languages to create an original oeuvre. Selected cases exemplify the practice as a pattern.

In 1984 Antoine Berman argued that the most urgent task for a genuinely modern theory of translation is a comprehensive history of translation (12). Here in the early years of the following century, as Piotr Kuhiwczak said in his introductory essay on Translation Studies in 2007, 'we might well be entering a period of gestation in which the discipline seeks a new understanding of itself by turning to history: be this its history as a discipline, the history of theories of translation, the role that translation has played in book and publishing history, or a social-cultural history of the translator' (5). By now many scholars have been pursuing each of those avenues in fruitful ways, in different combinations of languages. As I noted in *The Bilingual Text* (x), and as this volume attests, even the phenomenon of self-translation is gaining attention from historically minded scholars who can place the self-translator in his or her specific historical milieu, bringing social and political contexts to the bilingual text.

That broad rubric of 'turning to history', however, produces new questions. Are there identifiable constants linking those pursuits – can we get beyond individual self-translators and their publishers, theoreticians, even specific historical periods, in order to develop a panoptic view of whatever historical forces might drive or at least impel the phenomenon of self-translation through different moments of time and place? Are there such historical forces? Or drives? Or currents? If there are, how do we discern and identify them? If not, if the long history of self-translation seems more like a saltatory course of successive scriveners than a recurrent set of motives, what does that kind of randomness in turn imply?

After years of studying their history, it seems to me that self-translations can arise from the same sorts of socioeconomic conditions (such as exile or immigration) that have long prompted secondary translators to market their bilingual skills in a new land. If we look closely at self-translators as a group, however, as a subset of standard commercial translators as well as bilingual writers immigrating into a new literary language, it becomes apparent that across their different periods, languages and cultures, self-translators – as a group – have been largely motivated by certain private, artistic and literary ambitions of a uniquely dual nature.

The historical drives impelling or characterizing those ambitions are often a function of the degree to which canonical writers and genres reigning in one of the self-translator's literatures remain unknown in the other; that is, at some points in these bilingual writers' lives there is a perceived juncture of certain intercultural conditions which the practice of self-translation can serve or even exploit in highly creative ways. Bilingual writers as self-translators in dual discourse can infuse one literature with new materials from the other, using one to innovate in the other, and then reverse the process, thereby enriching and challenging the dominant in both. One way to evade, to supplant with a foreign rival, to challenge or (in some cases) to gleefully triumph over one's chief predecessors in either literature, is to create an original work in two versions that imports new discoveries into the old literatures or artistic forms, in two directions. The impetus is often the historic circumstance of a particular canon or a genre (along with the personal circumstances of foreign travel, exile, immigration, etc.). But in each case, and increasingly since the early modern period, the bilingual writer seems to begin self-translating as a means of exploring the relations between two literatures as a new source of original production. Equilibrating two sign systems freighted with different cultures enables the writer to pursue unfamiliar kinds of literary experiments. To my knowledge, from medievals to moderns, all literary self-translators in Europe and the Americas have seemed keenly aware of what we might call the mimetic boon of biculturality. As Tom Conley noted in another context, Joachim Du Bellay, 'one of the great bilingual writers and masters of Latin and French', 'exploited translation for the sake of rethinking the art of imitation' (11). At certain historical and intercultural junctures, such as Du Bellay's moment in the descent of Latin into vernaculars, or Ungaretti's battlefield conjunction of French symbolism and Italian modernism, certain bilingual writers seem to make a kind of absolute left turn into self-translation as their unique artistic means to rethink the legacies of mimesis as those obtain in both languages – indeed eventually to rework them into a new amalgam.

To test even that vague hypothesis would require an opus of encyclopedic detail. But I hope the following sketch will at least open the matter for discussion.

Differentiating self-translators as a group

The historical 'drive' metaphor is wobbly because it marks a problem of description. The discipline of Translation Studies is too new to have encoded its historical assumptions in the kind of bedrock on which most disciplines' historians and theoreticians ground their categories of analysis. Our foundations are still fluid. Our understanding of the global history of translated texts is still nascent and exploratory. Indeed one could argue that our most important contribution to the general study of history has been to deconstruct some of its more venerable presumptions – such as the textbook cliché that medieval elites were almost uniformly Latin-vernacular bilinguals or that Queen Victoria fairly incarnates imperial monolingualism. It is no small matter to have cleared such decks, showing the complexity of different Latins in the long Middle Ages or the social effects of the Queen's native German. Scholars in Translation Studies have already gone considerable distance in correcting the historical record, in national histories and period concepts. For Translation Studies has produced some extraordinarily deft and discerning period histories, from medieval to post-colonial. Such studies as Rita Copeland's *Rhetoric, Hermeneutics, and Translation in the Middle Ages,* or Antoine Berman's *Experience of the Foreign* on the Romantic era in Germany, are the true spadework for any foundation for this historical turn, and for the discipline itself in its historical dimension.

The construction of a panoptic view of the self-translator in the full sweep of history has to begin with sections, in this case the periods of history. Yet our histories have so far tended to be tailored to a theory of translation, assembling copious and often useful detail in service to a particularist view of what they purport to elucidate. That is a harsh and oversimplified take on the matter, abbreviated for the sake of space here. But few scholars of Translation Studies would disagree that our major foundation texts in comprehensive history, from such scholars as Steiner, Ballard, Vermeer, Venuti, from *After Babel* to *The Translator's Invisibility,* have adjusted their lenses to suit their view of history. As Santoyo put it in 2006, 'the reader cannot help thinking he or she is being presented with a distorted image of the translation panorama through the centuries' (12).

We all have our lenses, to be sure, and a young discipline needs multiple points of view. But, partly for such reasons, as an object of description, the historical figure of the self-translator seems ideally suited to help elude the snares of preconceptions by trying to focus on biographical data: Why did X self-translate? How do X's motives relate to Y's? How does the historical moment affect the motive? Can we discern any effects of those motives in their bilingual texts themselves? Only after reviewing case histories can we presume to diagram (or to x-ray history, in Proust's metaphor) the historical drives impelling self-translation through different times and places. The sequence of analysis would seem to lead from individual self-translators, then period clusters of them, then national, continental, hemispheric and global patterns. To begin with individual self-translators rather than period profiles is also a helpful way to sidestep the extraneous aspects of period contexts or, as Bandia puts it, to undo the often deceptive linearity of history.

A preliminary step is to recall some of the constants that general translation histories typically stress. First, we know for example that an immense amount of translative activity accompanies the founding of new political states. Cicero in the Roman Republic, the Pléiade in Paris, the Tudor translators in London, the Meiji translators in Tokyo, the young German Romantics, more recently the young Turks, all called overtly for theft: steal from the most prestigious foreign texts to enrich and modernize the native language. (See for example the encomiums on translation by Cicero, Dolet, Du Bellay, Schleiermacher.) As a result, as both Marc Bizer and J. W. Binns have shown with respect to Renaissance Latin-vernacular poetry for instance, or Sehnaz Tahir Gürçağlar on modern Turkish translators, their own translations are thus often densely layered sites of conflict and displacement, where national traditions and their tropes jostle uneasily against one another in discernible ways.

Second, royal patronage systems, like modern publishers' commissions, have similarly commanded vast amounts of translation. Post-colonial hybridities often replicate the language hierarchies and the power relations of earlier courts and urban centers, as in their different ways both John Adams and Leonard Forster on court societies and Edouard Glissant and Paul Bandia on post-colonial societies, have ably shown. Kings and popes, like colonial administrators and modern mega-publishers, have both nurtured and manipulated much of the world's translations. It has become something of a subset of Translation Studies to critique the political pressures and constraints embedded in the lexical interstices of such texts.

Third, exile is another leitmotif in general translation history, though still somewhat neglected as a parameter or general rubric. As one can learn from period histories, Huguenots in London, Spanish Jews in Venice, British refugees at the French Court in Versailles, tides of immigrants displaced to the New World by wars and pogroms, often put their language skills to work in translating their national texts into the literary and commercial contexts of the new land, for sheer survival. Such scholars as Anthony Pym on the Spain-Italy dialogue or Massimiliano Morini on Tudor translators, have detailed how, when migrating in sufficient numbers, they often changed the local literature (such as Italian), if not also the language (such as English), by such multiple injections of new modes and vocabularies. Those who managed to return home again in the next political generation (such as French refugees returning from New York in 1946), often did the same in reverse. One of the more fascinating branches of translation history today is the study of what they chose to translate and how the circumstances of exile impact their texts.

Fourth, religious reform movements and foreign proselytizing also figure prominently in translation chronicles. This is a more complex trope in our histories insofar as it entails admixtures of personal belief and/or institutional dicta, often indistinguishable. Yet it is pervasive even today. Missionary translators in Africa or the Americas, who used local interpreters to appropriate native rites and customs into evangelical translations, like modern televangelists on video-streaming in Moscow or Taipei, cast old foreign beliefs in new native dress, not unlike Luther appropriating the authority of Rome. Such scholars as Eugene Nida have tracked the history of Bible translations, others the translations of Buddhist sutras in China and later Japan, and in such texts we can see some deep tensions between orthodox and heterodox tones and conventions.

Other spurs or motives, as documented by period and regional historians, include the magnetic influence of a major patron of translation (as in the massive productions by teams of translators in ancient Alexandria or medieval courts), the comparable influence of a major text that circulates widely and invites successive retranslations (such as texts by Homer, Shakespeare, Murasaki), and the equally comparable influence of a transcontinental ideology like humanism or communism that entails a prized canon of texts to be adapted to local dialects and even pidgins. Glyn Norton's study of the spread of humanism, for example, tracks all three of these translative motives through Renaissance France, and most translation histories trace the effects (political, literary, economic) of such admixtures of patronage, canon and ideology or cultural moment.

Arising chiefly in period studies, all these rubrics are by now so commonplace in general translation criticism that there is no need to elaborate them here. The point is rather that we already possess a certain loose view of translation history against which we can try to sketch an historical profile of self-translators, as a subgroup of these general kinds of historical events or conditions. It remains to be seen whether the self-translator does enact these drives in translating, or pursues different trajectories.

Self-translators have not usually shared these motives, or participated in these historical endeavors through the centuries. Or they do so a bit differently, I would say, and their bilingual texts, while often serving such larger agendas, tend to spring directly from more personal and immediate motives, some unique but most largely shared among them. General histories of translation that stress exile, for instance, are usually not concerned with ongoing language change in the homeland, which inflects a great deal of exiled self-translators' concerns in bilingual work.

The second step, then, is to isolate the self-translator from these larger historical categories that have been seen to govern or elicit most second-hand translation and most bilingual writers' switch to a different language. We need to situate the self-translator as a singular figure in the historical interchanges between languages and between social milieus, in part by looking not only at the *what* and *how* of their work but also at *why* the translative practice was undertaken in the first place. Motive is not a common rubric in Translation Studies, even in the case of more recent lives documented in biographies. That lacuna is probably a legacy of the formalist and structuralist decades of the text dominant. Yet it is a loss, eliding an important constituent of translation history. If common or mutual drives to self-translate are identified, then a taxonomy of self-translators will be the richer for it.

Typically, when trying to abbreviate the complex interrelations of two domains, as in this endeavor to situate individual self-translators within the historical currents encircling them, contemporary scholars tend to use hyphens. We refer easily to the 'the social-cultural context' of writers, publishers, even periods, by way of suggesting overlap and mutuality, without pausing to clarify the relation. In his important book *The Theory of Social and Cultural Selection*, however, W. G. Runciman argues that that particular hyphen confuses what are really two unique and distinct realms, different in kind. The social entails the institutional forces which, on a macro-level, are imposed on an individual; they are impersonal, non-negotiable and can be coerced but are usually inherited unwittingly, such as government policies and requirements, or religion and education, or banking laws and the rise and fall of financial markets. Those are the 'forces', Runciman says, that historians usually use to explain peoples' behavior, whereas their individual motivation might be quite different – singular, incommensurate or defiant. The cultural entails those other more personal, micro-level forces that also shape behavior. As a Cambridge sociologist he is interested in whether there are ongoing causal chains by means of which social and cultural units circulate, shaping human evolution.

To look at self-translators' activity as thus dually shaped by macro – as well as micro – forces that have impelled them to create bilingual texts is a helpful perspective. Although it might seem a bit late in Translation Studies to redefine the term 'cultural' as Runciman would have it, he is echoing psychological anthropologists who locate cultural meaning in a similar split, in the interaction of two sorts of relatively stable structures, what Strauss and Quinn, for example, call extrapersonal, world structures and intrapersonal, mental structures (mental frameworks, understandings, assumptions) acquired by personal experiences (6; cf. Hannerz 192–4). For the moment one can simply use 'personal' to demarcate the individual – often psychological and artistic – domain of self-translating writers' motivations. In their case certainly, the macro-level of public behavior has often concealed private ideas and motivations that differ from those of the standard translators and immigrant writers of their era. Indeed as we will see, micro-level forces seem to be more common in their lives and more detectable in their texts.

Before turning to specific cases of self-translation, please note that the springs of art are notoriously difficult to define, and literary self-translators are all artists of language who undertake to recreate fictions as artwork in a second language. But with that caveat, one can at least begin to disentangle macro- and micro-levels of origin. Note also that the following cameos of specific writers abbreviate the extensive case histories in *The Bilingual Text*), which readers may consult for more detailed historical and biographical backgrounds to these self-translators and their positions in translation history.

Towards a history of self-translators

To the seventeenth-century Mexican poet and nun Sor Juana Inés de la Cruz, Latin-vernacular self-translation provided two different semantic fields for exploring her quite personal, almost heretical thematics of woman's place in Catholic theology. Although most of her correspondence was destroyed, it is clear from contemporaries' reports that she shunned the subservience of women in domestic life and entered the convent both because her faith was strong and because it was there that she could enjoy 'the freedom of my studies' (qtd. in Schons 45; see Paz 102) in the new sciences. Caught in a quarrel between rival Church officials, she indirectly attacked the new Bishop of Puebla (who held that if a women walked on the bricks in his hallway, the bricks must be removed) on behalf of her sex and her own literary writings, in baroque poetry and drama. Putting her Latin texts into Spanish allowed her to bend familiar Church Latin tropes to new Hispanic and new gender contexts, which she clearly relished. Under severe persecution, translating in both highly patriarchal regimens of Catholic Rome and Colonial New Spain, and in both directions, Sor Juana began in baroque conventions but developed a personal poetics of the feminine. She never lived in Spain (though her books were published there) but read copiously in Spanish literature and drama. She offended Church officials in Latin by gendering orthodox theological figures, just as in her Spanish texts she directly addressed the Hispanic social legacies of her own milieu, most particularly – as an outsider female of illegitimate birth – the institution of *onra*, or honor devolving upon high-born Colonial males and their women. Also, in her Latin texts melding pagan mythological with Christian references, she explicitly elevated women to divine status and, most notably, herself into the Latin literary pantheon. She positioned herself as the Virgil of New Spain. There is little doubt that in defiance of social forces constraining her, she felt impelled by personal pride, and probably no little anger, to self-translate for a second local, even more restrictive audience and thereby redouble the force of her claim that women inhabit equally the same realm as men (see Merrim 24–7). Self-translation allowed her to go beyond convent walls to engage her struggle with the second audience, in its own terms. Note that those terms include familiarity with the canonical writers of both literatures.

At the same micro-level, something similar occurs in the twentieth-century texts of Giuseppe Ungaretti, who self-translated literally in the trenches of the First World War, between Italian and French. Also a troubled Catholic, as Ossola has shown, he experienced his whole generation as a dispossession – a loss of faith and belief, and of literary tradition. With all certainties shattered, he thought he had to begin his poetry at zero, in the debris of inherited forms and voices. Until 1922 he could not decide on which language to use as a poet. Born in Alexandria of Italian parents, he had never lived in Italy or France at all, but he closely studied both languages and their literatures, finally moving to Paris for university study. Both Vegliante and Picon detail how, in war, moving between his languages as poet-translator, he devised a kind of pseudo-Mallarméan poetics in French and, striving to displace the shopworn Leopardi, he used those texts to inaugurate an original stanzaic form and strangely empty, hollow voice for his self-translations in Italian. To Ungaretti the quite personal experience of the bombings and bloody bandages of war drove him to develop a thematics of innocence, and in formal terms what he called his 'evocazione pure' ('Memoria d'Ofelia d'Alba', *Vita* 160) – like a French architect's *épure* – of stripped-down forms often in thin columns on the Italian page. His protest against the social machinery of war was less thematic than Sor Juana's, more formalist in its expression, but no less personally derived and pointed. His subtextual competitions with Mallarmé and Leopardi, like Sor Juana's with Virgil, resonate throughout his bilingual texts. Carlo Ossola calls his poetry from this period 'a constant linguistic to-and-fro' (27) between versions of his texts. As he translated and retranslated his war work, self-translation in Italian ultimately allowed him to escape the burden of Mallarmé's formal legacy in French poetics, and to use his French discoveries in pioneering in Italian. In both languages his texts sketch what he termed 'the metaphysical tragedy' of rootlessness in his time (qtd. in Cary 143). He believed that the writer had to assume his freedom from moribund traditions in an act of decisive aesthetic liberty ('una libertà estetica decisiva', *Vita* lxxvii), when left with only silence and a few bare, common words. Those he overtly manipulates on the page: he splays the French horizontally, and he stacks the Italian vertically, for comparable effects of unprecedentedly stark simplicity, shocking in each language and its attendant poetics.

Many male writers have experienced war, and many women writers oppression. Few undertake to transpose their accounts into a second language. In these two cases, we see writers volubly suffering under coercive social regimes, systematic constraints that are not personal, that is, not bound by local events, but institutional. The macro-institutions of repressive patriarchy and Great Power rivalries are also multilingual, spanning nations and continents. While they are by no means political poets in the common understanding of that term, Sor Juana and Ungaretti both develop their (quite different) contestatory poetics in one language and then develop new refinements, tonalities and figures in the second language, for a new audience which has a different sense of the traditions they are assailing and which needs to be addressed in different ways. They could leave the matter to translators but the results would be dim: only they can inject the Latin themes with the Spanish subtext of *onra* and set the French forms into an unprecedented formal spine in Italian, something standard translators would be loath to do. The bilingual text furthers their personal aims, as existants and as artists. In both cases, there is no mistaking the crystalline voice of these poets through their different languages, echoing and reechoing their experience of two social domains similarly flawed. Also, both writers gird their bilingual texts on a unique interfusion of canonical figures (names, styles, genres) in the two languages.

The eighteenth-century Italian dramatist Carlo Goldoni might seem to be a different type of self-translator, fired by sheer ambition to excel on the stage in two languages. Leaving Venice for Paris in 1762, a great admirer of Italian *commedia dell'arte* (although it was in decline as a comic genre), he became an official dramatist for a new Paris theater merging troupes from the famed Comédie Italienne, which had staged *commedia*-inspired plays in Italian (with Italian actors), and the French-language Opéra-Comique (with French actors). He was competitive. He was inspired by patriotic fervour for his nation and his language yet he knew that he must succeed in French to be awarded the laureates of a Paris playwright, and indeed he became one of the most famous bilingual playwrights in Europe. Initially, overwhelmed by a Molière performance in Paris, he set himself two ideals: 'either to be able to compose pieces for French actors, or to see my countrymen capable of imitating them. Which would be the most difficult to realize?' (369). In the end, through bilingual work, he managed both. Taking up the cudgels for the Italian actors (believing their honor to be at stake), he trained them to be less improvisatory (less *commedia* and more Molière or 'bourgeois' blending of farce and middle-class domestic comedy) and to be as well-rehearsed as their French counterparts. He soon wrote plays in French, explicitly for French actors and for those audiences who could not understand Italian. On the model of Molière, all his bourgeois plays in both languages are laced with farce and *commedia* hijinks, ending happily. Like most of his contemporaries, he saw French as a universal language, the 'home' of the educated elite of Europe, and indeed this charming Venetian moved rather quickly into the inner circles of the French court and intelligentsia.

Like Beckett and Nabokov two centuries later, Goldoni was appalled at a bungled translation of his work and he thereafter self-translated at least one major French play into Italian. Even in the age of *les belles infidèles*, his two versions struck critics as incommensurable. But Goldoni dismissed critics of his bilingual text by insisting that he was free to change whatever necessary in order to transpose the French material to fit 'the taste and customs of my nation' (257): 'to give us a knowledge of the literature of another country, the thoughts, imagery, and erudition must be transferred; but then the phrases and style must be adapted to the taste of the nation into whose language the translation is made' (396). Calques are 'insipid', he said, but 'I as the author of my own work' can sidestep the literal sense to fit the text to my other audience (257). He strenuously insisted that, if he wrote a text in French, 'it has the stamp of its origin in the thoughts, in the imagery, in the manner, and in the style' (417), all of which he brings into Italian in reworking these French components for Italian spectators in the theater.

Goldoni's bilingual work seems a fairly obvious function of the macro-level language politics of Europe in the age of Louis XIV, and of the theater in particular. Just as Sor Juana could not really be a Catholic poet then without writing in Latin, so Goldoni could not realize his ambition to conquer the European stage without working in Paris and writing in French. Beyond language emigration, however, is there also a discernible micro-level of forces impelling Goldoni further into self-translation? In the plays as in his memoirs, one discerns a deeply personal sense of rivalry with Molière, and Goldoni in his memoirs overtly admires the brilliant ways in which Molière had adapted *commedia* comic techniques to his French themes; certainly his own Molièresque subtexts are far more free or unconstrained in the Italian self-translation. Even though Italy was still a loose configuration of states, and though he himself spoofed Venetian and Tuscan dialects, powerful forces of national pride drove Goldoni towards bilingual production (and theater direction). Then his often extravagant efforts to display his own skills, as perfected in French, led him to suspect (or so he hints) that he could redouble his glory in two languages (see Colombani-Giaufret), by adapting his French discoveries to Italian poetics or dramatic conventions. His first English biographer reported that, while writing, Goldoni was known to mutter, 'good, but not yet Molière', and that Casanova described him to Voltaire as the legendary 'Molière of Italy' (Chatfield-Taylor 203). We should note the biographer's regrets: 'Indeed, that very sobriquet, "the Molière of Italy," has sorely blinded non-Italian eyes to his originality, his ultimate naturalism being peculiarly his own' (ix). When viewed as usual from only one of the two systems of poetics, the text's translingual originality dims. To view it stereoscopically, however, reveals how Goldoni and other self-translators uniquely web aspects of each in original work; it also enhances the striking creativity which characterizes each version.

Similar motives seem to underlie the immense bilingual oeuvre of Vladimir Nabokov. Because his case is so familiar, we need recall only a few points here. In a different era, the macro-level, social forces impelling him are of course distinctive, in his case the Russian revolution that forced him into exile, the twentieth-century American university as a wartime refuge for foreigners, and the international mega-success of his novel *Lolita*. After a botched commercial translation in London, he began translating his Russian texts into English, before adopting English as his literary language in 1938 and settling in the United States. He felt that the Russian language was the only thing that he had salvaged from his home country, and he believed that he was forced to abandon it (*Speak, Memory* 265). Although he feared that he might never bring his American English up to the level of his Russian, he strove to become an American writer, while taking jobs teaching Russian literature in translation, thus continuing to work in both languages. He felt intense loyalty to his Russian forbears (chiefly Pushkin and Lermontov) and an increasing rivalry with canonical English-language writers (especially James Joyce, and especially after he was called a 'wordsmith in the lineage of Joyce'; see his *Strong Opinions*, and Grayson 193). Wealth, upon the publication of *Lolita* in 1955, freed him from both the institution of the American university and from the United States, allowing him to indulge his desires – to construct intricate fictions laced with bilingual puns, to live in voluntary exile in Switzerland, and to resume his native language, as a self-translator of his recent English work into Russian.

Language nostalgia plays a great part in Nabokov's work, as in Goldoni's, but it is complex. All his texts feature polyglot characters and multilingual puns, pastiches, and code-switching, in which he overtly displays his skills as a dazzling wordsmith and master of the stylistic arabesque, in layer upon layer of reference and phonic play. The polylinguistic matrix of his work developed first in Russian (at university he translated *Alice in Wonderland* into a Russian version laced with pastiches of Pushkin and Lermontov, as Weaver has shown), then thickened a hundredfold in English, and then became through self-translations an increasingly intricate admixture of English and Russian echoes and references. Grayson and Beaujour have detailed the interaction of Nabokov's languages, and Rosengrant shows how Nabokov changes in translation the lexical terms, their meanings and their references while retaining the same principles of stylistic organization that are unique to his particular set of languages, canonical interests and artistic aims in prose. The young Nabokov who relished parody and pastiche as a novice writer at Cambridge became the master of 'the parodic character' of whole texts which can attain – often unbeknownst to the monolingual reader – a Russian tone, trace or 'emotional evocativeness' in English and vice versa (Rowe 21). It was as a self-translator that Nabokov most embellished: in either direction the translated texts are more sumptuous linguistic productions, cross-referencing his literary icons and shadings or cultural echoes in ever more complicated ways, many so subtle that the monocultural reader cannot detect the second aesthetic field being evoked.

As a two-way English-Russian self-translator, Nabokov's fervent patriotism entails not *patria*, like Goldoni's, but *lingua*, the grand linguistic territory of Lermontov and Pushkin. Yet, on a micro-level the two self-translators share common personal motives. Writing far from their homelands, both approached the second social domain like a battlefield, emulating the local stars and working hard to sweep the field. We should note that 'homeland' is never a static entity, of course, and that in this case 'Russian' and 'Italian' were not monolithic blocs but dynamic polyvocalities from which, for their part, Nabokov felt he had inherited the full European legacy of the Saint Petersburg nobility and Goldoni the vast comic repertoires of the itinerant theater troupes of Venice and Naples. Their translated texts are amalgams of the maternal social milieu (of the *commedia*, of Pushkin) and the new social traditions they strove to master. Though separated in time and cultures, the two writers were intensely conscious of both their literary legacy in the maternal language and of their new language's canon and audience's demands, and both were wary of missteps in what Nabokov called the magic act ('frac-tails flying', Afterward 307) of writing and translating for Americans. As Nabokov subtly insinuated in the final line of the Afterword, every writer tries to transcend the heritage of the language into which he was born – and the new one in which he writes – in his own way.

No standard translator worries about being as good as Molière or Joyce. The comparison does not obtain because the governing relation is that of the translator to the original author. Clearly, as all bilingual immigrant writers discover, to write a text in any language necessarily evokes, however faintly, at least some literary backgrounds of that language's history. Though overt rivalry with the local pantheon is rare among standard immigrant authors, however, self-translators as a group seem acutely conscious of writing in the language of venerable predecessors in *both* languages, those predecessors who established the dominant stylistic conventions in and against which they feel they must work, to create an original oeuvre.

Differentiating self-translators from second-language writers

Are the second-language versions of self-translators any different from the texts of typical immigrant writers who leave home and adopt a new literary language? Many critical studies of such writers' accounts or 'language memoirs' conclude that, like most bilinguals, immigrant authors hold their two languages in a binary relationship, because, as Miletic puts it, 'in essence they are moving away from their original culture towards the [new] language and culture which they embrace' (1). Such scholars track degrees of loss, whereas others stress gain. Mary Besemeres in *Translating Oneself* studies writers who have relocated into English and metaphorically 'translate' themselves by developing a bicultural self in a new land; following Genesee's categories, she finds that most suffer 'subtractive bilingualism' (162, 208) wherein the second language displaces the first and becomes the writing language. There is a great deal of disagreement among linguists and critics about this process and its directions, however, and indeed five years later Besemeres as editor of Australian language memoirs finds the opposite, that is, more 'additive' than subtractive experience by bilinguals, insofar as 'hybrids' have a rich range of experiences and values that monolinguals cannot share (*Translating Lives* xviii–xix). To avoid such quantification, in 2003 Georges Lüdi and Bernard Py called for replacing such emotive terms with simple degrees of 'multilingual' or 'polylectal' competence (referring to ideolect, sociolect, etc.). But the terminological confusion reflects deeper assumptions about bilinguality and translation (see my discussion of these issues in American immigrant writings, 'Intercultural Autobiography' 91–101). Historically, until around 2000, many scholars on immigrant bilingual writers, such as Courtivron, Lesser or Pérez-Firmat, subscribed to the loosely German Romantic paradigm whereby loss of the maternal language threatens identity and creativity, whereas many more recent studies tend to stress enrichment and adventure in the experience of bilinguality, and the overlap of the two languages, as in the compilations by Felici, Kroh or Kellman. The gradual shift of focus seems to be partly due to discoveries in neuro-linguistics, partly the product of closer attention by cultural-studies scholars to hybrid production, partly to the changes in attitude of contemporary bilinguals themselves towards their languages. Amid much overlap in their work, most scholars of emigré writings would probably agree that the horizon of the second-language writer's work is chiefly the new audience, not the old.

For such reasons, the rule of thumb obtains (and concerns not themes, of course, but only canons): bilingual writers who do *not* practice self-translation, those who immigrate into a second language and adopt it as their literary medium, tend to downplay the literary traditions of their homeland, as they become primarily focused on new materials and audience. In *European Immigration into the French Language*, for example, Miletic reviews the work of five loosely contemporary writers who came from abroad to settle in France, thereafter writing in French. She finds that despite different personal experiences and aesthetics, they all sought to build a literary identity and legitimacy in the new language and country of residence. They adopt French as their literary language 'for the specific and powerful ways in which it validates their European identity' (1), and their artistic choices too become a function of recreating themselves as Franco-Europeans entering and addressing the contemporary literary scene of Paris.

By contrast, all through social history, self-translators seem instead to juggle or equilibrate both the old and new literary languages and legacies at once, and usually together in frequent interliterary reference, in texts in either language. The sheer act of self-translating is an opening out onto both languages, rather than a binary tension or foreclosure.

This is not to suggest that immigrants do not often write about their homelands – such exotica has often been their subject, as well as their passport into royal courts and publishing houses – but only to stress that their new texts rarely any longer challenge the old legacy of the poetics and the canonical pantheon of the first language. Even those who continue writing about their homelands in the new tongue recognize that they are addressing a different audience in a discourse that must be tailored to them first of all. As Ha Jin says in 'Exiled to English', he took the path of Conrad and Nabokov when he decided to write only in English, 'to write in a language that was not my own' (31), because under its censorship he had no readers in China. Those two authors are not his literary models, far from it, but rather his acknowledged predecessors in turning away from his maternal tongue towards a quite different set of readers. (He is referring to Nabokov's legendary 'abandonment' of Soviet-era Russian; his own motive for not writing in Chinese is nuanced in his remark that 'I was also aware that I was forgoing an opportunity: the Chinese language had been so polluted by revolutionary movements and political jargon that there was great room for improvement', 31). Ha Jin typifies this particular posture of immigrant authors towards the lost or abandoned literary language. Self-translators by contrast, even Nabokov after 1955, tend to seize that opportunity, thriving in the overlap of their languages and continuing to address both audiences in their own languages.

To pursue the matter of self-translators' dual literary legacies for a moment, consider the late medieval, early Renaissance bilingual poet Charles d'Orléans. Grandson of a French king, he was taken prisoner by the English at Agincourt and held captive at the English court for 25 years (1415–40). There he wrote and self-translated lyric poetry in French and English versions, and his French texts circulated widely in France. As Coldiron notes, in his time the lyric genres were rigidly defined and codified with formal expectations, although those were quite different in the two languages. Charles conjoined them in extraordinarily original ways. His translated texts in either language interweave elements of the esteemed French *fin amor* tradition with the dominant English romance tradition as instantiated by Chaucer. Indeed Chaucer seems to haunt much of Charles' work even more than do the medieval *fin amor* poets (see Goodrich 42–8), yet they are indissociable in his texts in both languages. As detailed in *The Bilingual Text*, Charles' overt invocation of literary generics shows how he is deliberately positioning his text in the aesthetic field of the second language, through common stylistic properties in his French and English versions. As in Goldoni's interfusions of Italian *commedia* modes with French Molièresque ones, Charles' texts are amalgams of two literary legacies, which he seeks both to master and to conjoin in unprecedented ways. It is probably the fact that he succeeded so well that marks him, in literary histories, as more a modern Renaissance than a late medieval poet (Coldiron 183).

At the macro-level of social conditions in his time, Charles was impelled to self-translate because, on the one hand, as a poet in political captivity he felt driven into English; although he declined to relinquish his native language, he was required to adopt English for the royal audience (see Arn, '*Fortunes Stabilnes*'). But on the other hand, at the micro-level of personal choice and private artistic aims, his solution to such exile was to replicate the overlap of his languages in bilingual poetry. This is not a simple matter of transposing one text into the other language, but rather of transforming both sets of lyric genres by importing canonical materials from one language tradition into the other, gradually devising his own mode of mimetic biculturality in Anglo-French poetics.

Thus, in terms of the two languages and literatures, the subject position of the self-translating poet is not a serial function of the particular language in use, but rather transcendent and stereoscopic. I would argue that of course bilingual writers too seek 'to build a literary identity and legitimacy' in the social domain of the second language, like all literary exiles and transplants. Exilic texts that have been self-translated, however, seem to be more consciously crafted to occupy a dual position, as one original creation in both languages. Indeed by self-translating they often forego the probably easier option of getting known by only one set of readers. Very few readers or critics have ever read them in both languages, and to sustain self-translation as a literary practice requires powerful personal motives, knowledge banks and skills.

That particular micro-current of literary politics, jousting with one's forebears and amalgamating their legacies, can also impel writers into different kinds of bilingual work. In two-way English-Spanish self-translations, Puerto-Rican novelist Rosario Ferré says that she bridges 'such diverging cultural matrices' (44) through differential styles. She positions her narrator as a channel between cultures, her reader as a foreigner, and her text as a kind of literary-political ambassador between peoples. Ferré has no particular canonical figures in view, in either language, but rather she holds in creative tension the more general, broader legacies of the two sets of novelistic conventions (Spanish baroque and American colloquial, each with their long literary, philosophical and theological traditions). Is she the exception to the rule? Maybe more like a wrinkle in the pattern, insofar as she quite actively equilibrates both sets of poetics, while, like Nabokov, concealing each from the other.

The Irishman Samuel Beckett's bilingual texts also diverge somewhat from the pattern. He fled the literary heritage of English, finding even the 'Grammar and Style' in official English as 'irrelevant as a Victorian bathing suit' (171), and felt equally alien in the Proustian luxuriance of French. In wartime France he developed his aesthetics of impoverishment or 'insuperable indigence' (141), as he termed it, and claimed (in French) that for him as a foreigner 'in French it is easier to write without style' (qtd. in Gessner 32n), thus impoverishing himself still further as a writer. When he resumed writing in English he imported the same lean ironic style he had established in French. Expertly mocking both mimetic traditions, especially reigning dramatic and prose genres, Beckett stripped his texts of any obvious literary and philosophical allusions, leaving layers of covert ones in only faint traces of the European canon, like watermarks or ink washes. Where he overtly invoked the literary pantheon (Shakespeare, Dante, the Bible), puns and ironies ambiguate the aim, amid thematics of emptiness and loss.

Beckett exemplifies another strand of personal, micro-level artistic motives that a great many self-translators share. On the social level, Irish politics, self-exile and war clearly shaped his poetics. But more personally, like so many of his predecessors in this endeavor, while living abroad he used the second language as a kind of laboratory for creating original means (in French, but also drawing upon his Italian and German), and he then self-translated in order to bring those modes into the first language and literature, as he felt only he could. This kind of second-language literary, chiefly stylistic apprenticeship can be seen in Charles d'Orléans, Stefan George, Ungaretti and countless others. Thereafter, like such figures as Sor Juana, Nabokov, Julien Green, Rosario Ferré, for the rest of his life Beckett wrote dually and self-translated each language version. The stellar figures among self-translators succeeded: the resultant oeuvre is a singular crosscultural poetics in dual discourse.

Sum

The historical drives that impel authors into self-translation, then, seem to arise not only from the macro-level, social realm that often produces standard translators and second-language writers. For self-translators are certainly driven into the second language by similar events and (often political) circumstances. The historical drives towards self-translation originate also, if not chiefly, from micro-level, private and especially literary ambitions.

It might be objected that those micro-level, personal drives are notably historical forces too, insofar as a literary canon in any language is itself an historical artifact. Since that is true in one sense, we should stress that self-translators (as creative writers first and foremost) have a highly personal take on the canon, which is not primarily a social legacy but, to them, a dynamic personal inheritance and an artistic challenge.

Although noteworthy, such quibbles do not seem to me to change this composite profile of the self-translator as a writer fully conscious of what we might call the artistic advantage of mimetic bilinguality: the skill and the daring of wielding two literary languages and literary histories in his and her singular way. The springs of the text seem an admixture of occasion, the personal emotion the occasion produces in the writer (anger at gender inequality, wartime grief, etc., as we have seen), and a rare, striking ambition – not only to replicate the writer's own biculturality in the work, through self-translation, but also to situate the work with relation to the canonical figures, conventions and genres in both traditions. That aim can often produce overt interliterary reference, as in Goldoni or Nabokov, or amalgamated form, as in Charles d'Orléans or Ungaretti, or just percolate through the text as scattered, binocular allusion, as in Sor Juana and (her admirer) Beckett.

Is this simply a matter of tradition and the individual talent, or anxiety and influence? No. The historical drives that produce or characterize self-translation are not monocultural and are quite different from Eliot's or Bloom's sense of (usually monolingual) historical forces shaping writers' choices. If in general bilinguals tend to cast a rather cold eye on local traditions, self-translators in particular labour to construct texts in which we can often discern, stereoscopically, two social systems and their canons set into a unique relationship, inter-echoing. Thereafter, in its original modes, their bilingual text can then often seem to be flying free, in both languages, indebted but untethered to either canon.

We could probably detect this phenomenon, the self-translator's 'mimetic boon of biculturality', in hundreds of different writers in the West alone, from the Aramaic-Greek axis of Flavius Jospehus in the first century to the Danish-English of Isak Dinesen in the twentieth. (See the copious bibliography on self-translation at www.autotraduzione.com.) For example, Jacqueline Risset once noted that even when Joyce translated two passages from his *Work in Progress* into Italian, the self-translation was not a 'pursuit of hypothetical equivalents' but rather 'a kind of extension, a new stage, a more daring variation on the text in process' (Risset 6), opening the text out to the whole Italian system of phonic play and literary reference, which as we know also seeped back into the English in turn (see Ruggieri). The process is diverting for many bilinguals, who can practice it in short spurts, like Joyce, but it is foundational for the self-translators among them, who can make it the basis for an entire bilingual oeuvre.

In short, to my knowledge, most self-translators born before 1945 in Europe and the Americas have not participated in the macro-level historical currents that are known to have propelled translation activity. They have not served the founding of new political states. Instead of aiming singly to enrich the native language, they keep both the foreign and the domestic realms in equilibrium, working dually in both social domains. Nor has their self-translative work served to advance a religion among foreigners (despite John Donne's hilarious bilingual assaults on the Jesuits). Nor have they been impelled to self-translation in the service to a particular royal court or a particular publisher or administrative agent, since their bilingual production has entailed split allegiances, if any, and, certainly in the modern world, two publishers in two different capital cities.

Exile and war, on the other hand, since the Middle Ages, have indeed helped drive writers toward self-translation, though in myriad ways. Enforced exile like that of Charles d'Orléans, Nabokov or Green seems to have produced a bolder version of bilingual texts, more radically deploying the two literary traditions (or in Green's case the two languages on facing pages), than the voluntary exile of figures like Ungaretti, Beckett, Ferré, although such differences might be a function of their eras. Still, underlying even the macro-rubric of exile are a welter of private attitudes towards the homeland. What matters most, even in a sketchy topology like this one, is that exile has served to provoke self-translation among many different kinds of writers, each of whom thereby undertakes to remain in *active* relationship with the first literary language, its legacies and it readers.

There is no space here to track the effects of these self-translators' historic drives in the texts themselves, since that requires close comparative analysis (for the few writers mentioned above, see Hokenson and Munson, *The Bilingual Text*). The discipline of Translation Studies will gradually accrue such raw materials for more extensive histories.

The next step, then, is to unpack the monolithic terms for the various self-translators' historical periods: at each point in a lifetime, 'language' and 'literature' and 'tradition' are not static but multiply dynamic and complexly layered. What Hannerz calls 'the cultural flow' (4) of meaning at any moment entails the two loci of world and writer, in interaction. It is never easy to discern how those poles are bridged smoothly in any text, let alone a self-translation between cultures. But the effort will surely continue to help clarify the history of translation.

Works cited

Adams, James Noel. *Bilingualism and the Latin Language*. Cambridge: Cambridge UP, 2003. Print.

Arn, Mary-Jo, ed. *Charles d'Orléans in England (1415–1440)*. Cambridge: Boydell, 2000. Print.

—. 'Charles d'Orléans Translator?' *The Medieval Translator* 4. Eds Roger Ellis and Ruth Evans. Exeter: Exeter UP, 1994. 125–35. Print.

—. '*Fortunes Stabilnes*: The English Poems of Charles d'Orléans in Their English Context'. *Fifteenth-Century Studies* 7 (1983): 1–18. Print.

Ballard, Michel. *De Cicéron à Benjamin: Traducteurs, traductions, réflexions.* Lille: P U de Lille, 1992. Print.

Bandia, Paul. *Translation as Reparation: Writing and Translation in Postcolonial Africa.* Manchester: St. Jerome, 2008. Print.

—. 'The Impact of Postmodern Discourse on the History of Translation'. Bastin and Bandia. 45–58. Print.

Bastin, Georges L. and Paul Bandia, eds. *Charting the Future of Translation History.* Ottawa: U of Ottawa P, 2006. Print.

Beaujour, Elizabeth Klosty. *Alien Tongues: Bilingual Russian Writers of the 'First' Emigration.* Ithaca: Cornell UP, 1989. Print.

Beckett, Samuel. *Disjecta: Miscellaneous Writings and a Dramatic Fragment.* Ed. Ruby Cohn. London: Calder, 1983. Print.

Berman, Antoine. *L'Épreuve de l'étranger: culture et traduction dans l'Allemagne romantique.* Paris: Gallimard, 1984.

—. *The Experience of the Foreign: Culture and Translation in Romantic Germany.* Trans. S. Heyvaert. Albany: State U of New York P, 1992. Print.

Besemeres, Mary. *Translating Oneself: Language and Selfhood in Cross-Cultural Autobiography.* Bern: Peter Lang, 2002. Print.

Besemeres, Mary and Anna Wierzbicka, eds. *Introduction.* Besemeres and Wierzbicka iii–xxiv. Print.

—. *Translating Lives: Living with Two Languages and Cultures.* Brisbane: U of Queensland P, 2007. Print.

Binns, J. W. *Intellectual Culture in Elizabethan England: Latin Writings of the Age.* Leeds: Francis Cairns, 1990. Print.

Bizer, Marc. *La Poésie au miroir: imitation et conscience de soi dans la poésie latine de la Pléiade.* Paris: Champion, 1995. Print.

Bloom, Harold. *The Anxiety of Influence: A Theory of Poetry.* New York: Oxford UP, 1997. Print.

Cary, Joseph. *Three Modern Italian Poets: Saba, Ungaretti, Montale.* New York: New York UP, 1969. Print.

Chatfield-Taylor, Hobart C. *Goldoni: A Biography.* New York: Duffield, 1913. Print.

Cicero, Marcus Tullius. *De optimo genere oratorum/ The Best Kind of Orator.* Trans. H. M. Hubbell. *De Inventione, De optimo genere oratorum, Topica.* London: Heinemann, 1976. 354–72. Print.

Coldiron, Anne. *Canon, Period, and the Poetry of Charles d'Orléans: Found in Translation.* Ann Arbor: U of Michigan P, 2000. Print.

Colombani-Giaufret, Hélène. 'Goldoni écrivain français dans les *Mémoires*'. *Revue de littérature comparée* 67.3 1993 : 337–52. Print.

Conley, Tom. 'Translation "on the Line"'. *Profession 2010.* Ed. Rosemary G. Feal. New York: Modern Language Association, 2010. 9–17. Print.

Cope, Jackson. *Secret Sharers in Italian Comedy: From Machiavelli to Goldoni.* Durham: Duke UP, 1996. Print.

Copeland, Rita. *Rhetoric, Hermeneutics, and Translation in the Middle Ages: Academic Traditions and Vernacular Texts.* Cambridge: Cambridge UP, 1991. Print.

Courtivron, Isabelle de, ed. *Lives in Translation: Bilingual Writers on Identity and Creativity.* New York: Palgrave Macmillan, 2003. Print.

Dolet, Étienne. *La Manière de bien traduire d'une langue en aultre*. 1540. Dolet
    et al. *Quatre traités de grammaire*. Geneva: Slatkine, 1972. 11–16. *Critical
    Prefaces of the French Renaissance*. Ed. Bernard Weinberg. Evanston:
    Northwestern UP, 1950. 77–83. Print.
Du Bellay, Joachim. *La Deffence et illustration de la langue françoyse*. 1549. Eds
    Francis Goyet and Olivier Millet. Paris: Champion, 2003. Print.
Eliot, T. S. 'Tradition and the Individual Talent'. *The Sacred Wood and Major
    Early Essays*. New York: Dover, 1997. 27–33. Print.
Felici, Isabelle, ed. *Bilinguisme: enrichissements et conflits*. Paris: Champion,
    2000. Print.
Ferré, Rosario. 'On Destiny, Language, and Translation; or, Ophelia Adrift
    in the C. & A. Canal'. *Between Languages and Cultures: Translation and
    Cross-Cultural Texts*. Eds Anuradha Dingwaney and Carol Maier. Pittsburgh:
    U of Pittsburgh P, 1995. 39–49. Print.
Formigari, Lia. *L'esperienza et il segno: La filosofia del linguaggio tra
    Illuminismo e Restaurazione*. Rome: Riuniti, 1990. *Signs, Science, and
    Politics: Philosophies of Language in Europe, 1700–1830*. Trans. W. Dodd.
    Amsterdam: John Benjamins, 1993. Print.
Forster, Leonard. *The Poet's Tongues: Multilingualism in Literature*. Cambridge:
    Cambridge UP, 1970. Print.
Gessner, Niklaus. *Die Unzulänglichkeit der Sprache: Eine Untersuchung über
    Formzerfall und Beziehungslosigkeit bei Samuel Beckett*. Zurich: Juris, 1957.
    Print.
Glissant, Édouard. *Poétique de la relation*. Paris: Gallimard, 1990. *Poetics of
    Relation*. Trans. Betsy Wing. Ann Arbor: U of Michigan P, 1997. Print.
Goldoni, Carlo. *Mémoires*. 3 vols. Paris, 1787. Abridgment, ed. Guido Mazzoni.
    Florence: Barbera, 1907. *Memoirs of Carlo Goldoni, Written by Himself*.
    Trans. John Black. New York: Knopf, 1926. Print.
Goodrich, Norma. *Charles d'Orléans: A Study of His Themes in His French and
    in His English Poetry*. Geneva: Droz, 1967. Print.
Grayson, Jane. *Nabokov Translated: A Comparison of Nabokov's Russian and
    English Prose Works*. Oxford: Oxford UP, 1977. Print.
Gürçağlar, Sehnaz Tahir. *The Politics and Poetics of Translation in Turkey,
    1923–1960*. Amsterdam: Rodopi, 2008. Print.
Hannerz, Ulf. *Cultural Complexity: Studies in the Social Organization of
    Meaning*. New York: Columbia UP, 1992. Print.
Hokenson, Jan Walsh. *Japan, France, and East-West Aesthetics: French
    Literature 1867–2000*. Madison: Fairleigh Dickinson UP, 2004. Print.
—. 'Intercultural Autobiography'. *a/b: Auto/Biography Studies* 10.1 (1995):
    92–113. Print.
Hokenson, Jan Walsh and Marcella Munson. *The Bilingual Text: History and
    Theory of Literary Self-Translation*. Manchester: St. Jerome, 2007. Print.
Jin, Ha. 'Exiled in English'. *New York Times Book Review* 31 May 2009. 31.
    Print.
Kellman, Steven, ed. *Translingual Writers Reflect on Their Craft*. Lincoln: U of
    Nebraska P, 2003. Print.
Kroh, Aleksandra, ed. *L'Aventure du bilinguisme*. Paris: L'Harmattan, 2000.
    Print.
Kuhiwczak, Piotr. *Introduction*. Kuhiwczak and Littau 1–12. Print.

Kuhiwezak, Piotr and Karin Littau, eds. *Companion to Translation Studies.* Clevedon: Multilingual Matters, 2007. Print.

Lesser, Wendy, ed. *The Genius of Language: Fifteen Writers Reflect on Their Mother Tongues.* New York: Pantheon, 2004. Print.

Lüdi, Georges and Bernard Py. *Être bilingue.* Bern: Peter Lang, 2003.

Merrim, Stephanie. 'Toward a Feminist Reading of Sor Juana Inés de la Cruz'. Merrim. 5–37. Print.

Merrim, Stephanie, ed. *Feminist Perspectives on Sor Juana Inés de la Cruz.* Detroit: Wayne State UP, 1991. Print.

Miletic, Tijana. *European Literary Immigration into the French Language: Readings of Gary, Kristof, Kundera, and Semprun.* Amsterdam: Rodopi, 2008. Print.

Morini, Massimiliano. *Tudor Translation in Theory and Practice.* Burlington, VT: Ashgate, 2006. Print.

Nabokov, Vladimir. *Speak, Memory: An Autobiography Revisited.* New York: Putnam, 1966.

—. Afterword: 'On a Book Entitled *Lolita*'. *Lolita.* New York: Vintage, 1989. 311–17. Print.

Norton, Glyn P. *The Ideology and Language of Translation in Renaissance France and Their Humanist Antecedents.* Geneva: Droz, 1984. Print.

Ossola, Carlo. *Giuseppe Ungaretti.* Milan: Mursia, 1975. Print.

Paz, Octavio. *Sor Juana or the Traps of Faith.* Trans. Margaret Peden. Cambridge, MA: Harvard UP, 1988. Print.

Pérez-Firmat, Gustavo. *Tongue-Ties: Logo-Eroticism in Anglo-Hispanic Literature.* New York: Palgrave Macmillan, 2003. Print.

Picon, Isabel Violante. *'Une oeuvre originale de poésie': Giuseppe Ungaretti traducteur.* Paris: Université de Paris-Sorbonne, 1998. Print.

Pym, Anthony. *Negotiating the Frontier. Translators and Intercultures in Hispanic History.* Manchester: St. Jerome, 2000. Print.

Risset, Jacqueline. 'Joyce Translates Joyce'. *Comparative Criticism* 6 (1984): 3–21. Print.

Robinson, Douglas, ed. *Western Translation Theory from Herodotus to Nietzsche.* Manchester: St. Jerome, 1997. Print.

—. *Translation and Empire.* Manchester: St. Jerome, 1997. Print.

Rosengrant, Roy Judson. 'Bilingual Style in Nabokov's Autobiography'. *Style* 29.1 (1995): 108–27. Print.

Rowe, William W. *Nabokov's Deceptive World.* New York: New York UP, 1971. Print.

Ruggieri, Franca, ed. *Joyce's Feast of Languages.* Joyce Studies in Italy 4. Rome: Bulzoni, 1995.

Runciman, W. G. *The Theory of Social and Cultural Selection.* Cambridge: Cambridge UP, 2009.

Santoyo, Julio-César. 'Blank Spaces in Translation History'. Bastin and Bandia. 11–43. Print.

Schleiermacher, Friedrich. *Über die verschiedenen Methoden des Übersezens.* 1813. *Zur Philosophie.* 9 vols. Berlin: G. Reimer, 1835–46. 2 (1838): 149–495. 'On The Different Methods of Translating'. Trans. Douglas Robinson. Robinson. *Western.* 225–38. Print.

Schons, Dorothy. 'Some Obscure Points in the Life of Sor Juana Inés de la Cruz'. Merrim. 38–60. Print.

Strauss, Claudia and Naomi Quinn. *A Cognitive Theory of Cultural Meaning*. Cambridge: Cambridge UP, 1998. Print.

Ungaretti, Giuseppe. *Vita d'un uomo: tutte la poesia*. Ed. Leone Piccioni. Milan: Mondadori, 1969. Print.

Vegliante, Jean-Charles. *Ungaretti entre les langues*. Paris: Italiques, 1987. Print.

Venuti, Lawrence. *The Translator's Invisibility: A History of Translation*. New York: Routledge, 1995. Print.

Vermeer, Hans J. *Skizzen zur einer Geschechte der Translation*. 2 vols. Frankfurt: IKO-Verlag für Interkulturelle Kommunikation, 1992. Print.

Weaver, Warren. *Alice in Many Tongues: The Translations of Alice in Wonderland*. Madison: U of Wisconsin P, 1964. Print.

PART TWO

Interdisciplinary perspectives: Sociology, psychoanalysis, philosophy

CHAPTER FOUR

A sociological glance at self-translation and self-translators[1]

Rainier Grutman

Abstract: *Echoing the so-called cultural turn of the 1990s, Translation Studies is experiencing another, sociologically inspired turn. One of the more commonly evoked models is Pierre Bourdieu's field theory, which has resulted in a heightened emphasis on translators as agents occupying different positions in the cultural field(s) of one or, sometimes, several countries. The aim of the present investigation is to examine the trajectory of a particular category of such intercultural agents, namely self-translators, or writers who have translated (part of) their own work. The varied (and longer than expected) list of Nobel Prize laureates who were in this particular situation serves as a starting point for the development of a typology of twentieth-century self-translators. The crossing of two variables (exogenous vs endogenous bilingualism and symmetrical vs asymmetrical language pairings) yields four different categories, some of which had thus far escaped critical attention.*

A sociological wave is sweeping through Translation Studies. Over the course of only a few years, we have shifted from discovering that translation can be an 'object of sociological enquiry', as Johan Heilbron and Gisèle Sapiro (3) did, to 'constructing a sociology of translation' (which is the aim of a recent book by that title edited by Michaela Wolf and Alexandra

Fukari). The approach privileged in a good number of those investigations (by Casanova, Gouanvic or Heilbron) is Pierre Bourdieu's field theory, which may seem paradoxical, since Bourdieu himself barely, if ever, addressed translation (or intercultural phenomena in general, for that matter). He has nonetheless provided us with new and enriching ways of broadening the 'cultural turn' (Lefevere and Bassnett 4–6) that Translation Studies took some 20 years ago, leaving behind the field of Linguistics (applied or otherwise) to which it had been more or less confined since emerging after the Second World War.

One of the most striking effects of the introduction of Bourdieu's model in Translation Studies has been a move away from time-honoured, text-based approaches: sociologically inspired research instead privileges the individuals involved, notably identifying translators as 'agents'. Recall that in Bourdieu's field, agents seek to occupy positions by publicly *taking* position (in works of fiction, but also in prefaces, manifestos, interviews, etc.). They act in accordance with their socially acquired dispositions, which enable certain agents (authors, publishers, . . . but also translators) to recognize an impasse – or, conversely, a possibility for innovation – where others fail to do so on account of having less well internalized the structure of the field, having neither acquired the 'specific code of conduct and expression' nor discovered 'the finite universe of freedom under constraints and objective potentialities which it offers: problems to resolve, stylistic or thematic possibilities to exploit, contradictions to overcome, even revolutionary ruptures to effect' (Bourdieu 235). Therefore, thanks to their talent, but also (dis)advantaged by these social dispositions (which Bourdieu labels *habitus*, thereby giving new currency to a term that was fashionable in early twentieth-century German sociology), agents adopt a series of dominating and/or dominated positions, the temporal succession of which forms what he calls their 'trajectory'.

In the following, I shall examine more closely the trajectories of several agents that have two things in common. First, they themselves have translated some (inevitably variable) part of their oeuvre. Second, they were awarded the Nobel Prize in Literature, arguably the world's most important literary distinction, both because of its pedigree and because of its monetary value (10 million Swedish kronor (SEK), or 1 million Euros, according to the official website of the Nobel Foundation). Based on this sample, I shall seek to identify several characteristics of twentieth-century self-translators as social agents.

Resisting self-translation

Before I can describe the main categories of self-translators and explain the underlying criteria for distinguishing between them, however, some preconceived ideas about self-translation that emphasize its aporetic nature need to be revisited and reassessed. Curiously enough, these assumptions are sometimes shared by the very writers who have translated their own work or at least attempted to do so.

Received wisdom surrounding self-translation can be organized around two or three almost axiomatic ideas, the first of which states that self-translators are an extremely rare breed that became extinct almost as soon as it came into existence. Samuel Beckett, the one name everyone knows off the top of their head, is supposed to be as rare as Halley's comet (which, as we know, most human beings can only witness once in their lifetime). For all intents and purposes, Beckett is most often portrayed as the proverbial exception that confirms this rule, his genius being considered the best proof that self-translation is, in fact, impossible. He thus becomes a particular instance of the purported impossibility of translation in general (please insert here the hackneyed Italian adage all too frequently used in writing on translation). Hence the second axiom: self-translation is deemed impossible, or rather, it is only possible if it ceases to be a translation and becomes some other, supposedly nobler, form of rewriting. Judging from the critical literature, we notice that it apparently does not befit great writers to content themselves with 'simply' translating (whatever that is supposed to mean). We are thus regularly led to believe that they take significantly greater liberties with the original than 'standard' translators would (in accordance with an *Idealtypisch* and even skewed view of what translations should be, that is, not based upon actual analyses of existing 'standard' translations). According to this strange logic, self-translations, precisely because they do not measure up to a largely imaginary standard of 'fidelity', somehow end up belonging to another, paradoxically superior, category. Finally, a third axiom often encountered states that self-translation, even if it were possible (which it is not supposed to be, as we have just seen), would be far too time-consuming and altogether absurd, insofar as it forces writers to revisit texts they had regarded as finished.

Gallant, the non self-translator

Some authors simply refuse to engage in the exercise. Anglo-Canadian Mavis Gallant, who became internationally known through her short stories in *The New Yorker*, has made Paris her home since 1950 and feels perfectly at ease in French. However, she staunchly refuses to translate her work into this language: 'No, that what would be out of the question. Translating my own work would be like writing the same thing twice', she told Canadian translation scholar Judith Woodsworth (52) in 1988. In a more recent interview with the French daily, *Libération*, she supports her claim with a telling comparison: for her, self-translating seems as absurd as 'redoing a painting in another tone' (Devarrieux 15). It is important to note that Gallant believes in neither 'perfect' bilingualism nor the possibility of writing in more than one language. Languages are, in her estimation, too compartmentalized, each enclosing its speakers within a particular *Weltanschauung* (in the Humboldtian tradition of linguistic relativity). In Gallant's world view, a certain aura surrounds the English language (Woodsworth 52–4). Concerned about protecting her first language and preserving its 'purity', she has even gone so far as to erect 'a strong writing wall' (Gallant xvii) between herself and Parisian society. In defence of her attitude, the Montrealer likens herself to Marguerite Yourcenar, who knew how to maintain the quality of her French despite an extended stay in the United States.This is how Gallant made it through a temporary crisis that nearly breached her linguistic Maginot line: '*Je n'écoutais plus les nouvelles, rien, je ne lisais plus un seul journal en français, je bloquais le téléphone jusqu'à la fin de la journée, et, le matin, j'écoutais la BBC pour mettre ma pensée sur les rails*' (qtd. in Devarrieux 14–5; I stopped listening to the news, nothing, I did not read a single newspaper in French anymore, I left the phone off the hook until the end of the day, and, in the morning, I would listen to the BBC to get my mind on track. (my translation)).

Semprún, the occasional self-translator

If the case of Gallant – who has been fighting a war of attrition on French words and expressions that nonetheless infiltrate her English language – seems exceptional, then what of the recently departed Jorge Semprún? While he did not mind showcasing his bilingualism (born and raised in Spain, his oeuvre is almost exclusively written in what he often referred to as his 'other mother tongue', that is French), Semprún, too, balked at the idea of translating his own work. In 2004, when interviewed about *Veinte años y un día*, his first novel written directly in Spanish, he vehemently rejected the possibility of producing a French version himself. His objections were twofold.

On the one hand, as an author, Semprún did not feel 'obligated to be faithful', which he (somewhat naïvely) considered to be the task of the translator. By contrast, he added in a 2009 interview with Patricia López-Gay, '*la libertad del autotraductor es total*' (the self-translator's freedom is total). Hence the temptation to write a different book: '*Diferente, tal vez no en la estructura fundamental, narración o personajes fundamentales, pero diferente en miles de matices y quizá en el orden de las cosas* [. . .]' (Perhaps not different in its fundamental structure, its main narrative or characters, but different in thousands of nuances and maybe in the order of things [. . .] (my translation)). A self-translated book, he goes on to say, allows one to correct oneself ('*un libro autotraducido [. . .] permite corregirse*') (qtd. in López-Gay 161). This freedom to correct and rewrite – the exclusive poetic licence of writers since the Romantic era – explains the trust we intuitively place in self-translators: they know the author's intentions well, simply by virtue of the fact that they are their own (Grutman, 'Self-translation'). This same 'author function' (Foucault 107–13) helps us understand why, when awarding the Nobel Prize to Samuel Beckett, the Swedish Academy considered both his English and his French versions. As Academy member Karl Ragnar Gierow highlighted in his presentation, the 1969 Nobel Prize went 'to one man, two languages and a third nation [Ireland], itself divided'.

Semprún's other objection was more pragmatic in nature but no less important: at the advanced age of 80, he felt that he had a limited amount of time left: 'Je le dis sans aucune angoise, mais je préfère consacrer ce temps à un autre roman' ('Entretien'; I say so without any anxiety, but I prefer to dedicate that time to the writing of another novel (my translation)). Like Gallant, Semprún felt that the time required to produce a self-translation could be more effectively spent doing something else. In contrast to Gallant, however, he had actually tried his hand at translating his own writing: the experience had not proved conclusive . . . or rather it *had*, just not in the anticipated way. Following his stint as Felipe González's Minister of Culture (1988–91), Semprún symbolically bade his fellow Spaniards farewell in *Federico Sánchez vous salue bien*, a memoir he immediately translated as *Federico Sánchez se despide de ustedes*. Through this exercise, he came to understand that translation consists less of a linguistic transposition than of a reorientation towards a new audience, with different expectations and different political and cultural frames of reference (Tanzmeister 86–7, 96; López-Gay 160–1). Self-translation thus proved quite restrictive; contrary to expectations, it did not provide Semprún with an environment that was conducive to creative freedom.

Beckett (of course), the systematic self-translator

Even those writers who have practiced self-translation diligently, stress its repetitive, painful and painstaking nature. Vladimir Nabokov described the process as 'sorting through one's own innards, and then trying them on for size like a pair of gloves' (qtd. in Beaujour 90). Samuel Beckett, meanwhile, spoke in 1958 of the 'wastes and wilds of self-translation', a desert crossing that each time took 'many miserable months' (qtd. in Cohn 617). His opinion on the matter would scarcely change, if we are to believe an interview conducted two decades later, at a time in his career when he was writing more readily in English and subsequently translating into French. According to Charles Juliet, who interviewed Beckett in November 1977, '*c'est un labeur supplémentaire dont il* [Beckett] *se passerait volontiers: il n'aime pas revenir sur un texte après qu'il l'a conduit à son achèvement*' (49; it is an additional chore that he could quite happily do without: he does not like to go back over a text after having led it to completion).

Beckett did not necessarily enjoy translating. His biography tells of an incident that is particularly revealing in this regard. In 1950, he was mandated by UNESCO to translate into English an anthology of Mexican poetry edited by Octavio Paz. Beckett (whose command of Spanish left much to be desired) managed to honour the contract with the anonymous help of a friend who had a better grasp of the original's language, but he swore that he would never again take on a translation project, no matter how dire his financial straits (Bair 409–10). His decision to systematically translate his own work is therefore all the more surprising. Beckett was certainly not encouraged to do so by his editor at Minuit: Jérôme Lindon was 'disturbed by the time he [Beckett] insisted on lavishing on self-translation. Lindon felt that Beckett should content himself with a brief inspection of the translation someone else had made so that he could devote all his time to writing' (Bair 480).

Beckett's name invariably comes up in discussions about self-translation, an unwritten rule to which this chapter is no exception. Or so it seems, at least, for I would like to argue that it has become urgent to view him in a much broader perspective than in terms of the at once unique and typical linguistic encounter that his oeuvre provides us with. Beckett's case is by far the best documented: there are half a dozen books (and a myriad of articles) on his bilingualism. As a result, we are well-informed in the way in which he translated his own work, a way that of course changed over the years. We also know the chronology of his bilingualism, which helps us to identify key moments for self-translation. At the same time, however, I am afraid that by confining Beckett to the role of the great exception, these studies run the risk of considerably reducing their general explanatory potential, such that they end up revealing less than what we might have hoped about self-translation per se.

A sociological perspective

Without seeking to dwell on epistemological questions, I would like to recall a few observations made a century ago by Gustave Lanson, the founder of modern literary studies in France. In 1904, Lanson was invited by that other French powerhouse, Émile Durkheim, to reflect on the links between 'literary history and sociology' (the title of his talk). In a move typical of classical rhetoric, Lanson first takes considerable time to dissociate both disciplines on account of their incompatibility, in order to then better stress his main point, namely the 'close affinity between the sociological point of view and literary history' (225). This affinity stems, most notably, from the fact that 'every literary work is a social phenomenon' insofar as its 'essential, fundamental character [. . .] is to be a communication between an individual and a public' (226).

However, although literary historians 'bring out [. . .] the relation of the work to the author and to the various publics before which it has passed', their ultimate 'goal is invariably the individual' (225). In Lanson's view, 'the aim of literary history' is 'the precise description of [the exceptional writer's] literary individuality' (224). The more exact this description, the more it furthers our understanding of the specific: 'There is no knowledge but that of the particular', Lanson (225) retorts to those who, like the sociologists in his audience, subscribe to Aristotle's dictum that 'there is no science of the accidental' (6.1027a).

Sociologists are indeed by definition more interested in collective than in particular aspects. The stuff of their knowledge is society, not the individual, a philosophical concept that has become, Norbert Elias reminds us: 'one of the most confused concepts not only in sociology but in everyday thought too. As used today, [it] conveys the impression that it refers to an adult quite alone, dependent on nobody, and who has never been a child' (116). This image of the human being 'as a kind of closed box, as a *homo clausus*' (119) cut off from the social sphere, is at best 'questionable' (119), at worst 'a myth' (120), according to Elias, who understands humans as *energeia* (rather than as *ergon*), the ever provisional result of a long socialization process. But that is a different debate.

I think it is easy to see where I am going with this. By digging deeper into Beckett's work in terms of his biography (which no doubt contains relevant information for studying his linguistic choices), we know increasingly more about Beckett's 'literary individuality'. This is good – a lot even – but it is not everything. What of, for example, the 'figuration' (Elias 128–33) to which he belonged? What of his double 'trajectory' (in Bourdieu's sense) within the French and English literary fields?[2] Beckett sometimes seems something of a *hapax legomenon*, the most celebrated of a very small group of self-translators studied *in splendid isolation* (to use the parlance of British diplomacy). We have yet to move beyond the 'tradition of scientific atomism', as Elias (72) calls it, which in this particular instance yields only a partial and fragmented view of self-translation, in order to develop a truly holistic perspective.

Nothing guarantees that the problem can be resolved by simply expanding the corpus to include a larger number of 'cases'. By juxtaposing Beckett and Nabokov, Julian Green and Nancy Huston or Karen Blixen and Eileen Chang, for instance, independently of the societal and historical contexts they inherited, we run the risk of ending up with a portrait gallery that, although impressive, is rather limited in terms of model-building. Needless to say, this observation in no way tries to undermine the importance of these (or other) self-translators. What strikes me as more questionable, however, is the paradigmatic status they are often given. Is it for instance purely coincidental that each of the aforementioned writers has created a significant part of their oeuvre in English, and that half of them also published in French? These being the world's most widely *read* languages (which is something entirely different from the most widely *spoken* – a discrepancy that favours French against Spanish, for instance), we must ask ourselves whether their global reach – previously through colonization, currently through communication – has something to do with the critical popularity of superstars such as Beckett. I believe the time has come to heed Maria Fillippakopoulou's call for an historicizing focus, that is, an examination of self-translation that involves addressing 'pressures relating to constraints of systematic nature, related, for instance, to languages of limited diffusion and their role vis-à-vis majority languages; [to] power differentials, shorthand for the real differences in prestige and impact between major and minor languages and literatures' (24).

Exogenous versus endogenous bilingualism

It is very instructive to look at the list of self-translating Nobel laureates while bearing these questions in mind. A first glance (informed by Santoyo and Gentes) reveals that their number is significantly higher than commonly thought: it currently stands at eight,[3] or roughly one for every 13 laureates. Their names are: Frédéric Mistral (awarded the Nobel Prize in 1904), Rabindranath Tagore (in 1913), Karl Adolph Gjellerup (1917), Luigi Pirandello (1934), Samuel Beckett (1969), Isaac Bashevis Singer (1978), Czeslaw Milosz (1980) and Joseph Brodsky (1987). Even if it proved to be the case that self-translators were over-represented among Nobel Prize winners (but why should that be so?), this proportion invites us to revisit a number of preconceptions about the marginal nature of the practice.

A second observation: more than half of these authors self-translated *into* English, a language that was the mother tongue for but one of them, namely Beckett. The other ones (Tagore, Singer, Milosz, Brodsky) had to learn English, in some cases even quite late in life. It is equally telling that the three self-translators who did not choose English as a target-language – Mistral chose French, Gjellerup chose German and Pirandello chose Italian – are among the earliest laureates. Their careers had taken off (and in two out of three cases peaked) before the First World War, when English did not rank nearly as high on the linguistic hit parade . . . Unless, of course, one was a loyal subject of the 'Emperor' of India (a title George V had inherited from Victoria), like Rabindranath Tagore, who received the highest literary distinction shortly after translating a selection of his Bengali poems into the language of the British Empire (of which he would also, if briefly, become a Knight). The result, *Gitanjali*, is a kind of *best of* preceded by a glowing preface by William Butler Yeats, a poet endowed with enough symbolic capital to qualify as a 'consecrated consecrator' (Casanova 101). Far from being an early example of the metropolitan recognition of (post)colonial writers[4] (no more than awarding the 1921 Goncourt Prize to Martiniquan, and therefore French citizen, René Maran would prove to be), Tagore's success instead illustrates the paternalism of European elites during the Belle Époque.

The other three Nobel laureates who 'chose' to translate their own work into English, by contrast, were immigrants, not colonized subjects. Singer, Milosz and Brodsky all arrived in the United States from Eastern Europe: Singer in 1935 (at the age of 31), Milosz in 1961 (when approaching his fifties), and Brodsky in 1972 (shortly after turning 32), upon being deported from the USSR. The age at which they emigrated and the fact that, before leaving or being exiled, they had already launched their careers, explain why, once in North America, they continued to write in their respective mother tongue (Yiddish, Polish and Russian). Given how difficult it must have been to gain sufficient knowledge of and confidence in English, it is all the more remarkable (yet indicative of cultural pressures and underlying market forces) that they all insisted on self-translating their work so as to give it an 'afterlife' in the language of their adopted country.

Singer, Milosz and Brodsky belong to a specific category: that of bilingual writers for whom changing languages doubles as crossing borders (be these linguistic, national, religious or all of the above). George Steiner famously compared such writers to embassies: both are beyond local jurisdictions, both are in a state of 'extraterritoriality'.[5] Relative to their original speech community, their bilingualism seems external or 'exogenous' (Grutman, 'L'écrivain bilingue' 35–9): necessary to communicate with the outside world, it was neither widespread nor required back home. This is true for Beckett and Nabokov (Steiner's examples), for Nobel-Prize winners Milosz and Brodsky, as well as for many other self-translators: Julian Green, Jorge Semprún, Nancy Huston, Witold Gombrowicz. . . .

It would be incorrect, however, to label as 'extraterritorial' Mistral, Tagore, Gjellerup or Pirandello. None of them had to change countries in order to change languages. Their forays into self-translation were reinforced by a bilingualism that was not exogenous but rather internal or 'endogenous' (Grutman, 'L'écrivain bilingue' 39–41), a structural or systemic aspect of the (as a rule diglossic) speech community they grew up and were educated in. It is therefore necessary to identify a second category of self-translators, consisting of writers whose identity was marked from the very outset by linguistic diversity. In contrast to Beckett, Milosz or Brodsky, these self-translators grew up in societies that were characterized by a prolonged contact between different language varieties and the widespread, if unequally distributed, bilingualism in which that contact resulted. Difference was waiting for them on their doorstep. Mistral and Pirandello, whose native tongues were Occitan and Sicilian, could no more escape the sole official language of their respective countries (note that the French Republic is famously deemed *une et indivisible* in its Constitution), than Tagore could distance himself from English, the British Empire's steadfast and faithful companion, or Gjellerup could disregard German, Copenhagen's de facto *Kultursprache* for much of the nineteenth century. Such contexts of inescapable inequality make choosing a language, creating a bilingual oeuvre and translating one's own work, almost political questions or, at the very least, questions that are highly loaded on the symbolic level.

Singer's is a particularly complex case. He grew up in a diglossic community (the son of a rabbi and a rabbi's daughter, he knew Yiddish and classical Hebrew[6]), which, at face value, would put him in the same category as Mistral. Yet his later self-translations involved a language which he had neither heard nor learned in his native Poland prior to emigrating to the United States. Even if one day we were to discover that Singer also translated from Hebrew into Yiddish (or the other way around), it remains that the main thrust of his self-translational enterprise revolved around English, a language acquired later on in life but for which he would eventually claim the status of 'second mother tongue'. Though clearly exogenous to his original community and without historical links to either the *shtetlelkh* or the ghettos of Eastern Europe, English did allow him to reach out to many more readers (starting with the Gentiles of his adoptive country: Singer's self-translations have been likened by at least one critic to 'a simulacrum of conversion' (Lewi 224)). In general, his linguistic choices speak to the general dynamics of migration, which squarely puts him in the same category as Milosz and Brodsky.

Asymmetrical transfers in the linguistic galaxy

Taking a closer look at those two types of self-translators, one is struck by a second important difference. On the one hand, there are those whom Alexandra Kroh affectionately calls the 'aristocrats of bilingualism' (9): writers who can afford the luxury of using symmetrically, as it were, some of the world's most widespread and best established languages. For them, self-translation can represent the site of an individual venture, marked (and sometimes marred) by either their personal or family history but hardly fraught with difficulties resulting from a socially rooted power differential. Beckett, Nancy Huston and Julian Green (all rather famous French-English self-translators) are clear-cut examples, as appear to be Nabokov and Brodsky for the pairing of English and Russian.

Their aesthetic importance notwithstanding, it would be wise not to consider them as synecdoches of self-translation: as we have seen, they represent but one possible incarnation. As a matter of fact, among Nobel laureates, only Beckett and Brodsky fit the bill. The six others (Mistral, Tagore, Gjellerup, Pirandello, Singer and even Milosz) belong to an altogether different category, that of writers whose bilingualism reflects a social dominance configuration that puts systemic pressures on them and can force them to make painful choices (Grutman, 'Writing and reading diglossia'). Since the Romantic era, literary creation has been viewed as inextricably bound up with one's mother tongue, no matter how restricted its potential audience. This creates somewhat of a double bind for writers whose native tongue is (much) less widely used, symbolically dominated – or both – yet symbolically and emotionally so important that they do not want to forsake it in favour of an acquired, albeit 'major', language. Aware of not really having two equally *recognized* tools at their disposal, they do not cherish too many illusions about the rapport between them being symmetrical but accept the consequences of the symbolic (and sometimes even politically charged) differential between an unworkable 'universalist' position and an equally unworkable 'localist' position. The first stance encourages them to reinvent themselves for the centre of the (French/ British/Spanish/American) literary system, in the ever elusive hope of being adopted by it, a strategy that can backfire because of its very ambivalence in terms of identity politics. What they gain in authenticity by adopting a local stance and writing in their minority's language, on the other hand, they stand to loose in readership and recognition. I am thinking in particular of Rachid Boudjedra's Arabic, of Eric de Kuyper's Dutch, of Isak Dinesen (Karen Blixen)'s Danish, of Llorenç Villalonga's Catalan, of André Brink's and Breyton Breytenbach's Afrikaans and, of course, of Singer's Yiddish.[7]

The same issues cannot be said to be at work in the bilingual and self-translational practice of the aforementioned 'aristocrats', who juggle languages with less social baggage, their status being more a matter of international prestige than of local embedding. The challenges they face are therefore entirely different. For Samuel Beckett to be forced to choose between authenticity and universality, a decision that haunts all 'minority' writers, he would have had to grow up, like several of his catholic countrymen, in an environment that was much more open to and permeated with Gaelic – a language which instead he, as an Anglo-Irish Protestant, did not master at all (Bair 251; Arndorfer 42). Similarly, had Jorge Semprún belonged not to the bourgeoisie of Madrid but to that of Barcelona, he might very well have both inherited the Catalan language and interiorized the discrimination it was subjected to during Franco's regime, with all that this might have implied for his writing career and his choice (not) to translate himself. . . .

In addition to the particular sociolinguistic configuration of the endogenously bilingual community, the asymmetry underlying many instances of self-translation stems from the much broader unequal weight that languages carry in what Dutch political scientist Abram De Swaan has termed the 'global language system' or, more metaphorically, 'a galaxy of languages'(4–6). First, in terms of their exchange value on the linguistic market (which is something entirely different from their intrinsic value), not all languages are equal but some are more equal than others. Hence the disturbing fact that (half) a dozen of centrally positioned languages serve as source languages for the rest of the world, whereas several hundreds of other languages are hardly ever translated. Secondly, speakers of different languages occupy different hierarchical positions in society: many are forced to learn one or more foreign languages, whose native speakers are by that very fact invited to remain happily monolingual. In De Swaan's model, the relative weight of a language is calculated according to the number of bilinguals and polyglots using it, either by choice or by necessity. Thus, the global rise of English since the Second World War should not only be correlated with its more than 300 million native users but also, more significantly, with the 700 million non-anglophones whose first non-native language it has *de facto* become: let us not forget that there are probably more people who speak English on the Indian subcontinent than in Great Britain.

Applied to the matter at hand, this reasoning helps us understand the relatively light weight languages such as Milosz's Polish and Tagore's Bengali carry. Although their speakers number in the tens or even hundreds of millions, their geographical distribution and geopolitical influence are not buttressed by legions of polyglots. This is all the more true of smaller languages like Blixen's Danish or Brink's Afrikaans, to say nothing of Singer's Yiddish, which was nearly wiped out by the Shoah. By contrast, when first Samuel Beckett and later Nancy Huston relocated to France and started writing in that country's language, French was still sufficiently prestigious to resist the attraction of English and offer a viable alternative.

Carrying De Swaan's (and Bourdieu's) insights into the realm of Translation Studies, both Johan Heilbron and Pascale Casanova have stressed the key role played by translation in this global system of power relations, where writers from different nationalities compete for a place under the sun. '[F]ar from being the horizontal exchange and peaceful transfer' it is often thought to be, Casanova points out, translation is 'an important factor in the struggles for legitimacy [. . .] and one of the principal means of consecration for authors and texts' (86). Even aside from any deliberate strategies, translation is never an innocent intervention but an 'unequal exchange' defined by asymmetry.

Deciding to translate oneself can therefore become a truly Cornelian dilemma. Certainly, making their work known *urbi et orbi* without needing to wait for a translator to do so, can give bicultural writers with (near-)native access to a 'major' language competitive advantage. They can become their own ambassadors, agents and even career-brokers, but they will do so at their own risk. While it is true that autographic translations lend visibility, they can also conceal the fact that the work was originally created in a 'minor' source language, thereby reinforcing the dominant position of the 'major' target language. The more the latter gravitates towards or occupies a central position within the linguistic galaxy, the greater the danger of the minority language-original being ignored.

Highly symptomatic in this respect is the polemic surrounding Singer in the United States, as evidenced by Cynthia Ozick's novella *Envy; or, Yiddish in America* (for an in-depth analysis, see Seidman 243–55). While bilingual, Singer's oeuvre far from resembles a Rorschach card, given the considerable dissimilarities between its Yiddish and English versions (the latter often rewritten in close collaboration with anglophones). Singer's own claim, in his 1978 Nobel Lecture, that the 'high honour bestowed upon [him] by the Swedish Academy [was] also a recognition of the Yiddish language', may sound somewhat disingenuous coming from someone who asked his self-translated English stories be considered 'second originals'. This wish explains why they are used as source-texts for translations into third languages, a tendency that has the indirect effect of marginalizing the Yiddish text (already written in a language and script inaccessible to the vast majority of Singer's readership) a second time (Lewi 220–2).

Originals similarly run the risk of being disregarded in situations where the languages involved cohabit in a State that does not grant them equal status. Corinna Krause's (2005) research on Scotland has shown an increase in poetry anthologies that present readers with side-by-side Gaelic and English versions (each produced by the author). While enhancing the visibility of Gaelic writing, such initiatives also confirm the dominant position of the central/common language. By nature, indeed, bilingual editions have the unfortunate effect of creating a hierarchy between both versions, with one basically complementing the other, so that readers can end up concentrating on one page while more or less dispensing with the other. In this particular instance, English-language readers may well focus on the poems written in their language, and do little more than glance at the Gaelic text on the opposite page. This is why a militant writer like Christopher Whyte[8] prefers translating *into* Gaelic rather than *from* Gaelic, and condemns self-translations altogether: 'They tend to support the assumption that, since we have the poet's own translations, the originals can be dispensed with' (70).Therein lies the danger facing self-translators who work from smaller languages: by seeing their second text (chronologically speaking) granted the status of an entirely new creation, a 'second original', they run the risk of the original version being marginalized, disqualified or even effaced.

Conclusion

The preceding profile of modern self-translators was not only made possible but also deemed desirable by the sociological turn recently taken in Translation Studies. These reflections reveal, among other things, that there are several types of self-translators, some of whom had thus far escaped critical attention. Besides exogenous (or, in Steiner's words, 'extraterritorial') writers, who switch languages when switching countries and whose bilingualism tends to be coordinate (since they learned to write in their second language as adults), there is a second, less-known but no less important, category of endogenous bilinguals, who must juggle the languages of their native communities. Next, we can contrast self-translators who work in widely distributed languages that occupy comparable positions on the world stage, with those whose linguistic configuration rests on asymmetry, since it involves a language that is symbolically and/or socially dominating and one that is symbolically and/or socially dominated. Since these two divisions do not intersect perfectly, we obtain a 2 × 2 contingency table in which both variables (exogenous vs endogenous and symmetrical vs asymmetrical) are crossed. Classifying the eight Nobel Prize laureates in literature generates the following result:

	Symmetrical	Asymmetrical
Exogenous	Beckett Brodsky	Singer Milosz
Endogenous	Ø	Mistral Tagore Gjellerup Pirandello

Asymmetrical relationships predominate as much among self-translators who emigrated as among those who remained in their native country. Symmetrical or 'horizontal' transfers, on the other hand, are much rarer. The table clearly shows that their importance should not be overestimated for the study of self-translation as an historical phenomenon. From that perspective, Beckett's case – the most studied and the best known – seems in no way representative, even in a sample as marked by the mechanisms of institutional filtering as is a roll call of Nobel Prize laureates. Depending on the status granted to the Russian language (its global weight was significantly greater during the Cold War, when Brodsky penned his oeuvre, than today), Beckett ends up occupying an altogether separate category. He does so, less because he is the exceptional case of genius often referred to in critical literature than because the bilingualism underlying his consistent self-translations is unusually symmetrical, whereas most such transfers involve an unequal and asymmetrical relationship between languages. Another noteworthy observation in this regard is the fact that the sample has not yielded a single example of an endogenous horizontal exchange, that is, between languages sharing space within a given society. Without being excluded or theoretically impossible, this particular configuration proves much less probable in actuality. Most of all, looking at the contingency table above makes us realize that self-translation, in addition to representing a challenge for individual writers, who engage in a kind of linguistic balancing act, is a sociocultural phenomenon whose manifold manifestations have only just started to be investigated.

Notes

1   Parts of this chapter appeared in French (Grutman, 'Portrait') but have
    been extensively revised, updated and reframed for a different audience. My
    heartfelt thanks go to Trish Van Bolderen for translating the original essay, thus
    providing me with a canvas to work on.

2   I must therefore applaud Jürgen Siess's and Matthijs Engelberts's initiative
    to dedicate a special issue of the bilingual journal *Samuel Beckett Today/
    Aujourd'hui* to 'Beckett dans le champ littéraire/Beckett in the Literary Field'
    (scheduled to appear in 2013).

3   Nine, if we count Danish writer Isak Dinesen/Karen Blixen, who came
    very close to being honoured in 1959, according to a recent article in *The
    Copenhagen Post* ('Scandinavian Roots').

4   They would have to wait until 1986, when Nigerian Wole Soyinka was awarded
    the Nobel. It is important to note, however, that his work was published in
    English, not in Yoruba, and that Soyinka's country was part of the British
    Empire until its independence in 1960.

5   Like the shades of the dead in Greek mythology, who had to drink the waters
    of the river of oblivion, Lethe, in order to forget their earthly life so that they
    may be reincarnated, these writers left behind part of their old culture – the
    non-transferable, literally untranslatable, part – in order to begin a new life.
    This is what Nabokov complained of in his afterword to *Lolita*, where he
    described as a 'private tragedy' the fact 'that [he] had to abandon [his] natural
    idiom, [his] untrammeled, rich, and infinitely docile Russian tongue for a
    second-rate brand of English, devoid of any of those apparatuses [. . .] which the
    native illusionist, frac-tails flying, can magically use to transcend the heritage in
    his own way' (316–17).

6   As for Polish, Singer learned it only later in life, when he had already spent a
    fair part of his childhood in Warsaw (Weinstein 151–2).

7   Or that of Élie Wiesel, who translated *Night*, his first and most celebrated novel,
    himself: published in 1956 in Buenos Aires as a Shoah memoir called *Un di velt
    hot geshvign* [And the World Kept Silent], it appeared as a French novel two
    years later, in a much shorter text with a title chosen by editor Jérôme Lindon
    (him again): *La Nuit* (Seidman 219–24).

8   Francesc Parcerisas (120) mentions similar misgivings on behalf of Welsh author
    Ronald Stuart Thomas.

Works cited

Aristotle. *The Metaphysics: Books I–IX*. Trans. Hugh Tredennick. 1933.
     Cambridge, MA: Harvard UP and London: Heinemann, 1989. Web. www.
     perseus.tufts.edu/hopper/
Arndorfer, Martin. *Samuel Beckett : Fragen zur Identität eines zweisprachigen
     Schriftstellers*. Vienna: Praesens, 1997. Print.

Bair, Deirdre. *Samuel Beckett*. New York and London: Harcourt Brace
    Jovanovitch, 1978. Print.
Beaujour, Elizabeth Klosty. *Alien Tongues: Bilingual Russian Writers of the
    'First' Emigration*. Ithaca, NY: Cornell UP, 1989. Print.
Bourdieu, Pierre. *The Rules of Art: Genesis and Structure of the Literary Field*.
    Trans. Susan Emanuel. Stanford: Stanford UP, 1996. Print.
Casanova, Pascale. 'Consecration and Accumulation of Literary Capital.
    Translation as an Unequal Exchange'.*Translation Studies: Critical Concepts in
    Linguistics*. Ed. Mona Baker. Vol. 2. London and New York: Routledge, 2009.
    85–107. Print.
Chartier, Roger. 'Social Figuration and Habitus.Reading Elias'. *Cultural
    History. Between Practices and Representations*. Trans. Lydia G. Cochrane.
    Cambridge: Polity P, 1988. 71–94. Print.
Cohn, Ruby. 'Samuel Beckett Self-translator'. *PMLA* 76.5 (1961): 613–21. Print.
De Swaan, Abram. *Words of the World: The Global Language System*.
    Cambridge: Polity P, 2001. Print.
Devarrieux, Claire. 'Gallant: Paris est un jouet'. *Libération (hors série: les 80
    livres de l'année)* (March 1993): 14–15. Print.
Elias, Norbert. *What is Sociology?* Trans. Stephen Mennell and Grace Morrissey.
    New York: Columbia UP, 1978. Print.
Fillippakopoulou, Maria. 'Self-Translation: Reviving the Author?' *In Other
    Words: The Journal of Literary Translators* 25 (Summer 2005): 23–7. Print.
Foucault, Michel. 'What is an Author?' *The Foucault Reader*. Ed. Paul Rabinow.
    New York: Pantheon, 1984. 101–20. Print.
Gallant, Mavis. *Home Truths*. Toronto: MacMillan, 1987. Print.
Gentes, Eva. 'Toujours infidèle – Writing from the Midzone: Die literarische
    Selbstübersetzung im 20. Jahrhundert'. MA Thesis (*Diplomarbeit*) Düsseldorf
    U, 2008. Print.
Gierow, Karl Ragnar. 'Award Ceremony Speech [for Samuel Beckett]'.
    Translation. 1969. Web. http://nobelprize.org/nobel_prizes/literature/
    laureates/1969/press.html
Gouanvic, Jean-Marc. 'A Bourdieusian Theory of Translation, or the Coincidence
    of Practical Instances: Field, *Habitus*, Capital and *Illusio*'. *The Translator* 11.2
    (2005): 147–66. Print.
Grutman, Rainier. 'La autotraducción en la 'galaxia' de las lenguas'. *Quaderns*
    16 (2009): 123–34.
—. 'L'Écrivain bilingue et ses publics : une perspective comparatiste'. *Écrivains
    multilingues et écritures métisses. L'Hospitalité des langues*. Eds. Axel
    Gasquet and Modesta Suárez. Clermont-Ferrand: PU Blaise Pascal, 2007.
    31–50. Print.
—. 'Portrait sociologique de l'autotraducteur moderne: quelques réflexions à
    partir du palmarès des prix Nobel'. *Sprachen – Sprechen – Schreiben. Blicke
    auf Mehrsprachigkeit. Georg Kremnitz zum 65. Geburtstag*. Eds. Peter
    Cichon, Barbara Czernilofsky, Max Doppelbauer and Robert Tanzmeister.
    Vienna: Praesens, 2010. 209–24. Print.
—. 'Self-Translation. '*Routledge Encyclopedia of Translation Studies*.2nd edn.
    Eds. Mona Baker and Gabriela Saldanha. London and New York: Routledge,
    2009. 257–60. Print.

—. 'Writing and Reading Diglossia: Evidence from the French-speaking World'. *The Representation of the Spoken Mode in Fiction: How authors write how people talk*. Eds. Carolina Amador Moreno and Ana Nunes. Lewiston, NY: The Edwin Mellen P, 2009. 13–40. Print.

Heilbron, Johan. 'Towards a Sociology of Translation. Book Translations as a Cultural World-System'. *European Journal of Social Theory* 2.4 (1999): 429–44. Print.

Heilbron, Johan and Gisèle Sapiro. 'La Traduction littéraire, un objet sociologique'. *Actes de la recherche en sciences sociales* 144 (2002): 3–7. Print.

Juliet, Charles. *Rencontre avec Samuel Beckett*. Montpellier: Fata Morgana, 1986. Print.

Krause, Corinna. 'Finding the Poem – Modern Gaelic Verse and the Contact Zone'. *Forum: The University of Edinburgh Postgraduate Journal of Culture and the Arts* 1 (2005): 1–14. Web. www.forumjournal.org/site/sites/default/files/01/Krause_Gaelic.pdf.

Kroh, Alexandra. *L'Aventure du bilinguisme*. Paris: L'Harmattan, 2000. Print.

Lanson, Gustave. 'Literary History and Sociology'. 1904. Trans. Nicholas T. Rand and Roberta Hatcher. *PMLA* 110.2 (1995): 220–35. Print.

Lefevere, André and Susan Basnett. 'Proust's Grandmother and the *Thousand and One Nights*: the 'Cultural Turn' in Translation Studies'. *Translation, History, Culture*. Eds. Bassnett and Lefevere. London and New York: Pinter, 1990. 1–13. Print.

Lewi, Henri. 'Pourquoi IBS ne voulait pas être traduit du texte yiddish'. *L'Inconscient du yiddish*. Eds. Max Kohn and Jean Baumgarten. Paris: Anthropos, 2003. 219–44. Print.

López-Gay, Patricia. 'Conversación con Jorge Semprún. Sobre autotraducción. De los recuerdos y sus formas de reescritura'. *Quaderns* 16 (2009): 157–64. Print.

Nabokov, Vladimir. *The Annotated* Lolita, *Revised and Updated*. Ed. Alfred Appel, Jr. New York: Vintage-Random House, 1991. Print.

—. 'The Nobel Prize in Literature'. Nobelprize.org. 14 Aug. 2011. Web. http://nobelprize.org/nobel_prizes/literature/

Parcerisas i Vázquez, Francesc. 'De l'asymétrie au degré zéro de l'autotraduction'. *Quaderns* 16 (2009): 117–22. Print.

Prunč, Erich. *Entwicklungslinien der Translationswissenschaft. Von den Asymmetrien der Sprachen zu den Asymmetrien der Macht*. 2nd edn. Berlin: Frank & Timme, 2007. Print.

Santoyo, Julio César. 'Autotraducciones: una perspectiva histórica'. *Meta* 50.3 (2005): 858–67. Print.

—. 'Translation and Cultural Identity: Competence and Performance of the Author-Translator'. *Translation and Cultural Identity: Selected Essays on Translation and Cross-cultural Communication*. Eds. Micaela Muñoz-Calvo and Carmen Buesa-Gómez. Newcastle-upon-Tyne: Cambridge Scholars Publishing, 2010. 13–32. Print.

Sapiro, Gisèle, ed. *Translatio. Le Marché de la traduction en France à l'heure de la mondialisation*. Paris: CNRS, 2008. Print.

—. 'Scandinavian roots robbed Blixen of NobelPrize'. *The Copenhagen Post*. 28 Jan. 2010: 1. Web. www.cphpost.dk/news/135-science/48078-scandinavian-roots-robbed-blixen-of-nobel-prize.html.

Seidman, Naomi. *Faithful Renderings. Jewish-Christian Difference and the Politics of Translation*. Chicago: U of Chicago P, 2006. Print.

Semprún, Jorge. 'Entretien à l'occasion de la parution de *Vingt ans et un jour*'. Paris: Gallimard, 2004. Web. www.gallimard.fr/catalog/entretiens/01049083. htm

Singer, Isaac Bashevis. 'Nobel Lecture'. 8 Dec. 1978. Web. http://nobelprize.org/nobel_prizes/literature/laureates/1978/singer-lecture.html

Steiner, George. *Extraterritorial. Papers on Literature and the Language Revolution*. New York: Atheneum, 1971. Print.

Tanzmeister, Robert. 'Sprachliches Relativitätsprinzip und literarische Selbstübersetzung am Beispiel von Jorge Semprúns *Federico Sánchez vous salue bien* und *Federico Sánchez se despide de ustedes*'. *Quo vadis, Romania?* 7 (1996): 76–100. Print.

Weinstein, Miriam. *Yiddish: A Nation of Words*. New York: Ballantine, 2001. Print.

Whyte, Christopher. 'Against Self-Translation'. *Translation and Literature* 11.1 (2002): 64–71. Print.

Wolf, Michaela. 'Mapping the Field: Sociological Perspectives on Translation'. *International Journal of the Sociology of Language* 207 (2011): 1–28. Print.

Wolf, Michaela and Alexandra Fukari, eds. *Constructing a Sociology of Translation*. Amsterdam and Philadelphia: John Benjamins, 2007. Print.

Woodsworth, Judith. 'Writers and their Translators: the Case of Mavis Gallant'. *TTR* 1.2 (1988): 47–57. Print.

CHAPTER FIVE

The passion of self-translation: A masocritical perspective

Anthony Cordingley

Abstract: *Discussions of self-translation distinguish between writers who, for political, historical or cultural reasons, need to self-translate and those who decide to self-translate of their own free will. Criticism relating to this second group of writers often asserts and celebrates self-translation as an exploratory, creative act, a positive discovery or negotiation of multiple 'selves', even the emancipation of one or many identities within the self. However, many such writers experience self-translation as being particularly boring, unpleasant and even painful, a violence inflicted upon their texts and/or upon themselves. Rather than simply putting such claims down to self-directed expressions of the common fate of the translator, this chapter explores how psychoanalytic interpretations of masochism offer new ways of conceptualizing this form of reflexive transference or auto-translatory action. Viewed as such, the decision to self-translate is implicated in the desire for suspense and subversions of the ego, a resistance to completion and a deferral of gratification. Far from seeing the self-translator as a dupe to subconscious processes, I will consider how self-translation offers the 'social masochist' the possibility to square up to his or her dominant ego, or other. Self-translation is understood as a form of literary creation, but also of criticism, whose complex motivations are illuminated by Paul Mann's study of the masochistic dimension to professional literary criticism: masocriticism.*

In 1999 Paul Mann published a collection of essays entitled *Masocriticism*, a neologism which is also the title of the book's core chapter (19–49). Mann's essay is a psychoanalytic study of professional literary criticism: of the masochistic character of our submission to the texts we chose as the objects of our labour and our desire, and of our willingness to submit to the brutal arena of critical exchange and evaluation (peer review, publication, conferences, promotion . . .). The relevance of Mann's study to translation, and indeed self-translation, becomes apparent as he considers the translator to be prone to similar psychic impulses of affiliation and servitude as professional readers: 'The critic, the interpreter, the translator, wants to speak for the dead, to subject himself to a truth he instructs the dead to teach us' (48). Mann's thesis is that we choose the object of our identification, the master to whom we serve, sacrificing ourselves to a culture of violent scrutiny, inviting punishment for the 'sins' of those identifications. The justification we tacitly offer ourselves for this painful labour, a justification which we keep hidden from our daily thoughts, is that in the author or text we chose for our master we find the lessons we believe we should be taught. Writing within psychoanalytic readings of masochistic behaviour, Mann contends that the critic's and the translator's submission is but a complicated ruse for their redoubtable self-assertion: 'the cold lesson of masocritical science is that nothing is more aggressive than the desire to serve the other' (48).

Mann is able to couple the translator with the critic through the commonly held notion that the translator is a servant to an original text. While this might at first seem repugnant, given that literary Translation Studies is deeply invested in asserting the agency of both translator and translation, perhaps our instinct to quash such a 'retrograde' notion reveals how dearly held, perhaps fetishized, is our championing of the creativity, even autonomy, of the translator. I wonder if, in our desire to endow the translator with artistry, we are not at risk of overlooking the history of the labour of translation. In the current investigation, I will approach just one aspect of this question, and with reference to self-translation only, by confronting Mann's ideas with Theodor Reik's classic study of social, or cultural, masochism, *Masochism in Modern Man*. In exploring the decisions of those who are free to chose the works which they translate I am necessarily limiting my comments to a minority caste of cosmopolitan self-translators, without excluding the possibility that the comments I make about them apply to them and them alone. The issue at the heart of the present inquiry can be formulated in the following question: do these self-translators escape the definition of their behaviour as typical masochism (following Theodor Reik's definition) or is their textual servitude of the nature of Mann's masocriticism, and might they also be considered their own masters?

Masocriticism and translation

Mann considers the mechanisms of psychic displacement that come into operation when the critic (or translator) gives himself over to the object of his desire:

> To speak for the dead is to identify with the dead. In some sense to wish oneself dead. One assumes (in every sense of the word) the place of the dead, assumes their authority and their absence, their historicity and the fixity of their discourse [. . .] One gives oneself over, displaces oneself through some critical methodology, in order to represent the other, to speak the other's voice. (26)

Yet, with his typical irony, Mann adds in parentheses, 'No one really believes this for an instant' (26). His point is that criticism is impossible, and that no one can ever replace the dead, the absent object of one's intellectual identification. We engineer the fantasy of our submission, and the fact that we enter into this contract of submission is a fundamental and defining aspect of the masochistic nature of our work. When Mann mentions the translator in the same breath in which he mentions the critic and the interpreter, he is drawing not only on the received idea of the translator as the handmaid of the author but also on the fact that translation involves a reinterpretation of a source text. In a variety of ways, but fundamentally because differences between languages force a translator to decide which among the many possible translations for a word or idea is the best, translation is often said to offer a commentary upon its source. When it comes to literary *self-translation*, critics have tended to assert that a self-translated text assumes the status of a new original. This was not always the case, and during the early years of scholarship on the most intensively studied self-translator, Samuel Beckett, researchers were for a long time at pains to offer textual evidence which proved that one of Beckett's second 'versions' should not be considered secondary to its 'original'. This fact is today taken for granted and self-translation is generally understood to be a hybrid, paradoxical activity: it is both a reinterpretation of an original and the creation of a new original. It is therefore a privileged form of both translation and criticism. Contrary to Mann's assertion that all criticism is impossible, freed from the conventions of 'some critical methodology' (26) which might interfere with an author's interpretation of his own work, the recreation of that work in another language might in fact be the only possible act of criticism, or at the least the closest one might ever come to criticism.

Yet one is struck by the testimonies of many self-translators which suggest that such an ideal relationship does not exist, that they too find that they cannot speak for the dead, cannot articulate in another language the words of their absent, earlier self. While scholarship on self-translation often stresses the playfulness and invention of its practitioners, celebrating self-translation as an exploratory, creative act, as a positive discovery or negotiation of multiple 'selves', or even as the emancipation of one or many identities within the self, this is often at odds with testimonies given by those who devote their labour to it. A far greater number of authors have flirted with self-translation only to find the experience to be so tedious and/or difficult that they gave up than those who integrated it into their literary practice. Even rarer still are book-length studies devoted to this phenomenon, if one excludes studies of Beckett and Nabokov, and studies of the private motivations of the self-translator, or the collective motivations of a group of self-translators, are almost non-existent. Elizabeth Klosty Beaujour's *Alien Tongues: Bilingual Russian Writers of the 'First' Emigration* is an exception to this trend: her study finds a common and distressing 'discomfort' and 'struggle' (40) experienced by self-translators of the 'first' Russian emigration to Europe and the United States. Whether or not these writers found self-translation to be tedious, their resistance to self-translation stems, Beaujour argues, not from 'technical' or 'neurophysiological' factors, or even 'linguistic interference', but rather from 'emotional interference' (40). Her explanation for the source of this emotional trouble begins with the explanation that the self-translators of her study often express the feeling that what they are doing is illegitimate, an act of 'linguistic infidelity', which develops like a physical illness. However, the bodily metaphor soon gives way to a moral one when Beaujour finds that self-translators typically pass through a phase in which they 'express their linguistic situation in terms of bigamy, adultery, or incest' (41). She contends that when this sense of illegitimacy comes to be replaced with the knowledge that 'the bilingual writer has two avowedly *legitimate* output systems at his disposal [. . .] writing in the second language ceases to be a mere "fling" and the horror of bigamy sets in' (52). The subject is no longer just an exiled writer using a foreign language, but one who has developed into a bilingual self-translator. However, this too is but a stage, a phase which the exiled self-translator must cross before maturing into a healthy bilingual. This means having at one's disposal a 'third tongue', developing a 'personal idiolect' which one can use to address 'first and foremost, a small audience of fellow polyglots' (55). With two cultures at his disposal the bilingual self-translator is now free to exploit the 'polylinguistic matrix' to his advantage (55).

Beaujour offers Beckett and Nabokov as exemplars of those who have made their peace with self-translation, yet the complaints of both would suggest otherwise. Beckett's attitudes have been the most comprehensively documented, and his revulsion at the task had clearly not abated a decade into his intensive work as a self-translator. If his comments are to be believed, Beckett regarded translation as a chore, and a chore subordinate to his real 'work'. The comment in a letter to his friend Tom MacGreevy on 30 January 1957 is typical of his attitude: 'How sick and tired I am of translation and what a losing battle it is always. Wish I had the courage to wash my hands of it all, I mean leave it to others and try and get on with some work'. Here Beckett recognizes that to let go of his sense of obligation to self-translate would require more courage than to keep on translating, and that this is a weakness or defect. Beckett first began self-translating due to his dissatisfaction with the early work of the translation into English of his French novel, *Molloy*, coming to realize that it was easier to do the job himself than correct the work of another. He might have refused the collaborative model out of hand, but nonetheless laments his inability to accept seeing his texts rewritten differently (poorly) through the hands of others.

The lack of 'courage' which Beckett saw as his inability to let go of his works is different from his belief that his own translations were failures; not only did he fail *to give up* self-translation, but he failed *as* a self-translator. Indeed, Beckett's comments echo the clichés which some 30 years of Translation Studies have tried to debunk. Not only did he subordinate translation to real 'work', he was even prone to repeat hackneyed ideas about the 'impossibility' of translation, writing, for instance, on 22 November 1957 to Ethna McCarthy: 'I am supposed to be translating *L'Innommable*, which is impossible' (cited in Knowlson 441). When in mid-December 1958 Beckett began writing his last novel, in French, *Comment c'est*, he had already been self-translating for nearly a decade, and could not have anticipated that anyone other than himself was going to produce its English version, *How It Is*. But this knowledge certainly did not entice Beckett into making things easier for himself. On the contrary, he composed his most difficult work to date, and the subsequent effort to produce its English version was unprecedented. On 22 September 1961 he relayed to Barney Rosset that he was still 'plugging away grimly at translation of Comment c'est' (cited in Knowlson 495). In the most unequivocal of terms, Beckett expressed to Alan Schneider on 19 January 1962 not only the extreme difficulty of rendering the strange world and soundscape of *Comment c'est* into English, but his revulsion to the task: 'Translation of *Comment c'est* advances very slowly. It's the most distasteful job I ever took on and I'm often on the point of giving up' (Beckett and Schneider 119). On 22 January 1962 he wrote to his publisher, John Calder that the translation would be 'at the best, a most lamentable à peu près' (Knowlson 495). Even after one more year of work on the manuscript he wrote to Con Leventhal on 1 February 1962 that he was still 'struggling to liquidate' the translation of *Comment c'est*, that he found the task 'slow and obnoxious work' (Knowlson 555). The translation of *Comment c'est* was, even by Beckett's standards, extremely difficult: after 8 drafts and 18 months of work, it came to an end in February 1963. Such complaints must be balanced with the fact that Beckett is rarely on record as expressing positive, or even optimistic, sentiments with respect to his own writing. Yet, the fact remains that Beckett committed himself wholeheartedly to an activity which he consistently denigrated as an impertinent task, secondary to his real 'work'.

The masochistic in the mirror or the ventriloquist in furs?

For many Russian émigrés, for many Scandinavian writers, for many Indians or writers from the Maghreb, the decision to self-translate may be motivated by a myriad of practical, political or commercial factors. Without excluding such writers from the possibility that their practice might also be masochistic, those who write between major languages are clearer cases for the critic as analyst. At the very least, we must make a rather schematic distinction here between major and minor languages. For instance, the Scottish poet and novelist Christopher Whyte is a native Anglophone who writes in Scots Gaelic and has produced bilingual editions of his work. Yet, Whyte has written: 'self-translation has in my case always been done under duress. It has never been done with either pleasure or satisfaction' (67). Authors like Whyte who write in minority languages but who are proficient in major languages – especially English, French or Spanish – are subject to pressures from both publishers and readers to produce a supposedly definitive translation of their work, not to mention a more marketable bilingual edition. Such obligations, and the very different financial reality of publishing in a minor language, immediately set these authors apart from cosmopolitan self-translators.

The motivations to self-translate in a contemporary author such as Nancy Huston are very different. While she is an Anglophone Canadian who first published in French from necessity, she has since fashioned a practice of self-translation and bilingual writing out of her own free will. Yet, she has written of her experience of self-translation, comparing it to 'political torture' ('En français' 236).[1] While one might consider hers to be something of a bourgeois malady, and her comparison with torture somewhat misplaced, there is a remarkable propensity in authors like Beckett and Huston to express their practice of self-translation with a vocabulary of pain and suffering. In a talk she gave at the University of Toronto, Victoria College, 24 February 2003, Huston admitted to being 'unhappy' in her choice: 'Writing two versions of each book. Dying of boredom. Translating sentence after sentence after sentence, who else has endured this tedium? Beckett, but his books were usually shorter'. As a devoted masocritic, Huston could only write works longer than Beckett's. Indeed, when she speculates, 'God, how I long to say Okay, folks, enough of all this schtick. From now on, I'm gonna write all my books in . . . and choose one of the languages', Huston knows that this is exactly not what she is planning to do. If her practice results nonetheless in a form of healing, as Susan Bassnett's contribution to the present volume argues, then the scar is reopened, compulsively, every time Huston returns to the scene of writing.

Like freely circulating cosmopolitans, political exiles must choose whether or not to self-translate. Yet their experience of self-translation remains, if diminished, intimately and even imaginatively wedded to the forced separation from their country of origin and mother tongue. The peace which Beaujour's exiled self-translator finds in the development of the 'third tongue' is in fact the final stage of evolution within her teleological theory of self-translation, where the individual passes through multiple tests and phases before becoming accomplished in both cultures and at peace with his or her self:

> [. . .] self-translation is frequently the rite of passage, the traditional, heroic, psychic journey into the depths of the self (a version of Sigmund Freud's self-analysis or Joseph Campbell's archetypal voyage) that is a necessary prelude to true self-knowledge and its accompanying powers. Only when (and if) they have negotiated the hell of self-translation can bilingual writers proceed through the purgatory of the first years of writing in a second language and fully realize their bilingual potential. (36–7)

The 'journey' of the self-translator thus ends in an 'extraordinary reconciliation' where the self-translator has 'gone the whole course', and 'completing the full trajectory, a kind of constantly shifting balance or flexible synthesis is achieved' (53). This compelling and poetic account of the self-translator is curious in the way that it unashamedly inscribes itself into a metanarrative of heroic progress at the moment when such narratives were being systematically revised and critiqued across North American humanities departments – Beaujour's book was published in 1989 – and as debates around post-structuralism were being conducted with increasing vigour and acrimony. There is certainly a residual positivism in Beaujour's logic of the 'journey' of self-translation, something which equally compels her to find a rhetorically satisfactory conclusion to her own study. Her 'third tongue' (55) is a mysterious resolution to the problem of the self-translator's 'sin', and she sets her tortured souls along a self-perfecting Aristotelian-Dantesque path from 'hell' through 'purgatory' to 'peace' (36–56). Yet, during the earlier phase in 'hell' of the self-translator's *katabasis* (the transformative passage through the underworld in classical literature), indeed before their 'purgatory' of early, conflicted bilingual writing, Beaujour's self-translator displays a keen masocritical tenacity:

> Although the process of their linguistic metamorphosis was often *exquisitely painful* for Russian bilingual writers while they were undergoing it, many of them eventually came to realize that what at first seemed a sacrifice, a treason, almost a self-murder, was in fact merely a

step in a much more complex process that, over the long run, was not destructive or subtractive but, on the contrary, generative and positive. (6, my emphasis)

Although later in their careers bilingual writers frequently return to self-translation and may even become addicted to it, even these writers find self-translation *exquisitely painful* in the beginning. (51, my emphasis)

When one's pain is described as 'exquisite' one is led into to the semantic field of the masochistic. Yet for Beaujour this is incompatible with the mature, accomplished self-translator. But even if her narrative of self-translation is conditioned by the Judeo-Christian myths which permeate Western culture, following Theodor Reik's seminal account of social masochism there is no need to strip the self-translator of his masochism even if one wishes him to triumph. For many self-translators, their pain is not a stage in their development, but the constant condition for development itself.

In *Masochism in Modern Man* Reik develops a theory which champions the masochist as the hero of modernity. The masochist is supremely individual – 'By ordering his own punishment the masochist has made himself the master of his destiny' (161) – and successful – 'He always admits defeat, but in reality he is undefeatable. His complete surrender has more power than his wild rebellion' (164). However, the victory of the social masochist is not a wholly secular affair, for (in the West at least) this figure has internalized the eschatological religious paradigm which dominates his culture, the suffering on earth of one who waits for the Second Coming and the Day of Reckoning. For Reik, the ancient philosopher's 'old problem of suffering' (342) became in late Judaism and Christianity the means for accessing heaven. Christ defines the Western episteme: '[Christ] bore his punishment in order to ascend to heaven, he paid the highest prices so as to become God himself. He gained eternal life by death, he entered the glory of God by disgrace. He conquered through being defeated. He was victim and victor' (348). No one in the modern era has mastered Christ's lesson as well as the masochist.

In his *imitatio Christi* the masochist must, Reik stresses, conceive of sadistic fantasies which are essential to his capacity to fulfill the role of the victim, and thus suffer the requisite humiliations. In so doing, the masochist defers his supreme gratification, his judgement by the ultimate 'supernatural court of justice' (305) at his 'Day of Judgement': 'Then and there all sufferings, humiliations and ill-treatments will be justified and their purpose recognized. [. . .] his patience and his spiritual nobility will find the reward that had been withheld here below' (336). In his quotidian rituals as much as in his sadistic fantasies, the social masochist manifests a key figure in Reik's Freudian triangulation: the witness, or spectator, one who stands in waiting, menacing, ready to punish the individual. But this threat of punishment is conquered by the individual as he provokes his own punishment and thus inflicts this pain upon himself. Reik did not exclude the solitary individual from the possible configurations of masochistic submission. The fantasy in front of the mirror, for instance, generates a *witness* or *spectator* who figures in the realm of the imagination and remains essential in satisfying the conditions for masochistic pleasure. Considering the masochistic subject in front of the mirror, he writes:

> Such solitude is materially, but not psychologically, real. The masochist imagines a spectator whom he sometimes plays himself.[. . .] This second person cannot be eliminated in the phantasy because he is the carrier of the pleasure-bringing action [. . .] [S]uch beating scenes in front of a mirror [. . .] are attempts to realize phantasies in which one person has taken two parts by himself. (80)

If one considers that the suffering self-translator resembles Reik's masochist in front of the mirror, one also has to recognize that since St. Jerome's quarrel with Augustine – where Jerome affirmed the translation of scriptural 'truth' rather than word for word translation and regardless of the political consequences, thus inviting the censure of his critics – translators have long worked under the their imagined witness and ultimate Reckoner, God.[2] Psychoanalysis did not overturn the religious paradigm, but rather, as Reik acknowledges, 'Psychology with Freud brought the question of suffering out of the heavens and onto earth' (398).

One might speculate that many characteristics of Beckett's self-translation practice appear to be symptoms of the masochist. Certainly, his compulsive returning to the scene of his pain and failure recalls the central role of suspense and repetition in the masochistic situation. For Reik, suspense ensures the prolongation, the deferral, of the masochist's final gratification. The self's postponing its instinctual gratification in sexual masochism assumes a moral character in social masochism: 'The moratorium on satisfaction becomes a moralorium. [. . .] The sting of the flesh becomes a sting of the spirit. The masochistic suffering was endured originally for the aims of short-lived lust and acquires by and by the characters of depth, grandeur and ambition' (385). Repetition of the painful act is thus a formal necessity, one which the masochist must engineer for his own humiliation. Thus, contrary to popular belief, social masochism is not a practice focussed on the enjoyment of pain, it involves rather the constant deferral of the object of one's striving. To relish the object of one's journey would be its most profound failure. When Deleuze updated Reik's theory he added only one new element to Reik's list of factors in the masochistic situation, the contract: the masochist enters into an agreement to submit to the rules and conventions of the masochistic ritual. In 'Coldness and Cruelty' Deleuze writes: 'The masochist appears to be held by real chains, but in fact he is bound by his word alone' (72).[3] One might see Beckett operating in the sphere of social masochism when he refers to the pain of his contractual commitments on 3 July 1957, lamenting to Tom MacGreevy about his first attempts to translate *Fin de partie*: 'I find it [*Fin de partie*] dreadful in English, all the sharpness gone, and the rhythms. If I were not bound by contract to the Royal Court Theatre I wouldn't allow it in English at all'. While Beckett was certainly rushed by the tightness of the terms agreed with the Royal Court Theatre, his decision to create *Endgame* was not taken by the theatre: the contract of self-translation was signed by Beckett with himself.

One might conclude that Beckett's litany of self-denigrating comments about his self-translation manifest his sense of, first, the incapacity of his own translation, and second, his lack of courage in not being able to wash his hands of the whole business. As such he sins doubly against the author of his original, summoning his own punishment upon himself. However, in 'Masocriticism' Mann warns against an overly simplistic oedipal triangulation in the imagined relationship between the idealized text, the critic or translator and this witness or spectator. The witness, in this Freudian schema, is the imagined tormentor, one who will ultimately castigate the masochist for the sins of his fantasy. This person corresponds to the figure of the Greek who enters at the end of Masoch's *Venus in Furs* as the punisher, who occupies the place of the father in this oedipal triangulation. Yet Mann writes that such a father is never successfully integrated into the masochistic scene: 'The ritual thus both includes and excludes him; the masochist ritualizes his appearance within the fantasy and still suffers the disruption of the fantasy' (47). One can find this kind of ambiguously present and absent critic in Beckett's self-translations. Consider, for instance, the following translation Beckett made from his unpunctuated French novel, *Comment c'est*, published in 1961:

> [. . .] tant de mots tant de perdus un sur trois deux sur cinq le son puis le sens même proportion ou bien aucun j'entends tout je comprends tout et revis j'ai revécu [. . .]

> [. . .] so many words so many lost one every three two every five first the sound then the sense same ratio or else not one not one lost I hear all understand all and live again [. . .] (122–3)

Here, Beckett's narrator is searching for a formula which will explain his manner of narration. He implies that the voice in text is neither verbatim recitation, nor literal translation, but a repetition of the voice he hears in his head based upon form rather than sense by equating rhythm and sound.[4] Strangely, in this text the 'I' hears words from one he terms his 'voix ancienne', his former, or 'ancient' voice, which he also conflates with a figure he identifies as his own 'witness', an author figure who looks down on him named, 'l'autre dans la lumiere', 'the other above in the light'. His repetition of the words of his 'ancient voice' is in the above quote said to be controlled by a quantitative loss of words. However, the act of self-translation inscribes itself into this continuity of loss, with the addition of the English word 'lost' at the very moment when the apparatus (self-translation) breaks down once more, the rhythm of the translation becoming confused and provoking the question 'not one [?] lost[.]' Neither the question provoked by the dissonance between the sense and the rhythm, nor the reflexive 'lost' existed in *Comment c'est*. Beckett criticism often points to these sorts of disjunctions to highlight Beckett's playful metatextual writing. But more than this, the example is typical of moments when Beckett inscribes a *critical* voice into the translation. The narrator continues to dress himself in furs, striking the ludic pose of Reik's solitary masochist in front of the mirror, his text *en face*. His compulsion to comment on his translation performance publicizes his inadequacy as a translator, revealing elements of what Reik would term the 'demonstrative phase' or the 'narcissistic function' of the masochistic situation, that which encourages the ego through the publication (promotion) of its suffering.[5] Thus denying himself a 'successful' and seamless translation, the admission of what is 'lost' in translation maintains the masochistic suspense by demonstrating the collapse of the translating apparatus before the subject encounters its idealized object of desire (the master text). Reik's contention is that in masochism it is this collapse that was desired all along.

And if Beckett makes himself ridiculous in the process, mistranslating or posing as the suffering artist, he reminds us of Reik's insight that the clown is no less noble for his comic failures. Don Quixote is Reik's archetype of the indefatigable optimist in spite of his perpetual pessimism: 'The blows of fate mostly stage-managed by himself or provoked by himself, lay him low but he rises again. He is the jack-in-the-box of God' (324). Samuel Beckett, like Falstaff or Don Quixote, confesses his shortcomings before the world. His cunning strategy transfers his humiliation onto the reader: 'The production of laughter is a special means of masochistic gratification for the comical person', says Reik, 'That he makes a fool of himself, does not mean that he is a fool' (80). Beckett even might fulfil Reik's triumphant role for the masochist in the modern world:

> Instead of being afraid of humiliation, disgrace or punishment, he has brought it about himself, thus mastering a hard destiny. By anticipating all these sensations he deprives them of their terrors. The masochistic mechanism is – with regard to its direction – a flight toward the future. [. . .] [T]he masochist, by his perversion, succeeds in avoiding the development of his anxiety. (70)

Triumphant in the moral superiority of his 'flight toward the future', Reik's masochist nonetheless comes to resemble the teleological hero of Beaujour's positivistic journey; while the former is denied the attainment of his goal, sparing himself the pleasures of the naïve and base, it is this fact which opens an alternative route to the moral summit of Reik's estimation.

This situation produces some uneasiness in the masocritic, for as Mann writes: 'Whenever criticism poses as a solemn or sublime allegory, masocriticism exposes it as an over-literal parody' (40). Indeed by manifesting its witness-critic, Beckett's self-translated bilingual *œuvre* revels in a failure which resembles more Mann's masocriticism than Reik's masochism. For Beckett, the publication of failure anticipates the arrival of the narrator's imagined witness, the critic, who will reckon his translation performance. In 'Masocriticism', Mann holds that in their service to the texts they chose as their masters, critics and translators hide their desire to be castigated for this very identification: 'whatever one writes will fall short, mutilate the text, serve the master badly; and to do so is transgressive and hence punishable, and hence desirable' (37). Similarly, Beckett's failure to translate fulfils the prophecy of his inadequacy for the task. His failure is deliberate, and by inscribing the critical voice into his translation performance he even anticipates the judgements which he knows will be brought upon that performance by his imagined tormentor and witness. On the other hand, Beckett forces the actual critic to question if one can really criticize Beckett's translation performance. Indeed, when one becomes aware of Beckett's publicizing his own failure, when Beckett assumes the role of critic and intervenes into his text to identify precisely the moment when the translatory apparatus breaks down, can a critic really fulfil his or her role in the masochistic situation and punish Beckett for his sins? Beckett has equipped his text with a defensive strategy to defer the critic's censure. And what is true of Beckett is true also of his comic, self-humiliating characters: their behaviour and infantile antics make less of a parody of themselves than a simplistic diagnosis of their behaviour. If the reader is so dogmatic in his faith in the allegory of psychoanalysis as to fall for their *flaunted* symptoms then Beckett has succeeded in deflecting ridicule from himself, transferring it onto the reader/critic. One need look no further than the stage managed, all-too-perfect 'failures' in translation. One might indeed consider a text like *Comment c'est* to be a spoof on the suffering self-translator, a superlatively ironic piece of self-writing – it is difficult to consider it otherwise when its storyline involves Beckett straightjacketing his narrative 'I' into reciting and inscribing imperfectly and erroneously the voice it hears in its head, its 'voix ancienne', or former voice – which Beckett even felicitously 'mistranslates' into English as his 'ancient voice'. The tortured nature of this narrative dyad is replicated below as the text's 'I' traverses a hellish underworld of mud, provoking and being provoked by sadomasochistic rituals of grotesque torture and extreme violence. Yet the seriousness of this gruesome tale is but half-hearted, or rather it exists for the light hearted, because Beckett's correspondence from the period is testimony to his sense of the ridiculousness of his self-imposed 'wastes and wilds of self-translation' (Beckett, 'Beckett's Letters' 183). Similarly, a little too evident is the Freudian triangulation between the 'I' in text, it's 'ancient voice' – which does not miss its Judeo-Christian target when the 'I' confuses it with 'the other above in the light' – and its various manifestations of the projected 'witness', who is of course implicated in the scene of textual/scriptural reproduction/translation: 'the witness bending over me [. . .] the scribe [. . .] generations of scribes keeping the record' (103).

Such knowing masochism, one so aware of its easy psychoanalytic diagnosis, suggests that Beckett is less a martyr of his will than a purveyor of the masocritical arts. My aim is not to hold up Beckett as an ideal within Translation Studies or to celebrate a genius of self-translation. Yet perhaps it is inevitable that should future critics take up an investigation into the masocritical dimension to self-translation, the figure of Beckett will continue to loom large, assuming the role of witness and potential punisher, able to enter like the Greek at the end the *Venus in Furs*. If ever this situation comes about, or if it is presently the case, the lesson of Mann's 'Masocriticism' is that Beckett's arrival on the scene will never be the ultimate goal of a masocritical investigation. 'Beckett' is but a condition of the suspense which maintains our work. If he looms as a witness over our investigation it is because we require the possibility that he, or someone else, enter the scene and castigate us for our sins. And one need not be anxious about Beckett coming to dominate our thinking about self-translation, for if today he seems most qualified to fulfil the role of castigating witness, this is most likely the sign that tomorrow translation scholars will feel compelled to submit to another master, one different in kind or in number, a new body better adapted to our new objects of identification, a master who will be competent to teach us the next lessons we believe we need to be taught.

Notes

1 'L'autotraduction, c'est tout ce que je connais en matière de torture politique' ('En francais dans le texte' 236).

2 I thank Rainier Grutman for suggesting to me this link with St. Jerome.

3 '*Le masochiste n'est qu'en apparence tenu par des fers et des liens; il n'est tenu que par sa parole*' (Deleuze, 'Le froid' 76).

4 The Janviers make a similar account of Beckett's translating *Watt* into French: 'on le voyait compter sur les doigts. Les équivalences s'imposaient presque plus à cause du nombre que du sens' (58; [. . .] we saw him count on his fingers. Equivalent terms made themselves known almost more by their number than their meaning).

5 Stolorow argues that the influence of this feature of masochism is even stronger than Reik believed (441–8).

Works cited

Beaujour, Elizabeth Klosty. *Alien Tongues: Bilingual Russian Writers of the 'First' 'Emigration*. Ithaca and London: Cornell UP, 1989. Print.

Beckett, Samuel. *Comment c'est, How It Is* and / et *L'Image*: *A critical-genetic edition / Une édition critico-génétique*. Ed. Édouard Magessa O'Reilly. New York: Routledge, 2001. Print.

Beckett, Samuel and Alan Schneider. *No Author Better Served*: *The Correspondence of Samuel Beckett and Alan Schneider*. Ed. Maurice Harmon. Cambridge, MA: Harvard UP, 1998. Print.

Deleuze, Gilles. 'Coldness and Cruelty'. *Masochism*. *Venus in Furs*. London and New York: Zone, 1989. Print.

—. 'Le froid et le cruel'. *Présentation sur Sacher-Masoch, La vénus à la fourrure* (Leopold von Sacher-Masoch). Trans. Aude Willm. Paris: Minuit, 1967. Print.

Huston, Nancy. 'En français dans le texte'. *Désirs et réalités*. Montréal: Leméac, 1995. 231–6. Print.

—. Untitled. University of Toronto, Victoria College. 24 Feb. 2003. Unpublished transcript.

Janvier, Ludovic and Agnès Vaquin-Janvier. 'Traduire avec Beckett: *Watt*'. *Revue d'esthétique* (1986) 57–64. Print.

Knowlson, James. *Damned to Fame*: *The Life of Samuel Beckett*. London: Bloomsbury, 1996. Print.

Mann, Paul. *Masocriticism*. Albany: State U of New York P, 1999. Print.

Reik, Theodor. *Masochism in Modern Man*. Trans. Margaret H. Beigel and Gertrud M. Kurth. New York: Farrar, Straus, 1941. Print.

Stolorow, Robert D. 'The Narcissistic Function of Masochism (and Sadism)'. *International Journal of Psycho-Analysis* 56 (1975): 441–8. Print.

Whyte, Christopher. 'Against Self-Translation'. *Translation and Literature* 11.1 (2002): 64–71. Print.

CHAPTER SIX

Translating philosophy: Vilém Flusser's practice of multiple self-translation

Rainer Guldin

Abstract: This paper deals with the multilingual self-translation practice of the Czech-Brazilian writer and philosopher Vilém Flusser (1920–91). Flusser used up to four languages (Portuguese, German, English and French), systematically translating and retranslating all of his texts. He mainly used the technique of self-translation to distance himself from his texts in order to verify their inner coherence and formal qualities in a form of editorial recycling. After some general theoretical considerations about the practice of self-translation, the paper is going to focus on a particularly telling example from Flusser's work.

In this paper I would like to discuss Vilém Flusser's practice of self-translation, focusing first on its relevance within the general context of a theory and practice of self-translation and subsequently examining in detail a particularly telling example from his oeuvre.

Flusser was born in Prague in 1920 into a wealthy assimilated Jewish family and forced into exile in the spring of 1939 by the Nazi invasion of Czechoslovakia. While he managed to flee to Brazil in 1940, his whole family was wiped out in the Nazi concentration camps. In 1972 Flusser returned to Europe and spent the last years of his life in the village of

Robion, in Southern France, though his life was cut short by a car accident in 1991 when travelling back from a conference in Prague. Flusser became famous in the early 1990s as a 'digital thinker' and author of visionary texts on photography, video art and media theory.[1]

The originality of Vilém Flusser's multiple practice of self-translation

The uniqueness of Flusser's practice of self-translation lies in the fact, that he used up to four different languages (Portuguese, German, English and French), systematically translating and retranslating all of his texts, instead of rewriting them in the same language.[2] One can find at least a second version in another language of most of his essays and all of his books, but most of the time three or more versions. In some cases the number of versions of the same text can amount to ten or more. In this sense Flusser could be de called a 'multilingual writer', that is, someone who 'writes with competent or idiomatic skill in three or more languages' (Hokenson and Manson 14).

The second relevant aspect is that Flusser was writing as an essayist and philosopher, rather than as an author of literary texts. The practice of self-translation is relatively common among literary authors but remains an exception within philosophy or the social sciences. There are some authors of philosophical texts, like Walter Benjamin, Paul de Man and Jacques Derrida, to name only a few, who developed a particular sensitivity to language differences because of their interest in translation processes. And there is the German born bilingual author, Günther Gotthard, who migrated to the United States in the 1930s, where he developed a new Non-Aristotelian logic, which he called a polycontextural logic. Günther himself once stated that the very core of his work lies in the difference between his English and German publications. However, no one in the field of philosophy or social theory, as far as I know, ever made use of systematic plural self-translation the way Flusser did for over 40 years.

There is, moreover, another significant aspect to be taken into account with regard to the meticulous re-translational practice Flusser developed over the course of his writing career. Flusser's practice of an open-ended series of consecutive multilingual translations was usually followed by a final attempt at a synthesizing retranslation. In an unpublished typescript,[3] *Scribere necesse est vivere non est*, Flusser summed up the fluid border between translating and rewriting with the German word '*umschreiben*', which can be both read as '*umschreiben*', or rewriting, and '*umschreiben*', meaning literally to write around a specific subject matter, circling around it, in continuously expanding, concentric multilingual spirals.

Flusser also used the technique of self-translation to distance himself from his texts in order to check their inner coherence and formal qualities. By translating his own texts he could put his point of view in phenomenological brackets, and because of the rupture introduced by language-switching he could do this in a way that simple rewriting would not permit. In fact, rewriting a text in the same language generally does not entail the same radical reconsiderations that a translation demands, even if it is a self-translation.

Writing through translation is, moreover, a strategy that aims to accumulate as many points of view as possible. Each time a text is translated into another language a new standpoint is reached from which the original thought can be viewed. This is a strategy Flusser rediscovered in the Jewish interpretative technique of the *pilpul*, relating to the writing of the commentaries in the Babylon Talmud. 'In the middle of the page', writes Flusser, 'there is a word, or a few words, and around this kernel are drawn some concentric text-circles. [. . .] The circles do not only comment upon the kernel, but also comment upon each other' (my translation).[4] They are slowly forming around the centre like the rings of a tree trunk and are written not only by different authors over long periods of time – sometimes even centuries – but also often in different languages, mostly in Hebrew and Aramaic. The original thought, the *Ein-fall* as Flusser calls it in German, that which falls *into* something like a stone thrown into a pond, expands in wavelike ripples from the epicentre. These different commentaries make up a field of circling points of view attracting and repulsing each other. The object in the middle, beleaguered 'by an inexhaustible swarm of points of view' (my translation)[5] can be truly comprehended only when all of them have been exhausted. That is: *never*. Truth, thus, is a limit that we are striving to attain, but cannot possibly reach. The sacred word in the middle of the Talmud page always demands new attempts at interpretation and refuses at the same time to reveal its full essence. Comprehensive translation is, therefore, as Derrida put it, both necessary and impossible. In this sense the translatory movement is basically endless. It can be stopped at will or go on as long as the self-translating author wants it to.

Multiple-translation besides being a method of self-criticism is also a form of editorial recycling which depends on economic motives and publication opportunities. In the essay, *Retradução enquanto metodo de trabalho*, written in the mid-1970s in France, Flusser introduces the idea that the choice of a specific theme is dictated by its (un)translatability, that is, if it is especially well suited for the game of consecutive translations. 'The more difficult it is to translate a certain theme the bigger is the challenge it represents, because it will generate a dialectical tension between the different languages that inform me, forcing me to look for a synthesis of these contradictions' (my translation).[6] The creative principle is therefore activated by that which opposes itself to an easy transfer into another language, that which is not so much strictly untranslatable but which by its near untranslatability compels the translator-writer to find an original solution. Flusser uses the space in between languages to attain a new vision of his subject.

Creating palimpsests: Vilém Flusser's position within the wider field of self-translation

To better highlight Flusser's specific position within the field of self-translation in the twentieth century and the uniqueness of his writing career I would like, now, to discuss briefly some of the interpretative categories introduced by Michaël Oustinoff in his *Bilinguisme d'écriture et auto-traduction* in which Oustinoff tries to formulate a general theory of literary self-translation, setting out from the bilingual work of Julien Green, Samuel Beckett and Vladimir Nabokov. Oustinoff speaks of a palimpsestic logic of multiple overlappings, of a system of boxes within boxes, echoing Flusser's own definition of writing as a series of (re)translations. '*Pour moi*', he writes in the unpublished manuscript, 'Le geste d'écrire', '*c'est ça le geste d'écrire: faire des palimpsestes*' (9). To write is, therefore, to translate, in order to create a textual palimpsest.

Oustinoff distinguishes three stages of self-translation that differ only gradually from each other: the first one tries to cleanse the new text of all traces of self-translation, in an attempt to respect the purity of the original; the middle, decentring form, allows for single deviations from this rule; and the third extends this liberty to the whole text. The three forms mentioned can be associated with the work of certain bilingual authors, but can also coexist within a single text. Examples for the first, 'naturalizing' form can be met within the work of Julien Green (Guldin, 'Two Tongues' 193–214) and Joseph Conrad, both of whom also formulated a clear preference for one of their two writing languages. Beckett and Nabokov, on the other hand, represent the second, decentring type. Interestingly enough, Oustinoff does not propose any concrete examples for the third typology. Within Beckett's and Nabokov's oeuvre texts in different languages help illuminate each other, and the act of self-translation facilitates the unfolding of the still hidden potentialities of the original. Contrary to Julien Green, who painstakingly upheld a clear border between the two languages, Beckett and Nabokov moved back and forth between their two writing languages in the course of their career. This suggests that the use of different languages within single texts and the general attitude to these languages and their relationship basically correlate.

Into which of Oustinoff's categories does Vilém Flusser fit? Flusser's self-translation strategy, at least on a self-theorizing level, oscillates between a decentring and a completely free approach to the original. When it comes to the actual everyday practice of translation, however, Flusser also makes use of simple word to word translation, very much respecting the literal meaning of the original. As I have already pointed out, despite his strong sense of linguistic nuance and interlinguistic connections, Flusser is interested, above all, in systematically expanding and deepening the original thought that prompted his writing impulse. In this sense, his interest is primarily a philosophical and less a literary one. He, thus, never tries to recreate the original text, even if each writing act tries to reach back, from another point of view, to the first idea, the initial *Ein-Fall*.

In this sense, one could position him at the extreme end of Oustinoff's typology. In a way, Flusser represents a good example of a writer who radically strives to recreate each new text by amplifying and redefining it, without worrying too much about the conservation of the original content of the first version. If fidelity there is, then it is rather to the unreachable, vague, initially cloudy moment of inspiration that set the whole process in motion. '[. . .] [*J*]*e ne traduis pas comme un 'traducteur normal*', he writes in 'Le geste d'écrire'. '*Je n'essai pas d'être fidèle au texte* [. . .], *mais de le dépasser*' (9). To translate means, thus, not to be faithful to the original but to overcome it. To describe the presence of the first text *within* the second – and of all the different versions in the last synthesis, for that matter – Flusser uses the image of the palimpsest, suggesting in this way that in the empty spaces between the written lines, the intervals between the single words and letters of the new version, as well as in its overall textual arrangement, the previous texts are still living on in some sort of way. This palimpsest is 'not readily decipherable, but still in a sense effective' (Flusser, 'Gesture' 11). The new version will go beyond the older one, but between its lines persist the lines of the first text: '[. . .] *il aura, pour ainsi dire 'entre les lignes' du texte portugais, des vestiges des lignes allemandes*' ('Le geste' 9). There will be, so to speak, 'between the lines' of the Portuguese text vestiges of the German lines. The word 'vestiges', in its meaning of traces of an earlier civilization, points explicitly to the written page as a many-layered space of lines within lines within lines, which the reader is asked to dig up in an endless movement of deciphering. One has to look for the traces left by the process of translation and retranslation, the invisible plurilingual content hiding beneath the monolingual text of the last version, the different layers of the final multilingual palimpsest mirroring the manifold complexity of the original thought.

Contrary to Oustinoff's examples, Flusser never really wavered between his writing languages but used their differences throughout his writing career to fuel his productivity. In this spiralling ballet, languages can exchange their roles, subverting the essential opposition of source and target language. Flusser imagines his (re)translations as if they were a complex involuted system of Russian dolls within dolls.

> [T]he original relationship of the two codes is reversed: the object-code [the source language] becomes now a meta-code [the target language]. In other words: after the French code has swallowed part of the [. . .] English one, it is in turn swallowed by the English code, [. . .] so to speak with the English in its belly.[7] (Flusser, 'Kommunikologie' 343; my translation)

Thus, in the course of the translation and retranslation processes, a text ingests and digests another text that is in turn feeding on a text it has previously swallowed. Each new text is an 'invitation to a dance' as Flusser puts it in 'Retradução enquanto metodo de trabalho': 'Of course such recurrent coiled retranslation can be formalized. [. . .] But such a formalization of the problem of retranslation would get rid of the fascination of the game' (my translation).[8]

Flusser's retranslation strategy evolved over the course of his writing career. In the beginning, through the 1950s and 1960s, it was mostly a game played with two languages only, German and Portuguese. Over time, however, he added English and, after his return to Europe, also French, such that by the mid-1970s the complexity of the game had grown considerably and what was at first an attempt to survive as a German author within a foreign linguistic context had become a way of living. A survey of the two dozen major works written by Flusser in the course of his life shows that before his return to Europe he generally produced only two versions of his books, one German and the other Portuguese. After 1972, however, he started creating three to four different versions of each new book (Guldin, *Philosophieren* 313–15).

Discussing a significant example: 'The Ground We Tread'

The text I would now like to deal with, 'The Ground We Tread', was first written in the late 1970s and then translated several times into the early 1980s, at the very apex of Flusser's multilingual self-translating career. There are altogether eleven different versions of this text: two English ('The Ground We Tread:' A and B); five Portuguese ('O chão que pisamos:' C, D, E, F, G); five German ('Der Boden unter den Füßen:' H, I, J, K, L); and one French (*Le sol au-dessous de nos pieds*: M). Versions D and E, as well as J and L are identical, four were published (M, E, J and L), all the others are unpublished typescripts.

This short essay, dedicated to Hannah Arendt, is the first of a series of texts Flusser published in 1983 in São Paulo under the title *Pós-história*

(Post-history). This is the most extreme example of self-translation I have come across in Flusser's work. The insistence with which he kept rewriting this specific essay has certainly a lot to do with all the reasons mentioned before. But there are two other extremely significant motives to be considered: Auschwitz lies at the very existential and philosophical heart of Flusser's oeuvre. Auschwitz, according to Flusser, has changed our perception of the idea of history and progress; it has revealed the basic '*Bodenlosigkeit*', that is, the groundlessness of our culture. But Auschwitz symbolizes also the beginning of Flusser's own existential groundlessness. This very coincidence of the individual and collective historical destiny may account for Flusser's obsessive rewriting of the text.

The main problem with this textual series – and all the others, for that matter – is that, generally, Flusser neither put any date on his essays nor left any indication as to their position within the sequence of self-translations. All texts look the same: densely type-written numbered pages with no indication whatsoever as to the moment of their creation. In reconstructing the sequence, my two working hypotheses are that the thematic sequencing within the single texts and the fact that Flusser always switched languages when rewriting might help to reconstruct the actual sequence of the texts.

A comparison of the macrostructure of the texts, that is, the content of the opening paragraph, the sequencing of the single paragraphs and the aspects treated therein not only allow for the creation of two distinct textual lines but also help to determine which one was most probably written first. In fact, some of the texts had actually been published at some time permitting at least a partial definition of the time succession. The first series contains one for each language: Portuguese (C), English (B), German (K) and French (M). The second series contains nine texts: one in English (A), four in Portuguese (D, E, F and G) and four in German (H, I, J and L). All texts are about four pages long.

The first essential question to be answered regards the relationship of the two sequences. Why and when, in fact, did Flusser start writing a second series at all? The subsequent questions relate to the relationship of the single texts within the two series: What sequences can be detected? What happens when a text is rewritten in a new language? What changes does this lead to?

As far as the first question is concerned, practical reasons – such as, perhaps, the dissatisfaction with the texts written so far or the impossibility of finding a publisher for the versions already produced – should be considered along with the more existential response suggested above, the telescoping of individual and collective existence. In fact, only one of the texts in the first sequence was actually published. A closer comparison of the two main series, however, suggests that the main reason for the creation of the second series most probably lies in a significant thematic shift, a textual reorientation achieved by introducing a new central issue and by reshuffling the single paragraphs. The following overview of the main content of the single paragraphs – 12 in both variants – shall clarify this.

First text-sequence	Second text-sequence
1. The steps by which humanity advances towards progress sound hollow. Something unbelievable has happened to us in the recent past: Auschwitz. How was such a thing possible? How can we go on living after Auschwitz?	1. No refined hearing is necessary to perceive the hollowness of our steps toward the future, the hollowness of our progress. There is a historical period comparable to our own, because it has numerous traits which remind us of the present situation: the baroque.
2. Auschwitz expresses something absolutely fundamental about western culture.	2. We and the baroque. A comparison.
3. This is something we must refuse. We must look for counterarguments.	3. How was such a thing possible? How can we go on living after Auschwitz?
4. These objections are, however, insufficient.	4. Auschwitz expresses something absolutely fundamental about our culture. It is part of its program.
5. If one accepts this argumentation, however, our whole history basically leads up to Auschwitz.	5. Our idea of progress has, therefore, to be radically reconsidered. Is a second Auschwitz lying ahead?
6. Our idea of progress has to be radically reconsidered. Is a second Auschwitz lying ahead?	6. Auschwitz was not simply a 'crime' but the outcome of the apparatus with its resulting objectification of human life.
7. Those that reject their own culture end up in madness (Nietzsche). If you refuse your culture, the world loses all sense.	7. The very possibility of the existence of Auschwitz is shocking. Within apparatuses people operate merely as parts of a system.
8. But despite this we should not deny Auschwitz. It regards us all.	8. Those that reject their own culture end up in madness (Nietzsche). If you refuse your culture, the world loses all sense.
9. Auschwitz is the prototype of all future instances of Auschwitz.	9. Auschwitz is the first example of something written in our program.
10. We are not the first to have lived in an abyss. The baroque preceded us.	10. Black Boxes rapidly grow around us. Auschwitz is the first example of a perfect apparatus. The programmers lost control.
11. We and the baroque. A comparison.	11. The West is characterized by its ability to turn anything into an object. Apparatuses are instruments of objectification.
12. End of history. Embryos of Auschwitz rapidly grow around us. We try to ignore it and have a bad conscience.	12. Our existential climate: hoping that the ultimate totalitarian apparatus is not going to be actuated. The game is not over yet.

The main thematic shift from the first to the second version consists in the introduction of the concept of 'apparatus', which is for Flusser a technical, cybernetic and sociological category, a complex structure transforming everything into a mere object (Guldin, 'Golem;' Ströhl 216–20). Within an apparatus people tend to become operators functioning according to a set of pre-established rules. The very possibility of an apparatus like Auschwitz is, according to Flusser, part of the cultural project of western society, an essential inherent possibility of its programming, as he calls it.

In the first series the reference to the baroque is only used at the end (paragraph 10 and 11), whereas in the second it has been moved to the very beginning (paragraphs 1 and 2). Key words of the new reinterpreted sequence are 'program', 'apparatus', 'operator', 'function'.

The first thematically coherent text-sequence (C-B-K-M) must have been written in the late 1970s. Most probably the second sequence was started at about the same time or shortly after that. The French version (M) was published in April 1980 in the issue 3.4 of the French journal *Sgraffite*. A short introduction to the text announces that it has been translated by the author himself. A comparison with the German version K shows that it has most probably been translated word for word. There are, nevertheless, several deviations as far as style and sentence structure are concerned. Five short chapter titles have been added. Some passages in the German version have been deleted, but others, intended for a French speaking reading-audience, have been added. A word-play has been partially sacrificed. The German text uses the ambivalent '*Durchbruch*', breakthrough. Literally, however, it also means the opposite: values have splintered, broken apart and collapsed. This ambivalence is central to Flusser's interpretation of the apparatus. In the French version this has been rendered with the word '*cassures*'. A closer reading of the other three versions (C, B and K) shows that the general line of argumentation was not changed. On the word and sentence level, on the other hand, quite a few modifications can be made out. Some parts were translated word for word, but others stylistically altered through additions and deletions, as well as by changing the punctuation. All in all, the three versions are so similar that the question arises, what can they actually tell us about Flusser's method of self-translation. Did he write one version after the other, and if so, how long were the actual intervals between the different versions? Did he translate his texts from memory, or did he start out from the written variant as a normal translator would do? Some changes show that most probably Flusser produced the German text (K) combining the first two texts. Does this mean that he created his translations not one after the other but by using more than one variant at a time? In most cases the first Portuguese and the second English variant are so similar that they were most probably written before the others. It is, however, not clear which one was written first.

There is, moreover, still another more essential question to be dealt with regarding the very status of translation as a motor of textual transformation: which one of the two strategies is more important in terms of changes in content and form, beginning a new series or translating single texts within a series? If one follows Flusser's own view on the subject one would have to privilege the second interpretation. For Flusser, any translation amounts to a jump over an unbridgeable abyss. A closer look at the two series and their inner progression, however, suggests another possible answer. In fact, between the first and the second series a radical reshuffling of the paragraphs and a crucial change in point of view has taken place; a change that is more radical than the smaller shifts occurring when jumping from text to text within the two textual lines. Here one can identify only a series of micro-changes touching upon sentence structure, punctuation and above all the use of specific words. This, nevertheless, confirms Flusser's own suggestion that translation is above all something taking place on the level of the word, and not so much the text. It contradicts, however, Flusser's own theoretical conviction that any change of language automatically opens up a new perspective on the central issue. This evident inner contradiction can be partially solved if one considers that the second textual line also implies a jump into another linguistic universe. It is, nonetheless, only a partial solution. In fact, an analysis of Flusser's two sequences shows that other non-linguistic factors play a determining role in self-translation.

A comparison of the two textual sequences shows one specific aspect of Flusser's strategy of self-translation. The single paragraphs are used as textual blocks that can be moved around, changing the specific thematic accentuation of the essay. Sometimes single paragraphs are broken up along content lines and redistributed across the whole text. In this particular case the comparison between modernity and the baroque has been moved from the end to the very beginning of the essay. Furthermore, the concept of apparatus that was still missing in the first series gives the whole reflection a radically mediatic turn, suggesting a disconcerting connection between the extermination camp of Auschwitz and the modern technological world. In Flusser's eyes, both are expressions of the apparatus. These changes in the macrostructure entail, of course, several alterations within the microstructure.

A comparison of the single texts of the two lines shows, for instance, that the four texts of the first line are practically identical as far as the macrostructure is concerned. But there are many smaller changes that have taken place. Even if one comes across long stretches of word for word translations, sudden changes, probably made for stylistic reasons, can be made out: sentences have been reshuffled; punctuation has been altered; some elements have been deleted and others added. The first three versions are so similar that one wonders what method Flusser actually employed to produce them. Did he write one version after the other? How much time went by in between? Did he reproduce his texts from memory or simply rewrite them? Sometimes a later version comes back to a formulation used in a much earlier one, meaning that Flusser possibly collated different texts shifting back and forth between versions.

The second text-sequence (G-A-F-H-D/E-I-J/L) can be broken off into two major groups. In fact, the long initial paragraph of the first four texts (G-A-F-H) has been split into two smaller ones, moving the comparison with the baroque into the second section (D/E, I and J/L). These are also the versions that were finally published: *O chão que pisamos* (E) was included into *Pós-história*, whereas *Der Boden unter den Füßen* was published twice in *Nachgeschichten* (J) and in *Nachgeschichte* (L). There are, furthermore, three smaller multilingual groups to be made out suggesting that in this instance too Flusser systematically switched languages when rewriting his text, moving from Portuguese to English (G-A), to Portuguese and German (F-H) and finally to Portuguese and German again (D/E-I-J/L). Every text seems to be asking for what Hokenson and Munson term its 'partner version;' and instead of differences and unbridgeable gaps, Flusser's self-translation highlights 'continuities across language versions' (Hokenson and Munson 4).

> Bilingual analysis must [. . .] begin at a level more basic than current binary theoretical models of 'gaps' [. . .] One must start from a point closer to the common core of the bilingual text, that is, within the textual intersections and overlap of versions. [. . .] Again, turning the current critical practice around, to investigate the author as interculture and textual bilinguality as interliminality, will provide new means of analysis'. (Hokenson and Munson 4)

To convey an idea of what has been described so far and to allow such a 'stereoscopic reading' of the different texts I would like to quote the beginning of the first paragraph of the different versions one after the other and next to each other. This way the functional correspondences, the continuities across versions should become visible. Words in italics are to be found in all versions, words in small caps only in some of them. Finally, passages in square brackets call attention to words or sentences that were deleted in the passage from version to version.

Sequence 1: C-B-K-M:

C: O chão que pisamos	B: The ground we tread	K: Der Boden unter den Füßen	M: Le sol au-dessous de nos pieds
Os *passos* pelos quais a humanidade atual avança rumo ao PROGRESSO sôam ocos. [Alguma vacuidade,] algum *abismo* que se esconde debaixo do solo que pisamos, *ressôa* nos nossos passos. Todos os nossos *atos* traem, pela vacuidade que neles reverbera, que LHES FALTA AQUELA SOLIDEZ que carateriza todo ato fundado sobre DECISÃO vital [. . .].	The *steps* by which humanity advances toward PROGRESS sound hollow. Some *abyss* hidden beneath the soil *reverberates* in them. All our *acts* betray that vacuity: THEY LACK THE SOLIDITY which used to characterize acts and DECISIONS of previous generations.	Unsere *Schritte* in Richtung FORTSCHRITT klingen hohl. Irgendein *Abgrund*, der sich unter dem Boden verbirgt, *schwingt* in ihnen *mit*. Alle unsere *Handlungen* verraten diese Hohlheit: sie sind nicht so ,ENTSCHIEDEN', WIE SIE ES FRÜHER WAREN.	Nos *pas* en direction du FUTUR sonnent creux; un *abîme* quelconque qui se cache sous le sol *résonne* dans nos pas. Tous nos *actes* trahissent cette vacuité. Ils ne sont plus aussi DÉCISIFS QU'ILS NE L'ÉTAIENT DANS LES GÉNÉRATIONS PRÉCÉDENTES.

Sequence 2: G-A-F-H-D/E-I-J/L:

G: O chão que pisamos	A: The ground we tread	F: O chão que pisamos
Não é necessário dispôr-se de *ouvido* especialmente *apurado* para percebermos o quanto sôam ocos os nossos passos rumo ao progresso. No entanto para COMPRENDERMOS de que vacuidade se trata, qual O ABISMO que ressôa debaixo do solo, é preciso de alguma atenção mais refinada. Hà VÀRIOS TIPOS DE VACUIDADE, e a nossa pode ser compreendida somente se a compararmos com outras jà VIVENCIADAS PELA HUMANIDADE NO PASSADO.	*No refined hearing* is necessary to perceive the hollowness of our steps toward the future, the hollowness of our progress. But we need a trained ear to UNDERSTAND what sort of vacuity it is that vibrates underneath, to understand THE ABYSS we walk on. THERE ARE VARIOUS TYPES OF VACUITIES and ours can be understood only if we compare it to those which HUMANITY HAS EXPERIENCED IN THE PAST.	Não é preciso ter-se OUVIDO ESPECIALMENTE *afinado* para per-ceber-se quanto sôam ôcos os nossos passos rumo ao futuro, quanto sôa ôco o nosso ,*progresso*.' MAS é NECES-sàRIA ATENÇÃO CONCENTRADA para CONSTATAR -SE de que vacuidade se trata. PORQUE hà DIVERSOS TIPOS de vacuidade: o mais conhecido e o MELHOR ESTUDADO é o da vacuidade barroca.

H: Der Boden, auf dem wir gehen	D/E: O chão que pisamos	I: Der Boden unter den Füßen
Es ist kein besonders geschärftes Gehör nötig, um einen hohlen Unterton aus den Schritten herauszuhören, mit denen wir uns zur Zukunft hinbewegen: aus unserem ‚Fortschritt'. Hingegen ist es nötig, aufmerksam hinzuhören, wenn man FESTSTELLEN will, um welche Art von Hohlheit es sich dabei handelt. Es gibt nämlich verschiedene Hohlheiten, und die aus der Geschichte bekannteste ist die barocke [. . .].	Não è preciso de ouvido atento para descrobir-se que os passos pelos quais avançamos rumo ao futuro soam ocos. Mas è preciso concentrar o ovido se se quer DESCOBRIR DE que tipo de vacuidade se trata que ressoa no nosso progresso. Hà vários tipos de vacuidade, e a nossa deve ser comparada com outras, SE A META FOR COMPRENDê-LA. O INCOMPARÁVEL é INCOMPRENSÍVEL.	Es ist kein geschärftes Gehör nötig, um einen hohlen Unterton aus den Schritten herauszuhören, mit denen wir uns zur Zukunft hinbewegen: aus unserem 'Fortschritt'. Hingegen ist es nötig, aufmerksam hinzuhören, wenn man feststellen will, um welche Art von Hohlheit es sich dabei handelt. Es gibt nämlich verschiedene Hohlheiten, und wir müssen die für uns charakteristische mit anderen Hohlheiten vergleichen.

J/ L: Der Boden unter den Füßen	Kein geschärftes Gehör ist erforderlich, um einen hohlen Unterton aus den Schritten herauszuhören, mit denen wir uns der Zukunft entgegenbewegen: aus unserem Fortschritt. Hingegen ist es nötig, aufmerksam hinzuhören, wenn man feststellen will, um welche Art von Hohlheit es sich dabei handelt. Es gibt verschiedene Hohlheiten, und wir müssen die für uns charakteristische mit anderen Hohlheiten vergleichen, WENN WIR SIE VERSTEHEN WOLLEN.

Conclusion

As the above considerations have shown, in Flusser's use of self-translation, theory and practice do not always coincide but very often openly contradict each other. Add to this the fact that there exists a whole series of strategies that are used either singularly or in a combined way and that the reasons for choosing them are dependent on a complex set of conflicting factors and we find confirmation of Wittgenstein's verdict that there are always ways to solve translation problems but no systematic methods of solution. 'This distinction is [. . .] true', writes George Steiner in *After Babel*, 'not only of translation itself, but of the descriptions and judgements we can make of it' (223).

Notes

1   I published a book-length study on Flusser in 2005, *Philosophieren zwischen den Sprachen. Vilém Flussers Werk*, and co-authored with Anke Finger and Gustavo Bernardo *Vilém Flusser: An Introduction*, which appeared in 2011.

2   Flusser also used Czech at the beginning of his writing career, but only for his letters to friends and family.

3   All unpublished typescripts quoted in this essay can be consulted at the Vilém Flusser Archive, Universität der Künste, Berlin. The typescripts will soon be digitized and published at www.flusser-archive.org/.

4   'In der Seitenmitte steht ein Wort, oder einige wenige Worte, und um diesen Seitenkern drehen sich konzentrisch einige Textkreise. [. . .] Die Kreise kommentieren nicht nur den Kern, sondern auch einander. Das nennt man Pilpul' ('Pilpul' 144).

5   '[U]nerschöpflichen Schwarm von Standpunkten' ('Pilpul' 144).

6   'Quanto mais dificilmente traduzível determinado assunto, tanto mais me desafia. Porque vai provocar a tensão dialética entre as diversas línguas que me informam, e vai obrigar-me a procurar sintetizar as contradições entre elas' ('Retradução').

7   'Bei der Rückübersetzung dreht sich das ursprüngliche Verhältnis der beiden Codes um; der Objektcode wird nun zum Metacode. Mit anderen Worten: Nachdem der französische Code einen Teil [. . .] des englischen verschluckt hat, wird er seinerseits vom englischen verschluckt, [. . .] sozusagen mit dem englischen im Bauch'.

8   '[C]onvite para a dança'. 'Por certo: tal retradução recorrente em espiral é formalizável. [. . .] Mas tal formalização do problema da retradução levará a perder o encanto do jogo' ('Retradução').

Works cited

Finger, Anke, Rainer Guldin and Gustavo Bernardo. *Vilém Flusser: An Introduction*. Minneapolis: U of Minnesota P, 2011. Print.

Flusser, Vilém. *Pós-história*. São Paulo: Duas Cidades, 1983. Print.

—. *Nachgeschichten. Essay, Vorträge, Glossen*. Düsseldorf: Bollmann, 1990. Print.

—. *Nachgeschichte. Eine korrigierte Geschichtsschreibung.* Bensheim and Düsseldorf: Bollmann, 1993. Print.

—. 'Pilpul'. *Jude sein.* Mannheim: Bollmann, 1995: 143–53. Print.

—. *Kommunikologie.* Mannheim: Bollmann, 1996. Print.

—. 'Le geste d'écrire'. Upublished typescript.

—. 'Le sol au-dessous de nos pieds'. *Sgraffite* 3–4, (1980): 46–51. Print.

—. 'Retradução enquanto metodo de trabalho'. *Dubito ergo sum: cadernos de literature e folosofia.* Unpublished typescript.

—. 'Scribere necesse est vivere non est'. Unpublished typescript.

—. 'The gesture of writing'. Upublished typescript.

—. 'The ground we tread'. Unpublished typescript.

Guldin, Rainer. *Philosophieren zwischen den Sprachen. Vilém Flussers Werk.* Munich: Wilhelm Fink, 2005. Print.

—. "I believe that my two tongues love each other cela ne m'étonnerai pas': Self-Translation and the Construction of Sexual Identity'. *TTR* 20.1 (2007): 193–214. Print.

—. 'Golem, Roboter und andere Gebilde. Zu Vilém Flussers Apparatbegriff'. *Flusser Studies* 9 (2009). Web. www.flusserstudies.net/pag/09/guldin-golem-roboter.pdf

Hokenson, Jan Walsh and Marcella Munson. *The Bilingual Text. History and Theory of Literary Self-Translation.* Manchester: St. Jerome, 2007. Print.

Oustinoff, Michaël. *Bilinguisme d'écriture et auto-traduction. Julien Green, Samuel Beckett, Vladimir Nabokov.* Paris: L'Harmattan, 2001. Print.

Steiner, George. *After Babel. Aspects of Language and Translation.* Oxford: Oxford UP, 1998. Print.

Ströhl, Andreas. *Die Geste Mensch. Vilém Flussers Kulturtheorie als kommunikationsphilosophischer Zukunftsentwurf.* PhD Diss. Universität Marburg. 2009. Web. http://archiv.ub.uni-marburg.de/diss/z2009/0786/pdf/das.pdf

PART THREE

Post-colonial perspectives

CHAPTER SEVEN

Translated otherness, self-translated in-betweenness: Hybridity as medium versus hybridity as object in Anglophone African writing

Susanne Klinger

Abstract: *Post-colonial writing is often compared to or contrasted with translation. One of the differences between the two types of writing is that in post-colonial writing source and target language come into contact – and often merge with one another – not only in the process of creating the text but also in the reality portrayed in this text, as this reality constitutes itself an arena of past and ongoing translation. Translation is therefore not only the medium, but often also the object of representation.*

The distinction between translation as medium and translation as object forms the backbone of this chapter. Rather than conceptualizing post-colonial writing as a form of self-translation on the part of the author, as has hitherto been the case, it approaches the issue of hybridity by making a distinction between the self-translation of a character (or an embodied narrator) and other-translation in the form of narratorial intervention, and it investigates how hybridity – both as medium and as object – can be exploited in order to convey aspects of the characters' world-view.

Introduction

The Makerere Conference on Anglophone African Literature in 1962 and the subsequent publication of Obi Wali's contentious essay 'The Dead End of African Literature?' are often seen as the starting point of a heated debate over the use of European languages in African literature, which saw the crystallization of three schools of thought: the Neo-Metropolitans, the Evolutionists/Experimenters and the Rejectionists, to borrow Gabriel Okara's terminology ('Towards' 14). The latter school, as the name suggests, rejects the use of metropolitan languages as the medium of African literature; in their eyes, such a self-translation constitutes a betrayal of Africa, insofar as it contributes to the development of the metropolitan literatures at the expense of a development of African literatures and of a literary language within Africa's indigenous languages (see, for example, Wali 14–5). The Neo-Metropolitans and the Evolutionists/Experimenters, on the other hand, embrace colonialism's linguistic heritage in their writing. What differentiates them is the fact that the latter put their own distinctive African stamp on the colonial languages, shaping them according to their needs and purposes. This 'abrogation and appropriation' of the colonial language, as Bill Ashcroft, Gareth Griffiths and Helen Tiffin (37) call it, manifests itself on the page in a 'culturally marked English' (Ayo Kehinde 80): a hybrid English that fuses and juxtaposes European and African elements.[1] For the purposes of this chapter, hybrid English is consequently understood as an English that has roots in both worlds – the world of the former colonial centre, and that of the former colonies. The term is therefore synonymous with Ashcroft, Griffiths and Tiffin's coinage 'english' (8).[2]

The nature of the Evolutionists/Experimenters' culturally marked use of the metropolitan language has been studied most notably by Paul Bandia (especially *Translation as Reparation*) and Chantal Zabus, and, in the context of Francophone African literature, also by Kathryn Batchelor. One aspect that the studies of these three scholars share is their focus on analysing the language on the page, without systematically taking into account its relation to the language of the story-world. Zabus distinguishes between a 'synchronic' practice of hybridization that 'arises out of a need to "represent" linguistic usage and differentiation as it is found to exist in West Africa', and a 'diachronic' practice that 'corresponds to an artistic need to forge or create a new literary medium' (16). Both types of hybridization are therefore defined by their relation to the real world, not the story-world. Bandia and Batchelor categorize hybridity predominantly according to writing strategies (such as code-mixing, lexical innovation and elements of orality).

However, hybridity is not only a medium, but often also the object of representation in post-colonial literature. The post-colonial world constitutes an arena of past and ongoing (self-)translation, both in the metaphorical sense of assimilating the culture and/or language of the (ex-)colonizer – Cronin's 'translation-as-assimilation' (142) – and in the more conventional sense of linguistic transfer. It therefore seems essential to take into account the relationship between the language on the page and the language of the story-world, as hybridity on the page does not necessarily correspond to hybridity in the story-world, and vice versa. However, to my knowledge, no study of linguistic hybridity in post-colonial writing investigates this relationship in any detail.

Hybridity on the level of discourse and its relation to the story-world

Every narrative has two realities: the (fictional) reality of the world represented and the reality of the representation of this (fictional) world. In narratology, these two narrative levels are commonly referred to as the level of story and the level of discourse[3] respectively. Language is part of both levels: the illusion of a represented story-world is conveyed through the language or languages on the level of discourse (i.e. the language or languages on the page), and in turn, one or more languages are spoken in the represented story-world. Language is therefore 'both the medium and the object of representation' (Fludernik 64), and while we have direct access to the former, the latter can only be constructed from the former.

The relation between medium (discourse-language) and object (story-language) is not one-to-one; the same medium can represent different objects. Two examples will illustrate this briefly; both extracts are from Chinua Achebe's novel *No Longer at Ease*. Setting, speaker and addressee are identical in each case:

> 'Call it what you like', said Joseph in Ibo. 'You know more book than I, but I am older and wiser. And I can tell you that a man does not challenge his *chi* to a wrestling match'. (46–7; ch. 5)

> 'Look at me', said Joseph, getting up and tying his coverlet as a loincloth. He now spoke in English. 'You know book, but this is no matter for book. Do you know what an *osu* is? But how can you know?' (82; ch. 7)

On the discourse-level, both examples feature the non-standard collocation 'to know book' as well as Igbo lexis. However, on the story-level, two different languages are spoken: Igbo[4] in the first example, and English in the second. In the first example, therefore, story-language and discourse-language are not identical: translation from Igbo into English has occurred in the form of narratorial intervention and the foreign idiom and lexis signal this intervention. This practice of representing one language within another is known as 'translational mimesis', a term coined by Meir Sternberg (225).

According to Sternberg, translational mimesis can be achieved through the following four strategies:[5] (1) explicit attribution, that is, a direct statement regarding the language being used on the story-level; (2) selective reproduction, that is, the inclusion of scattered words and phrases of the story-language; (3) verbal transposition, that is, the creation of hybrid forms where the narrator deliberately mixes the code of the discourse-level with that of the story-level (see for example the expression 'You know more book than I' above); (4) conceptual reflection, that is, the retaining of 'the underlying socio-cultural norms, semantic mapping of reality, and distinctive referential range, segmentations and hierarchies' (230) of the story's language and culture in the discourse. One example of conceptual reflection would be Achebe's use of the Igbo time measurement of 'market weeks', lasting four days: 'It took the white man's ship sixteen days – four market weeks – to do the journey' (*Ease* 58). Other common examples include the use of elements typical for oral expression, conceptually reflecting oral cultures, or also the use of archaisms, creating a distance in time. According to Johannes Fabian, this 'denial of coevalness' (31 *et passim*) is one of the key elements of representing the other.

Thus, with the exception of explicit attribution, these writing strategies create hybridity on the discourse-level by juxtaposing or fusing two different codes. Yet, in the context of translational mimesis, they do not represent hybridity on the story-level. In the second example, on the other hand, story-language and discourse-language coincide. No narrator has intervened as translator: it is the character who fuses and juxtaposes different codes. The linguistic hybridity on the discourse-level therefore reflects story-level hybridity, both cultural hybridity (the speaker's in-betweenness) and linguistic hybridity (the speaker's hybridization of English).

To date we have no terminology that allows us to distinguish between (1) discourse-level hybridity that represents a different language on the story-level and (2) discourse-level hybridity that reflects 'english' on the story-level.[6] I propose to call (1) the former type 'symbolic hybridity' and (2) the latter type 'iconic hybridity'. The former type symbolically represents one language within another. The hybridization occurs only on the level of discourse and serves solely as medium. The term symbolic hybridity not only serves as an umbrella-term for Sternberg's terms selective representation, verbal transposition and conceptual reflection, but – unlike Sternberg's hybridizing writing strategies – symbolic hybridity is defined by its function of signifying translational mimesis, and is hence restricted to it. Iconic hybridity, on the other hand, represents hybridity as object. This representation purports to be immediate: it is iconic insofar as we, the readers, are expected to suspend our disbelief and imagine that these are the actual words spoken or thought by the character (or the embodied narrator); no mediator has intervened as translator.[7] The first example quoted above therefore features symbolic hybridity on the discourse-level, while the second features iconic hybridity.

Symbolic hybridity as ideational point of view versus iconic hybridity as mind style

While Fowler uses the two terms 'ideational point of view' and 'mind style' interchangeably, Elena Semino proposes making a distinction. She suggests using the former to 'capture those aspects of world views that are social, cultural, religious or political in origin, and which an individual is likely to share with others belonging to similar social, cultural, religious or political groups' (97). Mind style, on the other hand, should be reserved to 'capture those aspects of world views that are primarily personal and cognitive in origin, and which are either peculiar to a particular individual, or common to people who have the same cognitive characteristics' (97). Drawing on Semino's distinction, the following will argue that symbolic hybridity conveys the ideational point of view of an ethnic group, while iconic hybridity conveys the mind style of an individual or a group of individuals (who can, but need not, be of shared ethnicity).

Iconic hybridity, unlike symbolic hybridity, signifies not another language, but a particular language variety. More precisely, it represents a variety that in the narrative is not considered to be the standard variety and therefore is marked as such in the text. This feature can be exploited for characterization. For example, Ashcroft, Griffiths and Tiffin argue that in literature, Pidgin usually serves 'to install class difference and to signify its presence' (75). Often, Pidgin and non-standard varieties in general are used to signal a lack of formal education, as is the case for example in *No Longer at Ease* where a hawker distributes leaflets advertising a mixture against ailments such as 'Rheumatism, Yellow feaver, dogbight' (54; ch. 5), or where a musical performance is greeted with applause and cries of 'Anchor! Anchor!' (129; ch. 11). According to Zabus, Pidgin is 'still associated with a half-literate subculture', despite the fact that in Ghana and Nigeria, for example, it is more widely spoken than English (55). This is a point also observed by Bandia, who states that Pidgin 'has remained, for the most part, the contact language spoken by the "illiterate" and "semi-literate" masses of the urban centres' ('Code-Switching' 149). This notwithstanding, some novels have their characters or embodied narrators switch between metropolitan and non-metropolitan English, depending on context, thus highlighting their ability to adapt to different environments rather than portraying them as semi-literate. For instance, Pidgin can indicate an informal atmosphere or intimacy as is the case in *No Longer at Ease*:

> Whether Christopher spoke good or 'broken' English depended on what he was saying, where he was saying it, to whom and how he wanted to say it. Of course that was to some extent true of most educated people, especially on Saturday nights. (125–6; ch. 11)

Zabus observes a gradual 'shift in the use and status of pidgin in novels from baby talk to "the tongue of the people" or public patois on to the counter-prestige language of modernity' (56), yet is keen to point out that 'the linguistic behaviour of the pidgin locutor continues to be looked down upon' (83). In fiction, 'Pidgin is persistently stigmatized' and 'remains an "auxiliary" language into which a character slides, slips, lapses, as in a fall from a higher register' (83). Gane further points out that in West African literature, Pidgin often assumes the role of 'a kind of "underlanguage" or even what M.A.K. Halliday has called an "anti-language"' (137). In Achebe's novels, Pidgin is consistently associated with 'the underbelly of society' (Gane 137); in Wole Soyinka's *The Interpreters,* Pidgin hints at 'the seamy underside of official reality' (Gane 144). These examples show that pre-independence and early post-independence Anglophone African writing not uncommonly exploits the fact that iconic hybridity represents a language *variety* in order to conjure up negative connotations such as lack of education, moral dubiousness or corruption.

This is not to say that African 'english' is always marked as such in the text. In *The Interpreters*, Nigerian English constitutes the linguistic norm of the reality portrayed in the novel. Hence, it is not conveyed through iconic hybridity, but by means of unmarked English. What is conveyed through iconic hybridity instead is the speech of characters who deviate from the norm of Nigerian English. One example is Professor Oguazor, who strives to imitate the British and their pronunciation:[8] 'The whole centry is senk in meral terpitude' (249; ch. 18). Similarly, non-standard spelling indicates a Kenyan's boy imitation of an American accent ('beauddiful ciddy') in Ngugi wa Thiong'o and Micere Githae Mugo's play *The Trial of Dedan Kimathi* (Zuengler 118–22).

Iconic hybridity singles out its speaker. By foregrounding the speaker's linguistic idiosyncrasy it portrays him or her as departing from the norms of what is considered standard in the narrative. Symbolic hybridity, on the other hand, signifies not a language variety, but a language, or more precisely, it represents what is considered to be the standard variety of this language. Unlike iconic hybridity, it does not allow conclusions to be drawn about a speaker's level of education or his or her social class, but solely about his or her ethnic origin and therefore about his or her cultural values and beliefs. Hence, symbolic hybridity reflects the ideational point of view of a particular ethnic group, insofar as it represents a whole culture, and therefore does not tell us anything about the cognitive characteristics of its speakers as individuals, while iconic hybridity reflects either the mind style of a group of people or the mind style of a single person.

Furthermore, in the case of Anglophone African writing, symbolic hybridity usually marks an indigenous African language. It thus highlights African ethnicity. Iconic hybridity, on the other hand, more often than not identifies the speaker as African and as a speaker of English at the same time. It thus highlights in-betweenness. Due to this in-betweenness, iconic hybridity associates its speaker with other English speakers, namely the British ex-colonizers, and at the same time it locates the speaker in the local community of English speakers (as opposed to other communities of English speakers such as the British ex-colonizers). Hence, it can be employed to indicate that the speaker's allegiance has shifted or that it is split between both sides. Especially in pre-independence and early post-independence writing, this juxtaposition of ethnic belonging (signalled through symbolic hybridity) and in-betweenness (signalled through iconic hybridity) often serves to underpin the 'us/them' constellation of colonialism.

Self-translation as mind style: Traduttore, traditore

Although the Evolutionists/Experimenters defend their own self-translation (i.e. their writing in a colonial language), repudiating the Rejectionists' accusation of betraying Africa – Achebe for example makes the case that English is the only choice if Nigeria is to have a national literature, as its indigenous languages are confined to their ethnic boundaries ('African Writer' 56) – the self-translating characters in their stories are nevertheless quite often portrayed as cultural traitors. This is particularly the case in pre-independence and early post-independence writing that takes colonialism and its impact on traditional African society as its theme, and hence juxtaposes cultural self-translation (i.e. the assimilation of Western values) with cultural non-translation (i.e. the holding onto ethnic values). One such work that associates cultural self-translation with betrayal is *No Longer at Ease*, narrating the story of Obi, who is the first of his clan to be sent to the United Kingdom to study, and his subsequent transformation and assimilation of Western values that culminate in his betrayal of the trust, the hopes and the values of his kinsmen. As Gane puts it, 'Obi's very name is "Ibo" backwards: what he has come to be constitutes a reversal and a denial of his background' (140).[9]

The assimilation of Western values often goes hand in hand with the assimilation of the colonial language: cultural self-translation manifests itself in linguistic self-translation. Put differently, cultural self-translation manifests itself in the language of the story, and in turn the language of the story is reflected in the language of the discourse. On the discourse-level, linguistic self-translation can be signified through iconic hybridity, through non-standard symbolic hybridity and through metropolitan English. The following will look at each of these in turn.

In Nigeria for example, where English is the national language, Pidgin is especially prevalent not only among traders, but also among members of the police and the army (Todd 293). Pidgin is therefore associated with the institutional authority of the (post-)colonial world. Fiction reflects this reality: Bandia points out that 'In early West African novels dealing with colonial times, Pidgin was mainly used as a means of communication between characters depicted as native Africans working for the colonial administration and their white masters' (*Translation as Reparation* 125). Pidgin is therefore more than a *lingua franca* in these novels: it portrays its speakers as a sub-community of the occupying forces. The use of Pidgin thus mirrors the speaker's allegiance to the British and distances them from their own ethnic group. Self-translation becomes synonymous with betrayal. In the following example from Achebe's novel, *Arrow of God*, two African policemen working for the British rulers address local villagers in Igbo, while communicating with each other in Pidgin.

> Meanwhile the policemen arrived at Ezeulu's hut. They were then no longer in the mood for playing. They spoke sharply, baring all their weapons at once.
>
> '*Which one of you is called Ezeulu?*' asked the corporal.
>
> '*Which Ezeulu?*' asked Edogo.
>
> '*Don't ask me which Ezeulu again or I shall slap okro seeds out of your mouth. I say who is called Ezeulu here?*'
>
> '*And I say which Ezeulu? Or don't you know who you are working for?*' The four other men in the hut said nothing. Women and children thronged the door leading from the hut into the inner compound. There was fear and anxiety in the faces.
>
> '**All right**', said the corporal in English. '**Jus now you go sabby which Ezeulu. Gi me dat ting**'. This last sentence was directed to his companion who immediately produced the handcuffs from his pocket. (152–3; ch. 13; emphasis added)

The utterances in italics represent Igbo; the translational mimesis is signalled not only through the context (the village elders do not speak English), but also linguistically through the literally translated idiomatic expression ('I shall slap okro seeds out of your mouth'). The utterances highlighted in bold, on the other hand, represent Pidgin. The policemen use Pidgin to display their imagined superiority, thus distancing themselves from the villagers, and presumably also in order to have a secret code the villagers cannot understand. Bandia further argues that in this scene, Pidgin is portrayed as 'the new language of power and prestige' (*Translation as Reparation* 127). However, I would argue that Pidgin here is not so much an indicator for power and prestige as it is an indicator for betrayal and lack of real power. The use of English associates the policemen with the colonizer and hence underscores their opportunism, and simultaneously the hybrid nature of the English dissociates them from the colonizer, underscoring their inferior position in the colonial administrative hierarchy.

Achebe further highlights the policemen's assimilation of Western values through the lack of discoursal indirectness typical for verbal exchange in traditional Igbo society. In the eyes of the elders, the policemen are socially inferior. Not surprisingly, as Bandia points out, it was often the 'ordinary people at the bottom of the hierarchy of traditional society' who were collaborating with the British colonial administration – these are the people who are keen to 'undermine traditional authority and assume the mantle of the future' (*Translation as Reparation* 125). The elders expect to be addressed in a deferential manner. The policemen, however, express their disdain for the traditional society that does not respect their newly gained authority via their rude, straightforward manner (announced by the narrator with the words 'They were then no longer in the mood for playing'). The lack of discoursal indirectness is thus another indicator of the policemen's alliance with the British and therefore of their betrayal of traditional ethnic values.

Hence, Africans adopting British values can also express their allegiance – their self-translation – by violating the norms of their mother tongue. This violation can manifest itself in non-standard symbolic hybridity. The following extract, also from *Arrow of God*, containing a verbal exchange between the village elders and a court messenger who works for the British, will illustrate this in more detail. Both the messenger and the villagers speak Igbo in this scene:

'I salute you all'. He [court messenger] brought out a very small book from his breast pocket and opened it in the manner of a white man. 'Which one of you is called Ezeulu?' he asked from the book and then looked up and around the hut. No one spoke; they were all too astonished. Akuebue was the first to recover.

'Look round and count your teeth with your tongue', he said. 'Sit down, Obika, you must expect foreigners to talk through the nose'.

'You say you are a man of Umuru?' asked Ezeulu. 'Do you have priests and elders there?'

'Do not take my question amiss. The white man has his own way of doing things. Before he does anything to you he will first ask you your name and the answer must come from your own lips'.

'If you have any grain of sense in your belly', said Obika, 'you will know that you are not in the house of the white man but in Umuaro in the house of the Chief Priest of Ulu'. (137; ch. 12)

The elders perceive the court messenger as rude and disrespectful – the messenger behaves as if he were 'in the house of the white man', as Obika puts it. Like the policemen in the previous example above, traditional Igbo society considers the messenger as socially inferior to the elders. Like the policemen, the messenger has made the values of the British occupiers his own and expresses his disdain for traditional Igbo society by failing to respect the traditional rules governing conversation (see further Ngara 71–2; see also Bandia, *Translation as Reparation* 57–9 for a discussion of this scene).

The tension between the messenger and the villagers is reflected in the language. On the discourse-level, the language of the elders is marked by symbolic hybridity, mainly the idiomatic phrases signifying the underlying Igbo ('count your teeth with your tongue'; 'to talk through the nose'; 'if you have any grain of sense in your belly'). The messenger's language, on the other hand, is blunt and direct. The linguistic hybridity on the story-level – a merging of Igbo lexis with British norms of discourse – is marked by the absence of hybridity on the discourse-level in this short extract. The speaker self-translates by adopting the norms of the colonizer's discourse, and this self-translation manifests itself in a lack or lessening of discourse-level hybridity.

Of course, self-translation does not need to involve linguistic hybridity – neither on the level of story, nor on the level of discourse. Metropolitan English, when spoken by Africans, is often employed to the same effect as Pidgin, for example. When foregrounded against indigenous languages, it represents self-translation as object and can become associated with opportunism, or generally with turning one's back on one's own culture. One example in this vein is Abadi's opportunistic speech in Okara's novel *The Voice* (23–5; ch. 2), in which he aims to persuade the villagers of his plot to ban Okolo, whose non-conformism to the new society is perceived as a threat by those in power. Abadi switches to English in an attempt to attach more importance to his speech and himself. However, Abadi's switch to the colonial language – his self-translation – also stands both for a history of oppression and for the individualistic materialism the West has introduced to Okolo's (and Okara's) society.

Generally speaking, self-translation is an act of translation performed by individuals or groups of individuals: it sets the speaker apart from her or his ethnic group and therefore conveys the speaker's mind style (as opposed to the ideational point of view of the ethnic group). Self-translation connotes in-betweenness (regardless of the degree of linguistic hybridity both on the discourse-level and on the story-level) and can therefore indicate a shifted allegiance or a split allegiance. As the examples above have shown, in Anglophone African literature self-translation therefore often has negative connotations: the self-translating speaker has assimilated colonial values, at the expense of her or his traditional culture and community. *Traduttore* becomes synonymous with *traditore*. The self-translating individual is denounced and, by association, the (ex-)colonizing power and its values are denounced, too. And it is in this respect that a negative portrayal of post-colonial 'english' and post-colonial self-translation can ultimately serve a decolonizing agenda.

In conclusion

The aim of this chapter was to demonstrate the usefulness of taking into account the different narrative levels when analysing linguistic hybridity in post-colonial writing, and the necessity of having a terminology that can describe the relation between discourse-level hybridity and story-level language. As the discussion has shown, hybridity on the discourse-level can, but does not necessarily, correspond to hybridity on the story-level. Likewise, hybridity on the story-level can be, but is not necessarily, expressed by hybridity on the discourse-level. Approaches that do not take into account the different levels of narrative risk failing to notice – and to be able to account for – the difference between represented story-level hybridity and represented narratorial intervention and how their different characteristics can be exploited in order to convey aspects of the characters' world-view.

Furthermore, recognizing the relation between discourse-language and story-language is not only crucial for the critic but also for the translator of post-colonial literature. Symbolic hybridity is arbitrary in the sense that the discourse-language is not tied to the story-language, but serves solely as its vehicle. This separation between story-language and discourse-language is not possible in the case of iconic hybridity. Symbolic and iconic hybridity therefore pose different challenges to the target-text translator and call for different translation strategies. While a discussion of translational strategies for the rendering of the hybrid language of post-colonial literature is beyond the scope of this chapter, I hope to have demonstrated that an approach that is informed by the narratological distinction between story and discourse can yield fruitful insights for both critic and translator, and therefore can add to other approaches such as those put forward by Zabus, Bandia and Batchelor.

Notes

1   These elements need not be authentic. Nkem Nwankwo for example occasionally creates phrases 'which cannot be traced to any Igbo equivalents but ha[ve] an air of authenticity' (Zabus 151).

2   Incorporating influences from languages such as French and Latin into a Germanic language, English is, of course, itself a hybrid language; rather than being set in motion by the British Empire, the hybridization of English 'has been an ongoing phenomenon throughout history' (Ch'ien 4). Hence, an approach that views 'english' as linguistically hybrid and at the same time leaves aside the hybrid roots of metropolitan English, is doubtlessly Eurocentric. This notwithstanding, the term 'hybrid English' has been adopted in this paper as it underscores that 'english' has roots in both the metropolitan and the

colonized world. Other denominations include 'indigenized' English (Zabus 4), 'Africanized' English (Todd 299), 'decolonized' English (Salman Rushdie, qtd. in Dissanayake 233; Mwangi 67) and 'new English' (Achebe, 'African Writer' 62). The proliferation of terminology and the problem of finding one term that is value-free surely reflects the fact that the very making of a distinction between the 'language of the centre' (Ashcroft, Griffiths and Tiffin 37) and the 'english' of the former colonies is value-laden, as it inevitably posits metropolitan English as the original and the newer 'englishes' as derivatives and thus implies a hierarchy, rather than the parity of all forms of English.

3 Some narratologists, such as Shlomith Rimmon-Kenan, further subdivide the level of discourse into the level of text (also called the level of narrative) and the level of narration. A distinction between story and discourse however is sufficient for the present discussion.

4 Both spellings (Ibo/Igbo) are in use; with the exception of direct quotes, 'Igbo' is used throughout the article.

5 Like Lawrence Venuti's foreignization (*Translator's Invisibility*; *Scandals of Translation*), the goal of translational mimesis is not to imitate the other language, but rather to highlight the translatorial intervention through the mixing of different codes (see Jean Boase-Beier 68–9 on Venuti's foreignization and its 'virtually non-mimetic view of style'). However, although translational mimesis does not aim to mimic the foreign language, it nevertheless aims to *represent* the foreign language in the discourse-language. Herein lies a fundamental difference from foreignization.

6 It goes without saying that discourse-level hybridity does not need to be motivated by the story. For reasons of space, however, this paper focuses on story-motivated discourse-level hybridity.

7 For a discussion of the conventionalized representation of Pidgin in literature, see Rebecca N. Agheyisi (217). Nevertheless, despite this conventionalized representation, there is a strong link between signifier (the conventionalized representation of Pidgin) and signified (Pidgin as a spoken language).

8 West African English is based mainly on British norms; differences from British English are mostly reflected in vocabulary and pronunciation (Todd 285, 287). For a more detailed discussion of Soyinka's use of language in *The Interpreters* see Gane, 'Achebe, Soyinka, and Other-Languagedness'.

9 For a detailed discussion of the theme of betrayal and cultural self-translation in *No Longer at Ease*, see Philip Rogers, '*No Longer at Ease*: Achebe's "Heart of Whiteness"'.

Works cited

Achebe, Chinua. *Arrow of God*. 2nd edn. 1974. New York: Anchor-Random, 1989. Print.
—. *No Longer at Ease*. 1960. New York: Anchor-Random, 1994. Print.
—. 'The African Writer and the English Language'. *Morning Yet on Creation Day*. London: Heinemann, 1975. 55–62. Print.

Agheyisi, Rebecca N. 'Linguistic Implications of the Changing Role of Nigerian Pidgin'. *English World-Wide* 5.2 (1984): 211–33. Print.

Ashcroft, Bill, Gareth Griffiths and Helen Tiffin. *The Empire Writes Back*. 2nd edn. London: Routledge, 2002. Print.

Bandia, Paul. 'Code-Switching and Code-Mixing in African Creative Writing: Some Insights for Translation Studies'. *TTR* 9.1 (1996): 139–53. Print.

—. *Translation as Reparation: Writing and Translation in Postcolonial Africa*. Manchester: St. Jerome, 2008. Print.

Batchelor, Kathryn. *Decolonizing Translation: Francophone African Novels in English Translation*. Manchester: St. Jerome, 2009. Print.

Boase-Beier, Jean. *Stylistic Approaches to Translation*. Manchester: St. Jerome, 2006. Print.

Ch'ien, Evelyn Nien-Ming. *Weird English*. Cambridge: Harvard UP, 2004. Print.

Cronin, Michael. *Translation and Globalization*. London: Routledge, 2003. Print.

Dissanayake, Wimal. 'Towards a Decolonized English: South Asian Creativity in Fiction'. *World Englishes* 4.2 (1985): 233–42. Print.

Fabian, Johannes. *Time and the Other: How Anthropology Makes its Object*. 2nd edn. New York: Columbia UP, 2002. Print.

Fludernik, Monika. *An Introduction to Narratology*. Trans. Patricia Häusler-Greenfield and Monika Fludernik. London: Routledge, 2009. Print.

Fowler, Roger. *Linguistic Criticism*. 2nd edn. Oxford: Oxford UP, 1996. Print.

Gane, Gillian. 'Achebe, Soyinka, and Other-Languagedness'. *The Creative Circle. Artist, Critic, and Translator in African Literature*. Ed. Angelina Overvold, Richard Priebe, and Louis Tremaine. Trenton: Africa World Press, 2003. 131–49. Print.

Kehinde, Ayo. 'English and the Postcolonial Writer's Burden: Linguistic Innovations in Femi Fatoba's *My 'Older' Father and Other Stories'*. *Journal of African Cultural Studies* 21.1 (2009): 75–89. *Informaworld*. Web. 29 Sep. 2009.

Mwangi, Evan. 'The Gendered Politics of Untranslated Language and Aporia in Ngugi wa Thiong'o's *Petals of Blood'*. *Research in African Literatures* 35.4 (2004): 66–74. *EBSCO*. Web. 4 Aug. 2010.

Ngara, Emmanuel. *Stylistic Criticism and the African Novel*. London: Heinemann, 1982. Print.

Okara, Gabriel. *The Voice*. London: Fontana, 1973. Print.

—. 1964. 'Towards the Evolution of an African Language for African Literature'. *Chinua Achebe: A Celebration*. Ed. Kirsten Holst Petersen, and Anna Rutherford. Oxford: Heinemann, 1991. 11–18. Print.

Rimmon-Kenan, Shlomith. *Narrative Fiction: Contemporary Poetics*. 2nd edn. London: Methuen, 2002. Print.

Rogers, Philip. '*No Longer at Ease*: Achebe's "Heart of Whiteness"'. 1983. *Postcolonial Literatures: Achebe, Ngugi, Desai, Walcott*. Ed. Michael Parker, and Roger Starkey. Basingstoke: Macmillan, 1995. 53–64. Print.

Semino, Elena. 'A Cognitive Stylistic Approach to Mind Style in Narrative Fiction'. *Cognitive Stylistics: Language and Cognition in Text Analysis*. Ed. Elena Semino, and Jonathan Culpeper. Amsterdam: John Benjamins, 2002. 95–122. Print.

Soyinka, Wole. *The Interpreters*. 1965. London: Heinemann, 1970. Print.

Sternberg, Meir. 'Polylingualism as Reality and Translation as Mimesis'. *Poetics Today* 2.4 (1981): 221–39. Print.

Todd, Loreto. 'The English Language in West Africa'. *English as a World Language*. Ed. Richard W. Bailey and Manfred Görlach. Cambridge: Cambridge UP, 1984. 281–305. Print.

Venuti, Lawrence. *The Scandals of Translation: Towards an Ethics of Difference*. London: Routledge, 1998. Print.

—. *The Translator's Invisibility: A History of Translation*. London: Routledge, 1995. Print.

wa Thiong'o, Ngugi, and Micere Githae Mugo. *The Trial of Dedan Kimathi*. London: Heinemann, 1976. Print.

Wali, Obiajunwa. 'The Dead End of African Literature?' *Transition* 10 (1963): 13–15. Print.

Zabus, Chantal. *The African Palimpsest: Indigenization of Language in the West African Europhone Novel*. 2nd enlarged edn. Amsterdam: Rodopi, 2007. Print.

Zuengler, Jane E. 'Kenyan English'. *The Other Tongue: English Across Cultures*. Ed. Braj B. Kachru. Urbana: U of Illinois P, 1982. 112–24. Print.

CHAPTER EIGHT

'Why bother with the original?': Self-translation and Scottish Gaelic poetry

Corinna Krause

Abstract: This article looks at the phenomenon of self-translation in the context of literature written in a lesser-used language. It consults voices from within the world of Scottish Gaelic, Irish and Welsh poetry, offering a comparative study of their relationship to the English language, a language of far greater cultural prestige. This allows for an analysis of the impact which self-translation from a minority language into a majority language has on the reality of the source literature in terms of its appreciation and survival.

Self-translation and Scottish Gaelic poetry: A historical perspective

Self-translation has become a firmly established translation practice in connection with contemporary Scottish Gaelic poetry, so much so that the corpus of contemporary Gaelic poetry might be more realistically understood as a bilingual corpus of Gaelic originals and their English translations provided by the author. This was of course not always the case. Rather, today's situation has to be seen as the result of a steady development over the past 60 years or so, which began with initial attempts by Gaelic authors such as Sorley MacLean (known as Somhairle MacGill-Eain in the Gaelic world) and Derick Thomson (Ruaraidh MacThòmais) to enter into a professional dialogue with others involved with literary writing and its appreciation in Scotland and beyond. During the 1930s and 1940s, working most intensely towards the publication of his renowned poetry collection *Dàin do Eimhir*, MacLean had close friends in Hugh MacDiarmid, Douglas Young, Robert Garioch and other influential Scottish poets, all of them highly aware of the importance and potential of the linguistic diversity within Scottish society. As a result, we find some of MacLean's poetry translated into Scots by his literary friends and colleagues. *Dàin do Eimhir*, which was finally published in 1943, could well have been published with a selection of Young's translations into Scots. Indeed, the decision-making process was not an easy one (see Whyte, Introduction 37–8). Eventually, however, a selection of MacLean's own prose translations into English was included at the end of the volume. This choice indicates an approach to Gaelic poetry publishing which was to become established over the following half century, namely the author's being inclusive towards the Anglophone world while maintaining authority throughout the publication. Some years later, in 1951, the first collection by Thomson, entitled *An Dealbh Briste* (MacThòmais), appeared. Thomson, the founder of the highly influential Gaelic publisher *Gairm* and the associated Gaelic periodical of the same name, who was also later to become Professor of Celtic at Glasgow University, had a keen interest in placing contemporary Gaelic writing in the wider intellectual and aesthetic context of literary life in Scotland and beyond. His own poetry publications first offered a selection of English translations at the end of an otherwise Gaelic collection, evolving towards bilingual publications which give all poems *en-face* in Gaelic and English. These volumes used English only for most paratextual features (see Thomson's *Meall Garbh / The Rugged Mountain*), in other words signifying a steady departure from Gaelic as a literary medium for publication.

The literary space occupied by modern Gaelic poetry is that of a literature in a minority language, which means that writing and reading processes are subject to the friction that is present between languages of unequal status and prestige. Processes of translation cannot, therefore, be understood without reference to how language use dynamics affect lesser-used languages. In 1998, the Scottish literary magazine *Chapman* provided considerable space to a debate addressing the nature and consequences of translation activities in a Gaelic literary context. Wilson McLeod initiated the debate with an article aptly entitled 'The Packaging of Gaelic Poetry', in which he points towards the ever-increasing practice of *en-face* English translations in Gaelic poetry publication and anthologies. He also underlines the colonizing role of English, which finds its way onto spines and covers of books presenting Gaelic poetry as if English were their sole language of publication. The 'bilingual' in bilingual poetry publication therefore appears to be a relative and dynamic concept, with English increasingly gaining space, thus marginalizing the language of the original poetry and therefore declaring it incapable of presenting its original texts to a readership. McLeod's article is significant in that it was the first critical piece of writing to appear in an established Scottish literary magazine addressing the impact of translation in a Gaelic literary context. As such it interrupted the silent obedience of the Gaelic literary world in the face of translation dynamics which so forcefully informed its very being then and, as more recent poetry publications show, continue to do so today (see Mac an t-Saoir/MacIntyre's *Dannsam led Fhaileas / Let Me Dance With Your Shadow*; Bateman's *Soirbheas / Fair Wind*; MacNeacail's *Laoidh*).

From the language revival perspective, the concern is that within this particular literary space shared by Anglophone and Gaelic readerships the text in Gaelic is tamed: its presence does not interrupt habitual reading patterns by speakers of English and Gaelic alike. Neither does it challenge the reader's ignorance of inevitable poetic differences between the Gaelic and the English text and their appreciation within distinct cultural contexts. To adopt Michael Cronin's words, 'the colonial Other is translated into terms of the Imperial Self, with the net result of alienation for the colonised and a fiction of understanding for the coloniser' (92). This sentiment is expressed by the Gaelic poet, Christopher Whyte:

> I know that poets in both Ireland and Wales, not content with refusing to translate their poems into English, have forbidden any such translations to be published. Gaelic poets in Scotland do not feel themselves in a strong enough position to take up such a belligerent stance. ('Translation as Predicament' 182–3)

Indeed, the limited amount of critical concern by poets and critics about translation practices (see Krause, 'Eadar Dà Chànan') in Gaelic literature is remarkable given that neighbouring minority cultures, Irish and Welsh, show a high level of awareness regarding translation choices and their impact on the respective language of minority status.

Welsh and Irish poets: A comparative view on attitudes towards translation

In his article 'Sleeping with the Enemy' Grahame Davies points towards conscious choices among Welsh language authors to ensure the health and wealth of contemporary and future writing in Welsh. Such choices include delayed translation, where the Welsh original is considered for English translation only after a 'decent interval'; or the avoidance of self-translation 'to prevent the danger of adulteration' (61). 'Sleeping with the Enemy' was first published in 2004 in the *New Welsh Review*, and starts off with 'Adultery, bloodshed, war. Yes, it's the world of literary translation in Wales'. The same article published a year later in *Five Essays on Translation* opens: 'Adultery, addiction, bloodshed, war. Yes, it's the world of literary translation in Wales'. The addition of the word 'addiction' in the later version of his article might well suggest a kind of 'giving in' to the temptation of English publication. This case indeed exemplifies the sheer magnitude of the allure of English even though there is a considerable awareness among Welsh-language authors of the problematic relationship between their minority language and its translation into the dominant language. Furthermore, Gerwyn Wiliams, the Crowned Bard at the National Eisteddfod 1994, explained to me in a conversation on the subject of writing in Welsh, that those involved with Welsh literature perceive of Welsh poetry as:

> a defensive art form, since its very existence has been identified with the fate of the language. It is seen as the backbone to the Welsh language. Therefore attitudes towards English are all tied up with the fate of the Welsh language and for that reason it is not surprising that there are rather mixed feelings about English translation amongst those involved with Welsh literature.

Some poets go as far as refusing to have their work translated into English altogether, with Twm Morys arguably the most prominent example. He perceives of poetry as 'a discourse, sometimes with oneself, sometimes with others', explaining that:

> when I have occasionally wanted to reach an audience that does not speak Welsh I've written in English. Otherwise I write in Welsh because I'm speaking with Welsh-speaking people. If others would like to join in, well they can bloody well learn the language! The vast English-speaking world will be none the poorer for not being able to read the *cywyddau* of Twm Morys. But the little Welsh world, in my opinion, keeps a little more of its integrity if one or two of us elect to live out on the Craig Lwyd with Llywelyn ap y Moel. (55)

Consequently, his work remains invisible from a canon of Welsh poetry, as it is established in the English-speaking world, by not featuring in milestone publications such as *The Bloodaxe Book of Modern Welsh Poetry*, edited by Menna Elfyn and John Rowlands, or *The Adulterer's Tongue*, compiled by Robert Minhinnick.

In an Irish context, similar attitudes can be found. Biddy Jenkinson, for instance, refuses to translate herself into English; like Morys, she prefers her work to remain altogether untranslated. This she regards as 'a small rude gesture to those who think that everything can be harvested and stored without loss in an English-speaking Ireland' (34). Provocatively, she compares herself to a native bird: 'if I were a corncrake I would feel no obligation to have my skin cured, my tarsi injected with formalin so that I could fill a museum shelf in a world that saw no need for my kind' (34). Fellow poet, Cathal Ó Searcaigh contemplates the very practical implications of habitual self-translation: 'I would be listening to the whisperings of English when I was writing and if I were to use a saying or word play in Gaelic that I could find no equivalence for in English then I would be under pressure to leave it out entirely' (*Is Mise an Teanga*). Pól Ó Muirí observes a 'tendency to promote the translation over the original text', which he identifies as 'surely worrying'. He concludes that:

> The exchange of ideas between Irish and English is not an equal one. English is the dominant partner and has imposed translation on the weaker language. It is not an example of Irish being taken out of the ghetto (there is no ghetto) but of Irish being made to conform to the dominant language. (16)

From the published corpus of Irish language poetry it becomes apparent that in comparison to the situation with Scottish Gaelic, poets writing in Irish show a more experimental attitude towards translation and the bilingual edition. Nuala Ní Dhomhnaill's work in publication is a case in point. In addition to monolingual publications, we find her work published in English translation in bilingual *en-face* editions which all bear testimony to creative collaborative work. The front cover of her renowned collection *Pharaoh's Daughter* lists 13 translators, among whom we find Michael Hartnett, Seamus Heaney and Medbh McGuckianeach following their own idiosyncratic approach to translation. 1992 saw the publication of *The Astrakhan Cloak*, with Paul Muldoon providing English translations of Ní Dhomhnaill's poems in Irish and appearing as co-author on the title page. *The Water Horse* carries the names of Medbh McGuckian and Eiléan Ní Chuilleanáin as translators on its front cover. Nevertheless, self-translation also occurs in the context of Irish poetry publications, and Michael Davitt's *Freacnairc Mhearcair / The Oomph of Quicksilver*, published in 2000, relies on a mixture of self-translation and translations by others. Yet this publication, clearly aimed at an English-speaking readership, is only one amid the poet's otherwise monolingual Irish publications such as *Fardoras*, which has been celebrated as bearing witness to the healthy state of contemporary poetry in Irish. Similarly, the highly acclaimed poetry collection, *Sruth Teangacha / Stream of Tongues* by Gearóid Mac Lochlainn, published in 2002, includes self-translations as well as collaborative translations. What is more, throughout the publication, translation as a fact of life for Irish language poetry is acknowledged and even incorporated in the creative process of composing poetry, thus getting hold of its very subject matter. In 'Aistriúcháin/Translations', for instance, Mac Lochlainn uses English and Irish in both versions, thus catering for different anticipated readerships.

The result is a relationship between the two poems which arguably bears more the mark of adaptation than translation (62).

Debating translation and self-translation: Voices from a Gaelic literary world

As noted above, 1998 saw a small debate surrounding issues of translation and self-translation in a Gaelic literary context. Addressing translation practices which present Gaelic poetry in an otherwise English format, McLeod interprets the situation as a 'reflection of and metaphor for' the decline of Gaelic as a living language (151). Pointing towards the frail state of Gaelic in a community which is also always an Anglophone one, he contemplates that:

> in a sense, then, packaging Gaelic poetry in such a way as to push it into a kind of existential limbo is only appropriate. The utilitarian logic seems impeccable: Why bother with the expense of printing Gaelic introductions when everyone can read English? Why bother with printing Gaelic versions of the poems? And the inevitable last question: why bother with Gaelic at all? (151)

These questions become even more poignant in the light of the contrasting question 'why bother to translate at all', posed by Gaelic poet Aonghas MacNeacail during a literary symposium entitled 'English as a function for Gaelic', 20 years earlier (Thompson 6). In 1998, reacting to McLeod's article in *Chapman* (McLeod), MacNeacail incidentally answers his own question by stating that 'at the basic economical level, it makes our books more viable and we, surely, are as entitled as any other serious writers to seek viability' ('Being Gaelic and Otherwise' 155). This is somewhat in contrast to an earlier article published in 1990 where he states that 'the most popular Gaelic author will quickly recognise that writing solely in their native language is not a commercially viable venture. It's as well that Gaelic writers are not primarily motivated by the size of the potential audience, nor by the likelihood of any significant financial benefit accruing from their labour' (MacNeacail, 'Rage against the Dying of' 56). By the time the *Chapman* debate was printed, rather than perceiving of Gaelic poetry in translation as a cultural activity which takes from Gaelic to enrich English culture, he argues that 'we also offer yet another door, however narrow, for those who are curious about Gaelic to peer in, and perhaps eventually to step into our world' ('Rage against the Dying of' 55). Interestingly, while McLeod and MacNeacail hold opposite opinions, both arrive at the conclusion that the issue of translation cannot be divorced from spheres of politics. McLeod argues that 'the problem is fundamentally a political one: today's Gaelic denying approach needs to be recognised and named for what it is and what it says' (151). MacNeacail, on the other hand, asks, 'why shouldn't we argue that translation is also, and overtly, a political act, in that it offers a reminder to the outside world that "We are still here"?' ('Being Gaelic and Otherwise'155).

With respect to content rather than format, one finds contemporary poetry in Gaelic at times perceived as to be 'English verse in Gaelic' which 'loses something in the original' (MacInnes 342–3). The Gaelic original is clearly viewed as inferior to the English translation. Such an attitude, however, still considers the writing in Gaelic to be the original writing. This observation becomes important in view of Christopher Whyte's revelation: 'more than once I have been asked if I write the translation first, then put the poem into Gaelic' ('Translation as Predicament' 83). Indeed, with respect to reviewing Whyte's bilingual anthology, *An Aghaidh na Siorraidheachd* the critic Donald MacAulay admitted: 'I was concerned to find that with some poems I felt unable to determine, from reading them, which was the translation and which the original' (53). These two remarks epitomize the perceived collapse of the traditional distinction between the original and the translation, between original creative writing and translational activity. It is therefore not surprising that, as MacAulay notes, there is 'an assumption articulated (and defended) by some people in the literary establishment, and elsewhere in Scotland that the translation can somehow be an adequate substitute for the original [. . .] that the translation itself is somehow equally valued with the original' (53). Only the practice of self-translation makes such statements possible. '[P]resenting poetry in such a fashion has serious consequences', McLeod argues, 'The two texts can be understood as two functionally equivalent versions of the same thing, the same ideal "original"' (149). He elaborates:

> the two texts can be seen as two distinct and different compositions, two 'originals' of essentially identical legitimacy and importance, each the fruit of the author's labour, and not necessarily dependent on each other. What no longer seems a realistic interpretation is the most obvious one – that the Gaelic texts are the originals, and their English translations are ancillary and mediated compositions in whose production 'something has been lost'. (149)

Such an assumption becomes evident as soon as Gaelic texts are critically evaluated, as in the case of Aonghas MacNeacail, Scottish Writer of the Year in 1997, where, as McLeod notes, the judges 'took the translations at face value and read them as workable poetry' (149). Given the authority commonly attributed to self-translation, it is not surprising that the English text will be read as the version of the poem which allows for the most direct and transparent access to the poem in Gaelic. Consequently, the English version translated by the author acquires a canonical status.

To take the argument further, Whyte poses the question of whether the 'specific and peculiar' bilingual existence of Gaelic poetry today 'reveals a weakening of the Celtic language, a perceived need to help it along, to offer it completion' (*Modern Scottish Poetry* 227). The close proximity of original and self-translation denies the Gaelic poem a sense of completeness; in the case of contemporary Gaelic poetry, the translation process occurs more or less simultaneously to the original writing process, and is published accordingly in bilingual editions. As such, the poem in Gaelic has no independent existence, either as a process or as a fixed reference as original text preceding the translation in publication. The practice of self-translation can, therefore, be argued to have not only a significant impact on the status of the translation as canonical in terms of the author's corpus of work, but to be a shaping agent in the composition of an author's canon itself. With regard to the perception of MacLean's body of work, for instance, the impact is crucial. As Whyte points out:

> it brings about a distortion from which the 'Dàin do Eimhir' sequence of love poems has suffered notably. MacLean's poetic output is identified, to all intents and purposes, with his own translations into English. Those parts of the 1943 collection which where not available in English could, it seems, be ignored. (Introduction 40)

Therefore, translations resulting from self-translation do not merely succeed in having original status bestowed upon them, thus making the unique linguistic and stylistic features of the actual original writing invisible, they also succeed in making untranslated originals invisible altogether, thus erasing them from the canon. In this respect, the practice of self-translation in a Gaelic context reinforces invisibility, the very condition characterizing and concluding the existence of minority.

The year 2002 saw the publication of the highly acclaimed bilingual poetry collection *An Leabhar Mòr: The Great Book of Gaelic* (MacLean and Dorgan), which concluded a touring exhibition project of the same name combining Scottish Gaelic and Irish literatures and visual arts. In an article concerned with Gaelic language planning Alison Lang identifies prestigious cultural projects of this kind as branded Gaelic, and funded accordingly, while she criticizes them for failing to contribute towards reversing language shifts, given the use of English as the linguistic medium for communicating both the publication and associated events (239–56). Yet, as Calum MacLean states in the introduction to *An Leabhar Mòr*, the project is perceived by its makers as a 'modest, but significant and optimistic step' towards encouraging artists to 'recognise [the] acceleration in language death as an appropriate subject matter for literature, drama,

music and visual arts and as yet uncategorized artforms' so as to ensure
that 'the issue will come alive in the minds of the general public' (MacLean
and Dorgan 3). Noting the suggested role of the artist as mere mediator of
content rather than format, Lang poses the following question:

> Ma thig crìoch air dleastanas luchd-ealain agus sgrìobhadairean nuair a
> bhios iad air cunnart an t-suidheachaidh a chlàradh, a bheil e an uair sin an
> urra ri feadhainn eile – luchd-planaidh agus luchd-leasachaidh – fuasgladh
> a lorg gus stad a chur air crìonadh a' chànain agus ath-bheothachadh a
> chur an gnìomh, no a bheil uallach air an neach-ealain a bhith sàs anns
> an obair seo cuideachd? (201)

> If the artists' and writers' duty ends once they have noted the danger of
> the situation, is it then the responsibility of other people, planners and
> developers, to search for ways to stop language decline in support of
> revitalisation, or is it the responsibilities of artists also to engage in this
> work? (my translation)

Arguably, the artist who uses Gaelic as a label for his or her work moves
within the spheres of language politics, not necessarily in terms of
content but most certainly in terms of the format chosen, for every form
of artistic expression inevitably communicates with an audience through
the use of language. Talking from a Fishmanian point of view, that is,
from a point of view concerned with actively reversing language shifts,
Lang explains:

> Tha na Fishmanaich a' faicinn cunnart anns an teachdaireachd seo
> gu bheil Gàidhlig ceart gu leòr na h-àite fhèin, ann am bàrdachd is
> ceòl, ach gur i Beurla a bhios daoine a' bruidhinn agus a' sgrìobhadh
> gu h-àbhaisteach. Agus sin cnag na cùise [. . .] às aonais cleachdadh a'
> chànain, cha tig àbhaisteachadh, ann an raointean culturach is ealain no
> raointean cleachdaidh sam bith eile. (201)

> Fishmanians see a danger in this message that Gaelic is all right in its
> own place, in poetry and music, but that English is what is spoken and
> written habitually. And that is the crux of the matter [. . .] without
> language use there will be no normalisation, whether in the domains of
> culture and art or in any other domains of use. (my translation)

The argument is that practices which promote a minority language
mainly through the medium of the majority language further weaken an
underdeveloped language by denying it a development towards a habitual
medium for cultural communication. This in turn means the weakening of
the infrastructure to support such cultural communication, both in artistic
and commercial terms.

Gaelic poetry and self-translation:
An interpretative view

As Gaelic poet Rody Gorman notes, 'the world of Gaelic poetry is not in a healthy state, and the opportunities for publication are really limited', adding that 'publication outlets aren't that plentiful, there are a few in Ireland but they are virtually non-existent in Scotland' (Urpeth 1). This situation may well signify the concluding stages of a development of publication practices which saw Gaelic poetry accompanied by a selection of English prose translations by the author as with MacLean's *Dàin do Eimhir* in 1943 to original Gaelic poetry as the *raison d'être* for essentially English language publications, as seen from the 1990s onwards. No significant effort has been made during this recent past to develop a monolingual market for poetry in Gaelic. Consequently, today there is little else on offer than the continuation of this genre as essentially a bilingual self-translated literature. As already noted, latest contemporary Gaelic poetry collections – such as, *Dannsam Led Fhaileas / Let Me Dance with Your Shadow* by Martin MacIntyre, Meg Bateman's *Soirbheas / Fair Wind* and Aonghas MacNeacail's *Laoidh an Donais Òig / Hymn to a Young Demon* – rely on self-translation and the bilingual *en-face* format. While these authors certainly continue to seek appreciation from an English-speaking audience, it is interesting to observe, however, that in those recent publications Gaelic has made it onto pages dedicated to paratextual features. This might well be read as an attempt to 're-Gaelicise' the bilingual edition, at least to some degree. With these publications the authors are also introduced in Gaelic on the back cover. A similar approach is followed throughout the books, with Gaelic used in introductory notes on the authors and their poetry alongside English. In effect, Gaelic is re-evaluated as the natural linguistic medium for paratextual features, nevertheless confirming the need for English in order to communicate with a readership. Although any translation activity remains unacknowledged in all three publications, such practice can still be inferred by the reader of MacIntyre's edition from the comment on the very last page that one of the poems in Gaelic does not easily translate into English and therefore remains untranslated (Mac an t-Saoir/MacIntyre 124). In addition to this, we find a number of English poems in this collection untranslated into Gaelic. As a result, the bilingual nature of the author is emphasized, with bilingualism as an immediate reality resulting in self-translation which, nevertheless, remains unmentioned and generally unchallenged in the context of Gaelic poetry today.

If it is the paratextual spaces which inform the readership about to whom a particular publication is addressed and what it is aiming to achieve, a lack of paratext is just as revealing with regard to the purpose of any particular publication format to manipulate its reception and consumption (see also Wolf 115–31; and Genette 261–79). Incidentally, the insistence on the importance of paratextual features for the visibility of the translation process also raises the profile of the translator as creative and manipulating agent, which cannot fail to raise the visibility of the original literature *as* original literature. Highlighting the fact that we are reading literature in translation, therefore making the translation process, which is always a process of interference, visible, allows the reader to understand that the poems in Gaelic will necessarily be different from their English translations, even if translated by the author of the original. The mere fact of the visibility of translational activity in the context of minority languages ensures a conscious reading or non-reading of both source and target text for what they are. Moreover, given that an *en-face* publication format suggests equivalence by virtue of showing the text in one language as mirrored by the text on the other page, the Gaelic/English poetry publication allows for smooth consumption through the medium of English, suitable to raise the profile of individual authors and Gaelic poetry on the whole in an English-speaking world. Indeed, the ideologically driven exclamation, 'We are still here' (MacNeacail, 'Being Gaelic' 155), which suggests a loyalty to the language and thus a political positioning with respect to its maintenance and development, still confirms the desire to be culturally appreciated by the highly prestigious and globally powerful neighbour. Such a focus, however, diverts attention away from the minority source culture, which, after all, provides the linguistic and literary medium for the source texts. If the agenda, however, was more driven by the needs of the source culture, publication and translation choices would more likely reflect such needs. These would include translation into the minority language in support of a more robust corpus of literary texts or monolingual publications to enhance both confidence and pleasure in reading literary texts written in the minority language for a readership consisting of native speakers and learners alike. If self-translation from a minority language reveals the desire to communicate where communication through original writing is deemed to fail by not attracting a substantial readership, the contrary approach to translation, that is, non-translation, reveals a disregard for numbers and the intention to communicate with the readership of the minority language, however small it may be. This acute awareness of the literary space as a shared social genre leads some authors to abandon self-translation. Translation and publication choices are therefore a means of communicating a text within the spheres of the socially shared genre of literature. In that respect, translation and publication choices disclose where each text aims to position itself in the complex world of literary production and appreciation.

Returning to the established publication practice for Gaelic poetry today, one might also consider potential reading patterns which such a format invites. The bilingual Gaelic/English edition inevitably encourages a reading which views the Gaelic and the English text comparatively, with the word 'x' in Gaelic realized as the word 'y' in English. With a poem called 'samhla' (MacNeacail, *Oideachadh Ceart* 36), for instance, the reader unfamiliar with the Gaelic word '*cidhis*', a word which is not necessarily part of an active Gaelic vocabulary, will learn by glancing over to the English version of the text that it means 'mask'. In other words, Gaelic '*cidhis*' equals English 'mask'. Such reading practices, which interpret the Gaelic in terms of the facing English, are not merely restricted to the level of individual words (see Krause, 'Voicing the Minority' 135–7). This means that with regard to reading Gaelic poetry which is presented bilingually the meaningful engagement with the poem occurs more firmly with the English text, whereas with the monolingual text in Gaelic the denotative meaning remains supported by the surrounding words in the same language. What is more, inviting a parallel reading of the two different language versions might well end up in a linear reading of the English language version given the attractiveness of English as the habitual language for reading, even for speakers of Gaelic. As such, the mere presence of the English self-translated poem acts as a straitjacket for the poetry in Gaelic, concealing poetic dynamics as they unfold in each Gaelic poem. One could, therefore, argue that modern Gaelic poetry becomes most meaningful in the shape of its English 'doppelgänger', as McLeod calls it (151). Moreover, the continuous presentation of their 'native' literature along with the English back-up version poses a threat to the very willingness on the part of the Gaelic readership to make sense of the text in Gaelic. This in turn prepares the path for native Gaels to discard what is presented as a Gaelic text as not Gaelic in nature at all, thus denying the development of Gaelic literature within the global exchange of culture generally As mentioned earlier, recent Gaelic poetry has been described as 'English verse in Gaelic' (MacInnes 342). Similarly, in the introduction to *An Tuil*, a bilingual anthology of twentieth-century Gaelic poetry, Black states that 'items like "Fontana Maggiore" [by Christopher Whyte] [. . .] happened to read beautifully in English, but sprang entirely from non-Gaelic models and sensitivities, and appeared not to have an independent Gaelic existence, to the extent that the Gaelic versions could not easily be understood without reference to the English' (lxiv). In itself, statements of this kind are highly problematic in light of their recourse to the notion of 'cultural essence', which has been discredited in particular by postmodern and post-colonial cultural studies. In addition, they narrow the view with regard to the creative impulses which lead to the creation of a poem in Gaelic, which might well originate from a non-Anglophone world. After all, such creative impulses are essential to ensure the continuation and revitalization of literature in a minority language. It might well be that poetic innovation of this kind will lose many a reader along the way, but if the poetry is printed monolingually, at least it will not lose the reader to the English version. Rather, in the case of this language and literature it is more likely that literary innovation will win over support, as it has done with other languages and literatures throughout history. Failing this, if it continues to be published alongside the author's English translation, there will be no independence for Gaelic poetry as a published entity or as a literature in the making. If bilingual publication continues, one will still be left with the question, 'Why bother with the poem in Gaelic?', which inevitably implies, 'Why bother with Gaelic at all?'

Works cited

Bateman, Meg. *Soirbheas / Fair Wind*. Edinburgh: Polygon, 2007. Print.

Black, Ronald. *An Tuil. Anthology of 20th Century Scottish Gaelic Verse*. Edinburgh: Polygon, 1999. Print.

Cronin, Michael. *Translation and Globalization*. London and New York: Routledge, 2003. Print.

Davies, Grahame. 'Sleeping with the Enemy: the Tensions of Literary Translation'. *New Welsh Review* 64 (2004): 58–64. Print. *Five Essays on Translation*. Eds Katja Krebs and Christopher Meredith. U of Glamorgan P, 2005. 10–21. Print.

Davitt, Michael. *Fardoras*. Indreabhán, Connemara: Cló Iar-Chonnachta, 2003.

—. *Freacnairc Mhearcair / The Oomph of Quicksilver*. Ed. Louis de Paor. Cork: Cork UP, 2000. Print.

Elfyn, Menna and John Rowlands, eds. *The Bloodaxe Book of Modern Welsh Poetry*. Tarset: Bloodaxe, 2003. Print.

Genette, Gérard. 'Introduction to Paratext'. *New Literary History* 22 (1991): 261–79.

Is Mise an Teanga. Dir. Murray Grigor. Viz with Flying Fox Films, 2003. DVD.

Jenkinson, Biddy. 'A Letter to an Editor'. *Irish University Review* 21.1 (1989): 27–34. Print.

Krause, Corinna. 'Eadar Dà Chànan: Self-Translation, the Bilingual Edition and Modern Scottish Gaelic Poetry'. PhD Diss. Edinburgh U, 2008. Print.

—. 'Voicing the Minority: Self-Translation and the Quest for the Voice in Gaelic Poetry'. *Translating Selves. Experience and Identity Between Languages and Literatures*. Eds Paschalis Nikolaou and Maria-Venetia Kyritsi. London and New York: Continuum, 2008. 125–40. Print.

Lang, Alison. 'Cruthachadh is Cleachdadh: Ceistean mu Planadh Cànain agus na h-Ealain Ghàidhlig'. Ed. Wilson McLeod. *Revitalising Gaelic in Scotland*. Edinburgh: Dunedin Academic P. 239–56. Print.

Mac an t-Saoir, Màrtainn / MacIntyre, Martin. *Dannsam led Fhaileas / Let Me Dance With Your Shadow*. Edinburgh: Luath, 2006. Print.

MacAulay, Donald. 'Canons, Myths and Cannon Fodder'. *Scotlands* 1 (1994): 35–54. Print.

MacGill-Eain, Somhairle *Dàin do Eimhir agus Dàin Eile*. Glasgow: William MacLellan, 1943. Print.

MacInnes, John. Review of *Fax and Other Poems* by Rody Gorman and *All my Braided Colours* by Siùsaidh NicNèill. *Aberdeen Review* 58 (1998): 342–3. Print.

MacLean, Malcolm and Theo Dorgan, eds. *An Leabhar Mòr: The Great Book of Gaelic*. Edinburgh: Canongate, 2002. Print.

Mac Lochlainn, Gearóid. *Sruth Teangacha / Stream of Tongues*. Indreabhán, Connemara: Cló Iar-Chonnachta, 2002. Print.

MacNeacail, Aonghas. 'Being Gaelic and Otherwise'. *Chapman* 89–90 (1998): 152–7. Print.

—. *Laoidh an Donais Òig / Hymn to a Young Demon*. Edinburgh: Polygon, 2007. Print.

—. *Oideachadh Ceart agus Dàin Eile / A Proper Schooling and Other Poems*. Edinburgh: Polygon, 1996. Print.

—. 'Rage against the Dying of'. *Chapman*, 35/36 (1990): 54–8. Print.

MacThòmais, Ruaraidh / Thomson, Derick. *An Dealbh Briste. Gaelic Poems, with some Translations in English*. Edinburgh: Serif Books, 1951. Print.

McLeod, Wilson. 'The Packaging of Gaelic Poetry'. *Chapman* 89–90 (1998): 149–51. Print.

Minhinnick, Robert, ed. and trans. *The Adulterer's Tongue: An Anthology of Welsh Poetry in Translation*. Manchester: Carcanet, 2003. Print.

Morys, Twm. 'A Refusal to be Translated'. *Poetry Wales* 38.3 (2003): 55. Print.

Ní Dhomhnaill, Nuala. *Pharaoh's Daughter*. Oldcastle: The Gallery P., 1990. Print.

—. *The Water Horse*. Trans. Medbh McGuckian and Eilean Ní Chuilleanáin. Oldcastle: The Gallery P., 1999. Print.

Ní Dhomhnaill, Nuala and Paul Muldoon. *The Astrakhan Cloak*. Oldcastle: The Gallery P, 1992. Print.

Ó Muirí, Pól. 'A Desire to Scavange'. *Fortnight* (supplement) 316 (1993): 15–17. Print.

Thompson, Frank. 'English as a Function for Gaelic'. *Books in Scotland* 3 (1978–9): 6–8. Print.

Thomson, Derick. *Meall Garbh / The Rugged Mountain*. Glasgow: Gairm, 1995. Print.

Urpeth, Peter. 'Bridging the Gàidhlig-Gaelige Gap'. *Northings*. 2004. Web. www. heritagenorth.org.uk/HI-Arts/Features/2004/mar04_interview-rody-gorman. htm

Whyte, Christopher, ed. *An Aghaidh na Sìorraidheachd / In the Face of Eternity: Ochdnar Bhàrd Gàidhlig / Eight Gaelic Poets*. Edinburgh: Polygon, 1991. Print.

—. Introduction. *Dàin do Eimhir / Poems to Eimhir*. Somhairle MacGill-Eain / Sorley MacLean. Ed. Christopher Whyte. Glasgow: Association for Scottish Literary Studies, 2000. 1–41. Print.

—, ed. *Modern Scottish Poetry*. Edinburgh: Edinburgh UP, 2004. Print.

—. 'Translation as Predicament'. *Translation and Literature* 9.2 (2000): 179–87. Print.

Wiliams, Gerwyn. Personal Interview. 24 Oct. 2005.

Wolf, Michaela. 'Feminist Thick Translation: A Challenge to the Formation of Feminist Cultural Identity'. *Tradução e Comunicação* 12 (2003): 115–31. Print.

CHAPTER NINE

Indigenization and opacity: Self-translation in the Okinawan/ Ryūkyūan writings of Takara Ben and Medoruma Shun

Mark Gibeau

Abstract: *As with many post-colonial writers, contemporary Okinawan writers are faced with a language dilemma. There is no single, neutral language upon which they can unthinkingly draw. Instead they must choose between variants of their native, local or ancestral tongues, the tongue of the colonizer (standardized Japanese) or some combination thereof. This paper examines how two contemporary writers, the poet Takara Ben and the novelist Medoruma Shun, integrate the language dilemma into their works and employ it as a mechanism for redefining contemporary Okinawan subjectivity vis-à-vis mainland Japan.*

The paper examines how both writers use Okinawan/Ryūkyūan languages in their texts to resist the hegemonic dominance of mainland Japanese culture, language, historical narratives and identity. Through an analysis of the writers' use of language, self-translation, historical narratives and local culture I argue that the works function on a performative level to introduce a 'strategic opacity' into the texts in order to delimit the gaze of the mainland reader, to reject Japanese ethnocentrism and assert the existence of Okinawan difference.

In an article discussing post-colonial writing as translation Paul Bandia outlines the paradoxes facing the post-colonial writer of a minor literature. Building upon Deleuze and Guattari's concept of a 'minor literature' (16) Bandia writes of 'the impossibility of writing in the language of the oppressor [. . .] as well as the impossibility of doing otherwise' (353). Forced to write in an environment where language itself is an object of contention and where 'everything is political' (Deleuze and Guattari 17) the writer of a minor literature 'turns the literary machine into a revolutionary machine, claiming the right to difference' (Bandia 354).

The need to reclaim such a 'right to difference' is particularly important in the case of contemporary Okinawa. Subjected to a highly aggressive assimilation policy for over 100 years, Okinawa has been redefined as a 'branch' or variant of Japanese culture. In examining how contemporary Okinawan writers utilize translation to reassert their right to difference and to navigate a new form of cultural identity, the present investigation takes its cue from Bandia's application of Deleuze and Guattari's concept of 'minor literature' to the realm of translation in post-colonial literature. This investigation will focus primarily on two contemporary writers: the poet, Takara Ben (born in 1949) and the novelist, Medoruma Shun (born in 1960), though other important literary figures – Sakiyama Tami, Ōshiro Tatsuhiro and Yamanokuchi Baku – will be discussed briefly in the final section.[1] Specifically, this article will look at the ways in which these two writers integrate Ryūkyūan[2] languages into their works and how strategic use of language serves the dual function of rendering Okinawa simultaneously visible and opaque to a mainland Japanese readership. The significance of this characterization of language will then be assessed in terms of what it holds for the translator.

The language dilemma

Okinawan writers face a dilemma common to many post-colonial writers in that there is no neutral language on which they can draw. They must choose between variants of their native, local or ancestral tongues, the tongue of the colonizer or some combination thereof. This decision carries with it a range of connotations that reflect back on the writer, the work and the work's stance vis-à-vis Okinawan political and cultural identity. To write in one of the many Ryūkyūan languages is, among other things, to convey the rhythm and concrete daily existence of the islands; it is to preserve what Wa Thiong'o calls the 'collective memory bank of a people's experience in history' (15), and to resist the 'passive colonial alienation' (28) that distances colonial subjects from their histories, cultures and languages. Furthermore, as many Ryūkyūan languages are being driven to extinction by the overwhelming presence of the Japanese education system, mass media and popular culture, the act of writing keeps the language alive, if only just. In a sample of approximately 200 Okinawans surveyed, none identified themselves as speaking Okinawan languages 'very well' or 'fairly well', and most indicated that they could speak it only very little or not at all (Osumi 75–6). While the sample size is quite small in relation to the total population of Okinawa (approximately 1.31 million), the results are confirmed by the UNESCO online Atlas of Endangered Languages, which lists three Ryūkyūan languages as 'definitely endangered' and two Ryūkyūan languages as 'severely endangered'. To write in a Ryūkyūan language is to delimit the size and diversity of one's audience; in many respects, to write into a void (Molasky and Rabson 7–8; Cather 55–7).

Writers thus face the unsavoury choice of either 'betraying' their Ryūkyūan heritage by writing in the dominant language or of relegating themselves to a narrow readership and reducing the potential impact of their writings. Medoruma Shun, among others, has been criticized for using an 'impure' form of Okinawan dialect to gain a broader Japanese readership (Cather 55–6). However an either/or choice does not reflect the reality of contemporary Okinawa. After over a hundred years of assimilation, it is impossible to expunge all traces of Japanese and Japanese-ness and return to a pre-colonial utopia. Japanese language and culture are integral parts of Okinawan life and the works of these two writers – both of whom are fervent supporters of Ryūkyūan languages – are written mostly in standardized Japanese. This is not to say, of course, that there is no place for 'pure' Ryūkyūan languages in Okinawan literature or that standardized Japanese should be uncritically adopted. Okinawan identity and culture are defined by their hybridity and to fail to recognize that is to engage in cultural essentialism.

Before Okinawan writers can reclaim and redefine difference they must first render that difference visible. In Okinawa the campaign of assimilation has been so successful that not only do most Japanese see Okinawa as a natural part of Japan, the majority of Okinawans also see Okinawa and Okinawans as Japanese (Molasky 22; Lie 95). This view of Okinawa in relation to mainland Japan, coupled with the widely held (and deeply flawed) perception of Japan as an ethnically homogenous nation, results in Okinawans being relegated to the category of a largely invisible minority.

To be characterized as 'different' often means to be subjected to ethnocentrism, to be dehumanized and discriminated against. Accordingly, much post-colonial writing seeks to reclaim and redefine difference and employ that difference to undermine the hegemonic order of ethnocentrism. In Okinawa, however, the universalizing logic of colonialism has been taken to such an insidious extreme that Okinawans are not recognized as non-Japanese even as they remain objects of exclusion and discrimination.

Oscillating identities: Redefinitions of Okinawan otherness

The position of Ryūkyū islanders as a invisible minority is a modern development. During the Tokugawa period (1603–1868) both the ruling Tokugawa shogunate and the Satsuma domain, the Ryūkyū kingdom's closest Japanese neighbour, emphasized the kingdom's 'foreignness'. The kingdom's position as a foreign state enabled the Satsuma domain – which invaded the kingdom in the seventeenth century and forced it to pay heavy tributes and taxes – to circumvent the prohibition on foreign trade as proscribed in the 'closed country' policy of the Tokugawa government (Oguma 18–19). The Tokugawa government, keen to represent itself as a central power dominating lesser states, wanted to maintain the visibility of difference between Japan and the Ryūkyūs. Thus, Ryūkyūans were forbidden to adopt Japanese dress or the Japanese language and assimilation was actively discouraged (Oguma 19). Tributary missions to Japan were required to wear suitably 'foreign' garb to ensure that the members of the mission not be mistaken for Japanese (Morris-Suzuki, *Reinventing* 19).

Far from being assimilated as Japanese, the difference between Okinawans and Japanese was specifically insisted upon until the late nineteenth century. When the Ryūkyū kingdom was annexed and reconfigured as 'Okinawa Prefecture' in the new modern nation-state of Japan the differences between Okinawa prefecture and the rest of Japan were remapped onto the temporal axis. That is, the Okinawans could not be seen as fundamentally different from Japanese – for they were now part of a single, homogenous nation state – so their difference was attributed to backwardness, superstition and the unfortunate influence of China. Okinawans were fundamentally the same as mainlanders, only a bit behind the times (Morris-Suzuki, 'A Descent' 81–94; *Reinventing* 28). Similarly, in *Okinawa no gengoshi* Hokama Shuzen demonstrates that Ryūkyūan languages are often seen not as separate languages but as dialects of Japanese frozen in the distant past. Folklorists and ethnologists such as Yanagita Kunio, Shibusawa Keizô and artists such as Okamoto Tarô characterize Okinawa as a 'treasure house' of Japanese culture that has vanished from the mainland (Christy 623; Lie 95).

To not be considered 'non-Japanese' is, of course, very different from being treated as an equal. Though the most blatant forms of discrimination to which Okinawans were subjected over the course of the nineteenth and twentieth centuries have largely disappeared, the prefecture remains the poorest in the country, it has the lowest percentage of students going on to university and the highest divorce rates. Unemployment is double the national average and, to the great resentment of many Okinawans, the prefecture houses approximately three-quarters of all the US forces stationed in Japan, despite the islands constituting less than one per cent of Japan's overall landmass (Molasky 22; Lie 100; Tanji 1).

As Tomiyama notes, the historical relationship between mainland Japanese and the Ryūkyū islanders has been characterized by a frenetic oscillation between the desire both to assimilate and to other the Ryūkyūan (168). Historically the Ryūkyūan served to define, by means of contrast, what it meant to be 'Japanese', while at the same time being placed within the realm of Japanese (albeit at a temporal remove). This oscillation – what Tomiyama calls an 'incomprehensibility' that emerges from the 'inaccessible reality' of the Ryūkyūan – bears within it the potential to 'shake and rattle the relationship that defined "the Japanese" and "the Ryūkyūan", thus triggering a crisis into which the uniformity known as "the Japanese" would plunge' (168). While Tomiyama is referring primarily to the early twentieth century, the works of Takara Ben, Medoruma Shun and other contemporary Okinawan writers can be seen as trying to revive and amplify this oscillation for their own purposes. By pushing the 'incomprehensibility' of the Ryūkyūan to a crisis point, they may force a contemporary re-evaluation of the very meaning of 'the Ryūkyūan' and 'the Japanese'.

Takara Ben: Writing from the in-between

Takara Ben is a prominent Okinawan intellectual, former high school chemistry teacher, editor of various Okinawa-related journals, literary critic, political activist, proponent of Ryūkyūan independence and a poet. In his poetry, Takara employs both Ryūkyūan language and self-translation, and juxtaposing this linguistic strategy with the historical and cultural trauma of the islands, he cultivates that 'inaccessible reality', or strategic opacity, which pushes the mainland reader to the brink of Tomiyama's 'crisis point'.

Before commencing, however, it is important to note that the bulk of Takara Ben's poetry is written almost entirely in standardized Japanese. Only poems that focus specifically on events or themes that are inextricably tied to Ryūkyūan culture, history and identities employ Ryūkyūan languages in a prominent manner. The relatively small number of such poems, nevertheless, does not reduce their significance but rather emphasizes the larger, metatextual significance of the poet's choice of language. It is because the poet is trying to negotiate a space for Ryūkyūan identity and subjectivity within and against the dominant Japanese language and culture that language and translation come to the forefront.

'Cape Kyan' is representative of this smaller subset of Ryūkyūan poems. Whereas his other poems freely interject Ryūkyūan terms into standardized Japanese verse – employing various cushioning devices to make their meaning clear to the mainland reader – his self-translations do not allow

Ryūkyūan and Japanese to intermingle: the two poems are presented as two separate versions, with the Ryūkyūan text running across the top of the page and, carefully separated by a blank space, the Japanese version below. Rotating the text to the horizontal axis, romanizing its script and adding Takara's own English translation (*Koeru* 105), an excerpt of 'Cape Kyan' appears as follows:

(Ryūkyūan)	(Japanese)
うらみん・あわりん・ちむむげーいん Uramin, awarin, chimumugeein	怨み・悲しみ・怒りを Urami, kanashimi, ikari o (To break Grudge, Grief)
てぃちなーてぃちなーわてぃくだち Teichinaa teichinaa watei kudachi	一つ一つ打ち砕き hitotsu hitotsu uchi kudaki (And rage one by one)
胸内ぬ底なかいしじみーんとぉー Muni uchinu sukunakai shijimiindoo	心の奥深く沈める kokoro no okufukaku shizumeru (Sink into my soul deeply)
ちゃんざちょー Chanzachi yoo	喜屋武岬よ(Takara 1994, 101) Kyanmisaki yo (Oh CAPE KYAN)

The eye goes to the Ryūkyūan version first – it being at the top of the page – and the reader of standardized Japanese is immediately struck by its almost complete unintelligibility. Only a handful of scattered words can be understood. Thwarted by the Ryūkyūan version, the reader must turn to the Japanese texts at the bottom of the page. When reading the poem in public, the poet adopts a similarly disorienting approach, reading only the Ryūkyūan version of the poem while those who are not proficient in Ryūkyūan (usually the entire audience) are left to follow along using a bilingual written version.[3]

Why publish a poem in a language that very few readers know and read a poem in a language that none of the listeners can understand? In readings given on the mainland to an audience of non-Okinawan listeners the poet is almost invariably the only person who can understand what he is saying. The significance of the two versions is further complicated by the fact that there is no 'Ryūkyūan original' or 'Japanese translation' at all. Rather, the poet composes the Japanese version first and then writes a Ryūkyūan version, neither one neither being a simple translation of the other nor being completely independent (Takara, 'Interview'). The processes of composition and performance indicate that the object is not primarily to bridge the gap between languages – in that case the softer approach he adopts in his other poems would be more appropriate. Rather, the poem itself constitutes a performance of difference and the gap between the languages becomes a central component of the poem. The Ryūkyūan version delimits the mainland reader's gaze, rejecting attempts at assimilation and acculturation, while the Japanese version enables the reader to understand just enough to realize how much of that Ryūkyūan reality remains inaccessible. The poem revives the 'incomprehensibility' that once threatened the stability of 'the Japanese' while simultaneously carving out a space in which Ryūkyūan subjectivity can be explored.

Just as the languages of the poem alienate the reader, the content of the poem reveals the gaps between the historical narratives of the mainland reader and the Ryūkyūan poet. Cape Kyan is the southernmost point of the island of Okinawa and also a site of one of the many 'group suicides', or what Norma Field terms 'compulsory group suicides' (61), that were one of the more tragic consequences of the Battle of Okinawa.[4] A Memorial to Peace stands at the Cape commemorating those who died. Located approximately 15 kilometres from Takara Ben's birthplace, the Cape functions as an important symbol of the modern Okinawan experience in Takara Ben's writing.

As with many Okinawan writers, the Battle of Okinawa, and the suffering incurred by the civilian population, is critical in defining Takara Ben's understanding of 'the Ryūkyūan' and 'the Japanese'. The Okinawan islands were the site of the largest land battle on Japanese 'home' territory during the Pacific War. Although it was clear by early 1945 that the war was lost, the emperor refused to consider surrender, instead insisting that one more major victory first be won in order to wrest concessions from the Allies – the foremost of these concessions being the preservation of the imperial throne. The Battle of Okinawa was intended to delay attacks on the mainland and to inflict heavy casualties upon the Allies. This would give Japan more time and more leverage to negotiate surrender. Okinawa was deliberately positioned as a 'sacrificial pawn' despite the knowledge that military and civilian casualties would be devastating (Bix 487–93; Ienaga 229–31; Ishihara 89–91; Arasaki 2–3).

In late 1944, the allies dropped incendiary bombs on the city of Naha, destroying approximately 90 per cent of the city and killing or wounding nearly 8,000 people. A few months later, the air raids were followed by a seemingly endless naval bombardment known as the 'typhoon of steel', which left hardly a single building standing, and in some cases even altered the shapes of mountains (*Heishitachi no sensô*). While exact figures vary, approximately one-third of the entire population – some 65,000 soldiers from the Japanese mainland, 30,000 soldiers conscripted from Okinawa and 94,000 civilians – was killed in the battle. Those who survived were left homeless and severely malnourished (Arasaki 2–3; Molasky 17–18; Ienaga 199).

Compulsory group suicides were one of the more horrific aspects of the battle; many civilians and Japanese soldiers committed suicide when capture by the Allies was imminent. However these suicides were not necessarily acts of fanaticism. Indeed, many were coerced by a Japanese military that did not want to see potential sources of intelligence fall into the hands of the enemy. Furthermore, both civilians and soldiers had long been subjected to propaganda campaigns designed to convince the populace that various atrocities, tortures and abuses awaited any Japanese so unfortunate as to be captured by the Allied Forces – beliefs reinforced by what some of the Japanese soldiers had done themselves in China. The act of suicide was thus more often than not a result of desperation and terror (Yakabi 164–71; Field 61; Ienaga 185). Cape Kyan is one of many such sites where civilians and military personnel committed 'group suicide' or 'compulsory group suicide'. Groups of Japanese soldiers and civilians, driven to the southernmost point of the island by the Allied advance, leapt from the cliffs of Cape Kyan.

The poem, of which the above is only a small excerpt, is structured as a series of images: farmers tilling the red earth of the Cape; the timelessness of the waves; the bright sun on the memorial; traces of blood washed out to sea; prayers offered to the dead. The Cape – a synecdoche for the Ryūkyū islands – is an image of an unchanging natural purity that transcends human grief. It stands amid the waves, the rocks below and the blue sea, each the same as they have always been, but to the narrator this 'pure' nature will always be stained with the blood of those who threw themselves into the sea. Even as he prays for the souls of those killed, he struggles to contain his rage towards those responsible.

While all Japanese suffered during the war, there is something qualitatively different about the experience of the Okinawans. Used as pawns by the Emperor and military command, bombarded and attacked by the Americans, Okinawans were also threatened and attacked by their own army. Japanese soldiers murdered civilians for their food, their hiding spots, for surrendering to the enemy (and being subsequently released), for making noises that might give away their position and so on. Of the officially verified 298 executions of Okinawan residents by the Japanese military – the actual figure is thought to number in the thousands – the most common reason for execution given was suspicion of spying (Yakabi 165). Orders for regiments stationed in Okinawa treated the mere act of speaking in the local language as evidence of spying and ordered that such people be 'disposed of'(*Heishitachi no sensô*; Yakabi 165). In some instances civilians were lined up and executed for no discernable reason whatsoever (Molasky and Rabson 22). Medoruma Shun's hometown of Nakijin was the site of one such 'spy hunt' (Yakabi 167) and the sudden disappearance of men figures in his novella *Mabuigumi*.

The narrator of the poem is more than simply grief stricken. Not only was Okinawa colonized by Japan, it was then betrayed by the military and an emperor, whose duty it was to protect them. The narrator is on the verge of being overcome by his rage.[5] This rage is not an abstract deception provoked by the injustice of war or the Americans. It is anger at mainland Japan's betrayal of Okinawa. While they may empathize with the Okinawan, this rage no doubt provokes in the mainland reader a sense of alienation no less substantial than the wall of Ryūkyūan text running across the top of the page. Mainland readers can thus experience the poem and feel its emotions in 'translation', but they are confronted with a linguistic barrier designed to 'other' them, to make them aware of their delimited experience of the poem. Use of the local speech, which was once a capital crime, is thus resurrected to drive home the consequences of difference: recognizing how subjects are positioned differently by historical narratives makes one aware of 'other' experiences and traumas of war and its aftermath.

Insofar as translation is considered to be a communicative act, Takara Ben's poem is perhaps best interpreted as an act of anti-translation instead of self-translation. His deliberately 'self-othering' approach does not attempt to convey a message to the reader so much as it attempts to emphasize the reader's inability to understand that message, occupying the gap between the poem's language and the reader. It highlights the limits of the mainland reader's gaze and, through its opacity, signals the depth of cultural and historical experience that the mainland reader cannot share. The poem is not a communicative act but an untranslatable 'surplus' of meaning lost in translation, what Venuti calls a 'remainder' which '[. . .] exceed[s] communication of univocal meaning and instead draw[s] attention to the conditions of the communicative act, conditions that are in the first instance linguistic and cultural but that ultimately embrace social and political factors' (471). This 'remainder' constitutes the poem's raison d'être. It must not be domesticated or supplanted by the target language, lest the critical historical dimension of the text be lost (Venuti 472).

In Takara Ben's poem the 'remainder' the historical, linguistic and ongoing political conditions of the communicative act overpower the communicative component of the Japanese version, making the 'meaning' of the poem secondary to the display of that which cannot be communicated. There is no original or translation in Takara Ben's poem, rather the poem itself exists in the tension between the two – in the white space between the Japanese and Ryūkyūan poems, between Japanese and Ryūkyūan histories and identities, between 'the Japanese' and 'the Ryūkyūan'.

Medoruma Shun: Writing in the margins

Medoruma Shun first came to national prominence in 1997 when he won the prestigious Akutagawa Prize for the combination of his anti-realist tone, the strong sense of the '*locale*' and his unflinching treatment of the Battle of Okinawa (Maruya et al. 427–8). Since then he has gone on to win numerous other literary prizes and in 2004 his story 'Fūon' or 'The crying wind' was made into a film and received the Innovation Award at the 2004 Montreal World Film Festival.

As with many Okinawan writers, Medoruma Shun is highly attentive to the range of island languages and the subtleties conveyed by the employment of each. In his article, 'Uchinaaguchi to Yamatoguchi no aida de' (between Okinawan language and Japanese language) he discusses not only the significance of using Okinawan (or Japanese) but also the sociopolitical nuances conveyed by the extent to which people speak the creole – uchinaayamatoguchi – that exists between the two languages (see Bhowmik 131–2). Indeed, the linguistic hybridity of Medoruma's 1997 novella, 'Suiteki' ('Droplets', translated in 2000) is a compelling example of how multilingual writing offers a mode of self-translation with strong political implications. In this work the dialogue of the villagers – the older residents in particular – is written largely in the Okinawan dialect native to the author's hometown of Nakijin. As Ikeda notes, language becomes a mechanism to delineate and stratify the social structure of the village itself: outsiders, characters affiliated with the mainland and/or its institutions, tend to speak in standardized Japanese; on the other hand, the protagonist Uta, as the shamanness or 'yuta' of the village, speaks in the local dialect of Okinawan; whereas the speech of younger characters tends to be less heavily inflected (118–19, 143). Critical attention has been devoted to how this choice of language plays an important function in the delineation of characters within the novel. Yet little has been said with respect to the effect of Medoruma's use of Okinawan languages on the reader of standardized Japanese.

When Medoruma writes a dialogue in Okinawan, he writes in something very close to standardized Japanese, appending a gloss which provides the Okinawan rendition. Excerpts from his novella, 'Droplets', Romanized and translated, appear as follows:

「珍しいこともあるものやさ」

mijira   kuto
mezurashii koto mo aru mono ya sa (Medoruma, 'Suiteki' 11)

'Mighty strange' (Rabson translation, 256)

「何が、我っ達徳正や見せ物るやんな。」

nuu   watta   mishimun
Nani ga, wattatchi Tokushou ya misemonoru yan na (Medoruma 11)

'What do you think this is, some kind of freak show?' (Rabson, 256)

「<ruby>何<rt>ぬー</rt></ruby>しが<ruby>来<rt>ち</rt></ruby>ゃーが」

n u u   ch
Nani shiga kyaa ga (Medoruma 23)

'What in hell's name you doin' here?' (Rabson, 265)

The technique employed here is a combination of self-translation and what Zabus, referring to techniques in African writing, has called 'cushioning' (7). The main line of dialogue – that which appears below the superscripted gloss – while much closer to standard Japanese than the glossed version, is nonetheless inflected. The author appears to bend the language in the main line of dialogue and, once he reaches a breaking point, shifts the Okinawan language into the gloss. If only the gloss were provided the dialogue would be extremely difficult, if not impossible, for the reader of standard Japanese to follow.

The constant presence of Okinawan language on the margin of the reader's vision has the effect of jarring the reader out of the flow of the narrative. The gap between what is 'said' and written – the space between Okinawan and Japanese – is reinforced throughout the text. As such, Medoruma's glossing diverges from the conventional function of glossing in intercultural texts. While considered to be a less-than-ideal explanatory apparatus which suffers from the defects of being both bulky and distracting, glossing is one mechanism by which transcultural texts can resist complete domestication by the target language – allowing for the inclusion of 'native' terms while retaining intelligibility for non-native readers (Ashcroft et al. 60–5). In Medoruma's case, however, Okinawan words are not glossed with Japanese equivalents; it is the other way around and the Okinawan language lurks in the spaces between the lines. The gloss does not serve an explanatory function as the meaning is already clear in the body of the text, rather, it disrupts the flow of the narrative and forces the reader to consider what has been omitted, serving as a visible reconstitution of the 'domestic remainder', that which played such a critical role in Takara Ben's poetry. By insisting on the visibility of the gap between languages the gloss enables the text to retain that which cannot be fully expressed in either language, but only through the tension and ambiguity that exists between them. The function of the gloss is thus not so much one of translation as it is of transculturation. The distinction between the two lies, for Maria Tymoczko, in that transculturation may involve the transportation of 'a culture [. . .] a language, a cognitive system, a literature [. . .], a material culture, a social system and legal framework, a history [. . .]' (20).

Writing and translating contemporary Okinawa

The writers discussed thus far are only two of a large number of Okinawan writers who have grappled and continue to grapple with the problem of Okinawan-Japanese relations, language, identity and representation. Motohama's dissertation on Ōshiro Tatsuhirō, the first Okinawan novelist to attain widespread recognition in Japan, shows how Ôshiro tries to navigate the difficulties involved in constructing an Okinawan subjectivity while continuing to engage with Japan. More radically, Sakiyama Tami adopts an approach somewhat reminiscent of Tawada Yōko, in which language becomes a tool to fracture and disrupt calcified meanings and structures. Sakiyama's desire for her writing and her languages to behave like Bandia's 'revolutionary machine' (354) of post-colonial translation is evident in her portrayal of her writing strategy:

> [. . .] island language will detonate an explosion in the solid, high rise bulding, steeped in history, we call Japanese. When it comes into contact with suicide bombing island language, this Japanese building will break into smithereens. (qtd. in Bhowmik 166–7)

In 'Shell-Shocked Island', Yamanokuchi Baku offers a different image of this complex intersection of language, history and politics. Yamanokuchi is Okinawa's most prominent poet and has been a powerful influence on Takara Ben, who even devoted himself to a study of Yamanokuchi, *Boku wa bunmei o kanashinda*. In 'Shell-Shocked Island' the poet's attempts to engage islanders in the local language is met with their awkward smiles, causing him to wonder if even the local language had been destroyed in the war. Indeed, this situation is emblematic of the tension between languages which preoccupies contemporary Okinawan writers and which often governs the tropes within their works. Furthermore, the scene in Yamanokuchi's 'Shell-Shocked Island' exemplifies an inescapable component of much Okinawan writing: the need to inscribe the tension between the writer of the minor language and the culturally dominant Japanese readership.

This critical and complex relationship between languages in Okinawan writers presents a daunting challenge to the translator. How to translate translations that are anti-translations, disruptions, explosions and laments? How can one replicate the tension and contested identities that emerge out of the hybridity of the text? The translators of Medoruma Shun and Takara Ben, and other Okinawan writers, have deployed a variety of strategies. Michael Molasky's English translation of Medoruma's 'Suiteki' ('Droplets') in 2000 renders the language into a somewhat equivalent dialect in the target language. On the other hand, Kyle Ikeda's English version of Medoruma's 'Mabuigumi' leaves the dialect intact, providing parenthetical translations in English. Alternatively, translating Takara Ben, Norma Field chooses to leave key terms in their (Romanized) original, relying on footnotes to convey the nuances of the original to the reader (Takara, 'Dream' 51–5).

Regardless of the strategy adopted, it is essential that the translator be aware of the presence and significance of the tension between Okinawan and the 'official' language, its historical contexts and, at least in the works addressed here, this tension's important, performative function. To return to Bandia, it is essential that the translator be committed to 'an ethics of difference whose main objective is to safeguard [. . .] linguistic and cultural specificity' (359).

Notes

1   All Japanese names are listed in Japanese order, surname followed by given name.

2   One of the first issues encountered when studying Okinawa is that of nomenclature. There is no politically neutral term for the region, culture, history, language and people. Independence activists – Takara Ben among them – prefer the term Ryūkyūan over Okinawan as a means to highlight the region's past and its distinct history. Furthermore the terms 'Okinawan' or 'Ryūkyūan' conceal the enormous amount of diversity between the various islands contained in 'Okinawa'. Accordingly, while this will necessarily generate some degree of confusion itself, the terms Ryūkyū, Ryūkyūan, Okinawa, Okinawan, islands and islanders will be used as appropriate to the particular context.

3   I was fortunate enough to attend two public readings of this poem, once on 14 May 2004 and again on 30 September 2006. In both cases, the poet read the Ryūkyūan version of the poem only.

4   The term 'group suicide' (集団自決) is problematic as it conceals the various forms of compulsion – direct, indirect, physical and psychological – that drove groups of civilians and soldiers to end their lives rather than be captured. Norma Field has proposed the term 'compulsory group suicide' (61) as a more accurate alternative, a term that has since been adopted by Japanese scholars.

5   It should be noted that while the Okinawans were undoubtedly victimized by the Japanese military they were also active participants in the military campaign and, as one-third of the military personnel were recruited from Okinawans, they were also victimizers (Yakibi 149–77).

Works cited

Arasaki Moriteru. *Okinawa gendaishi*. Tokyo: Iwanami shoten, 2005. Print.
Ashcroft, Bill, Gareth Griffiths and Helen Tiffin. *The Empire Writes Back*. London: Routledge, 1986.
Bandia, Paul. 'African Europhone Literature and Writing as Translation: Some Ethical Issues'. *Translating Others*. Ed. Theo Hermans. Vol. 2. Manchester: St. Jerome, 2006. 349–61. Print.

Bhowmik, Davinder. *Writing Okinawa: Narrative Acts of Identity and Resistance*. New York: Routledge, 2008. Print.

Bix, Herbert. *Hirohito and the Making of Modern Japan*. New York: Perennial, 2001.

Cather, Kirsten. 'Dilution or Diversification – Okinawan Works and the Akutagawa Prize'. *Issues of Canonicity and Canon Formation in Japanese Literary Studies*. Ed. Stephen Miller. Vol. 1. Boulder: U of Colorado P, 2000. 47–58. Print.

Christy, Alan. 'The Making of Imperial Subjects in Okinawa'. *Positions* 1.3 (1993): 607–39. Print.

Deleuze, Gilles and Félix Guattari. *Kafka: Toward a Minor Literature*. Minneapolis: U of Minnesota P, 1986. Print.

Field, Norma. *In the Realm of a Dying Emperor*. New York: Pantheon, 1991. Print.

Heishitachi no sensō: Okinawa sen jūmin wo makikonda higeki no senjō. Nihon Hōsō Kyōkai. NHK Entâpuraizu, 2010. DVD.

Hokama Shuzen. *Okinawa no gengoshi*. Tokyo: Hosei daigaku shuppankyoku, 1971. Print.

Ienaga, Saburô. *The Pacific War*. Trans. Frank Baldwin. New York: Random House, 1978. Print.

Ikeda, Kyle. 'Unspoken Memory and Vicarious Trauma: The Battle of Okinawa in the Second-Generation Survivor Fiction of Medoruma Shun'. PhD Diss. U of Hawaii at Manoa, 2007. Print.

Ishihara, Masaie. 'Memories of War and Okinawa'. *Perilous Memories: The Asia-Pacific War(s)*. Eds T. Fujitani, Geoffrey White and Lisa Yoneyama. Durham: Duke UP, 2001. 87–106. Print.

Lie, John. *Multiethnic Japan*. Cambridge: Harvard UP, 2001. Print.

Maruya Saiichi, Hino Keizô, Kurio Senji, Takubo Hideo, Kôno Taeko, Miyamoto Teru, Ikezawa Natsuki, Furui Yoshikichi and Ishihara Shintarô. 'Senpyō'. *Bungei Shunjū* 75.11 (1997): 426–31. Print.

Medoruma Shun. 'Droplets'. Trans. Michael Molasky. *Southern Exposure: Modern Japanese Literature from Okinawa*. Eds Michael Molasky and Steve Rabson. Honolulu: U of Hawai'i P, 2000. 255–85. Print.

—. 'Mabuigumi'. *Mabugumi*. Tokyo: Asahi Shimbunsha, 1999. 5–45. Print.

—. 'Mabuigumi'. Trans. Kyle Ikeda. *Fiction International*. 40 (2007). Web. 29 Jan. 2010.

—. 'Uchinaaguchi to Yamatoguchi no aida de'. *Bungei* 37.5 (1998): 192–3. Print.

—. 'Suiteki'. *Suiteki*. Tokyo: Bungei Shunjū, 1996. 9–50. Print.

Molasky, Michael. *The American Occupation of Japan and Okinawa: Literature and Memory*. London: Routeledge, 1999. Print.

Molasky, Michael and Steven Rabson. Introduction. *Southern Exposure: Modern Japanese Literature from Okinawa*. Eds Molasky Michael and Steven Rabson. Honolulu: U of Hawai'i P, 2000. 1–36. Print.

Morris-Suzuki, Tessa. 'A Descent into the Past: The Frontier in the Construction of Japanese Identity'. *Multicultural Japan: Palaeolithic to Postmodern*. Eds Donald Denoon, Mark Hudson, Gavan McCormack and Tessa Morris-Suzuki. London: Cambridge UP, 2001. 81–94. Print.

—. *Reinventing Japan – Time, Space, Nation*. New York: M. E. Sharpe, 1998. Print.

Motohama, Hidehiko. 'Writing at the Edge: Narratives of Okinawan History and Cultural Identity in the Literary Texts of Ôshiro Tatsuhiro'. PhD Diss. U of Pennsylvania, 2005. Print.

Oguma Eiji. *'Nihonjin' no kyōkai – Okinawa, Ainu, Taiwan, Chōsen shokuminchi shihai kara fukki undō made*. Tokyo: Shinyōsha, 1998. Print.

Osumi, Midori. 'Language and Identity in Okinawa Today'. *Studies in Japanese Bilingualism*. Eds Mary Goebel Noguchi and Sandra Fotos. Clevedon: Multilingual Matters, 2001. 68–95. Print.

Takara Ben. *Boku wa bunmei o kanashinda: Okinawa shijin Yamanokuchi Baku no sekai*. Tokyo: Yayoi Shobō, 1997. Print.

—. 'Dream Revelations'. Trans. Norma Field. *Southern Exposure: Modern Japanese Literature from Okinawa*. Eds Michael Molasky and Steven Rabson. Honolulu: U of Hawai'i P, 2000. 51–5. Print.

—. Personal interview. 30 Sep. 2006. Print.

—. *Koeru – Beyond*. Naha: Niraisha, 1994. Print.

Tomiyama, Ichiro. 'The Critical Limits of National Community: The Ryūkyūan Subject'. *Social Science Japan Journal* 1.2 (1998): 165–79. Print.

Tymoczko, Maria. 'Post-Colonial Writing and Literary Translation'. *Post-Colonial Translation*. Eds Susan Bassnett and Harish Trivedi. London: Routledge, 1999. 19–40. Print.

UNESCO. 'UNESCO Interactive Atlas of the World's Languages in Danger'. 1 Sep. 2011. Web. www.unesco.org/culture/languages-atlas

Venuti, Lawrence. 'Translation, Community, Utopia'. *The Translation Studies Reader*. Ed. Lawrence Venuti. London: Routledge, 2000. 468–88. Print.

Wa Thiong'o, Ngugi. *Decolonising the Mind: The Politics of Language in African Literature*. Oxford: James Curry, 1986. Print.

Yakabi Osamu. 'Okinawa sen ni okeru heishi to jūmin'. *Ajia, taiheiyō sensō*. Vol. 5. Ed. Kurazawa Aiko, Sugihara Tôru, Narita Ryûichi, Tessa Morris-Suzuki,Yui Daisaburô, Yoshida Yutaka. Tokyo: Iwanami Shoten, 2006. 149–77. Print.

Zabus, Chantal. *The African Palimpsest: Indigenization of Language in the West African Europhone Novel*. Atlanta: Rodopi, 1991. Print.

PART FOUR

Cosmopolitan identities/texts

CHAPTER TEN

Self-translation, self-reflection, self-derision: Samuel Beckett's bilingual humour

Will Noonan

Abstract: This chapter aims to explore the links between Samuel Beckett's activity as a self-translator, the sense of linguistic self-consciousness that permeates his writing in both French and English, and his peculiar brand of multilingual and intensely reflexive humour. Beginning with a survey of Francophone and Anglophone scholarship on Beckett's bilingualism, it will go on to argue that self-translation functions as a driving force of Beckett's aesthetics that can be observed not only between the different versions of his texts but also within individual texts in either language. The effect is one of intertextual and translingual knowingness but also, paradoxically, of self-effacement: humour arises here not only out of the situational absurdity and bilingual wordplay that are especially prominent in his earlier texts, but also out of Beckett's undermining of realistic representation and of the stability of the subject. The ultimate interpretation of such humour remains open, but this combination of reflexivity and indeterminacy offers a useful framework through which to approach Beckett's self-translated oeuvre.

A rare combination of canonical author and systematic self-translator, Samuel Beckett owes part of his notoriety to having produced almost his entire creative work in both French and English versions. The bilingual, double nature of his oeuvre has become something of a critical commonplace, although details like the plethora of Dewey numbers under which his works are classified and the competing 2006 Beckett centenary celebrations in Dublin, London and Paris encapsulate an ongoing sense of confusion about how to approach an author claimed as the cultural property of at least two linguistic and literary traditions.[1] Beckett's activity as a bilingual writer and self-translator has interested scholars since at least the early 1960s, and one of the aims of this chapter is to offer a survey of Francophone and Anglophone scholarship on the topic. Concentrating mainly on texts from the earlier part of his career, it will go on to contend that Beckett's presence as a self-translator is evident not only in comparisons between French and English versions of his works but also within individual texts irrespective of the language or order of composition. As an activity that involves a transition between nominally distinct texts in different languages, self-translation can be considered both as a cornerstone of and a framework for exploring Beckett's radical linguistic and textual self-consciousness. While recent scholarship has articulated this claim in a number of productive ways, this chapter seeks more specifically to explore how bilingual writing and self-translation give rise to a particular brand of self-conscious humour, a form of discourse whose notorious resistance to analysis offers an apt metaphor for Beckett's work as a whole.

Bilingualism and self-translation have become increasingly prominent fields of Beckett criticism since the 1980s, though a recurring point of consensus is that accounting for this aspect of his work is a slippery task. Writing in 1987, bilingual novelist and critic Raymond Federman argued that:

> an urgent need exists for a solid, thorough, definitive study of Beckett's bilingualism and his activity as a self-translator. But not merely to compare passages in the twin-texts, not merely to note differences or variants, but to arrive at an *aesthetic* of bilingualism and self-translating, or better yet to arrive at a *poetics* of such activities. (9; emphasis in original)

The call for an integrated 'poetics' of self-translation has marked Federman's essay as something of a critical watershed, although the underlying question remains of how adequately to account for Beckett's work within the framework of a single critical and linguistic tradition. In a slightly earlier essay, Ann Beer notes a reluctance among critics to address the bilingual tensions permeating the English text of Beckett's novel *Watt*, whether because the predominance of philosophical and psychoanalytical interpretations have for the most part 'remained firmly within a unilingual framework and have also tended to diminish the novel's humor or emotional power', or because the New Critical and Structuralist rejection of biographical criticism has tended to mean that 'bilingualism cannot be accepted as a consideration, for Beckett's different-language texts meet only in Beckett'

('*Watt*, Knott' 41–3). Also writing in the 1980s, bilingual Canadian critic Brian Fitch notes a tendency among both Francophone and Anglophone scholars to focus on whichever version of Beckett's texts corresponds to the language of criticism ('Problématique' 91–2). Fitch argues that treating Beckett as a purely Francophone or purely Anglophone writer may, to some extent, reflect how he is perceived by a monolingual reading public in each language, although this type of approach fails to account either for the genetic process of self-translation or for the importance of bilingualism within individual versions of his work (*Beckett and Babel* 12–15).[2] Even assuming substantive similarity between the two works, there is also the problem of accounting for the different literary and philosophical contexts in which Beckett's works have been inscribed: 'to oversimplify the situation', Fitch suggests, 'one might say that the anglophone Existentialist writer and the francophone New Novelist are barely on speaking terms with one another' (16). Even if a double corpus of French and English texts were to be elaborated, 'neither [. . .] would correspond to the reality of the works as they have been and continue to be perceived and experienced by the public' (16). Fitch goes on to argue that the only approach able adequately to account for Beckett's work is one in which the critical metalanguage is itself bilingual (viii–ix). Written mainly in English but incorporating a chapter of bilingual commentary that is interspersed with passages of Beckett's own writing (141–61), *Beckett and Babel* provides an intriguing, if unconventional, demonstration of such a methodology. While Fitch amply demonstrates the importance of accounting for Beckett's bilingualism, the present chapter will explore both French and English texts, as well as the growing corpus of Francophone and Anglophone scholarship, from within the confines of English expression. As Beer notes, writing in the 1990s, works like Federman's and Fitch's 'show how central to Beckett criticism this once marginalized aspect of his work has become' ('Beckett's Bilingualism' 210). Conversely, Pascale Casanova, writing in French at a point slightly later than Beer, describes a 'double critical tradition' of largely insular Francophone and Anglophone scholarship, dominated since the beginning of Beckett's career by works in English (9). However, recent years have seen a marked growth in Francophone scholarship as part of an increasing interest in the effects of self-translation among scholars in both languages.

One of the difficulties in assessing Beckett's oeuvre lies in the peculiar status of self-translation, which undermines the traditional Romantic distinction between creative, original authorship and secondary, derivative translation by investing both activities in the same person.[3] Labelling either version of a self-translated text according to a conventional taxonomy of 'originals' and 'translations' is, at best, problematic; as Michaël Oustinoff argues, a text translated by its author must be considered both in a positive light, as a separate, authorized version of an antecedent text, and in a negative light, in the traditional manner of a translation judged by its shortcomings in faithfully recreating an original work (24). The task of classifying the French and English versions of Beckett's works is complicated by his use of both languages for initial composition (and consequent habit of translating in both directions), by the varying delays between the first and second versions of his works (extending to over two decades in the case of *Mercier et/and Camier*), and by the close genetic links between different works in his gradually evolving oeuvre. As Oustinoff has discussed (68–72), Beckett's habit of translating his own work can sometimes be ascribed to pragmatic publishing considerations, but it also offers obvious analogies with the questioning of conventional notions of authorship, language, representation and subjectivity that is widely seen as characteristic of his oeuvre. As Sinéad Mooney argues, self-translation affords Beckett 'a welcome opportunity for both textual self-effacement and a form of textual ventriloquism' ('A Roving Cancellation' 226).

Beckett's switch to composing in French from 1945 offers an easy analogy with the distance from Romantic authorship implied in traditional notions of translation; scholars like Linda Collinge have remarked on Beckett's reported comment that writing in French allowed him to 'écrire sans style', writing in what might be imagined as the colourless language of a translator, as a way to escape the stylistic baggage of his native English ('Auto-traduction' 64). But critics have also drawn attention to Beckett's comment that writing in French allowed him to 'faire remarquer moi' (roughly 'make known me') in what amounts to an aesthetic of self-conscious play that consists, in Gilles Deleuze's formulation, of 'faire bégayer la langue' (135; making language stutter) through 'une création de syntaxe qui fait naître la langue étrangère dans la langue' (141; syntactic creations that give birth to a foreign language within a language).[4] Especially in his early works, Beckett's claims about writing 'without' style can be taken as disingenuous or playful; as Harry Cockerham noted in the 1970s, Beckett is renowned for his stylistic distinctiveness in both languages, and his 'voice and accents are seen as so characteristic as to rise above whichever language he writes in' (143).

Many of the examples Cockerham discusses (see esp. 143–7) display both a sense of self-consciousness towards language and a distinct propensity for bilingual humour. At the beginning of the second act of *En attendant Godot*, Vladimir hesitatingly delivers a comment about the onstage tree involving a complicated French grammatical construction: 'Il s'en est fallu d'un cheveu qu'on ne s'y soit pendu. *(Il réfléchit)* Oui, c'est juste *(en détachant les mots)* qu'on – ne s'y – soit – pendu' (76). Whereas the equivalent passage in *Waiting for Godot* simply renders the basic meaning of the sentence ('We nearly hanged ourselves from it' 61), Vladimir has to repeat the sequence 'qu'on ne s'y soit pendu' in order to check the complex sequence of pronouns and particles and the correct use of the subjunctive. The overall effect is that of an absurdist language learning exercise in the style of Ionesco's *La Cantatrice Chauve*. While this particular joke works in the French but not in the English text (though it is, at least arguably, funnier for native English speakers competent in French than it is for native French speakers), Cockerham notes that Beckett's self-translated texts often try to reconstitute untranslatable jokes in other ways. Shortly after the sequence just quoted, the text of *Waiting for Godot* incorporates a new bilingual joke that is absent from the French text:

Estragon	Que voulez-vous?
Vladimir	I beg your pardon?
Estragon	Que voulez-vous?
Vladimir	Ah! Que voulez-vous. Exactly. (65)

Here, Estragon's unassuming insertion of the French expression 'Que voulez-vous' into the English dialogue works as a metalinguistic joke on two levels: first, as a stock phrase of French origin that Anglophones with pretensions to high culture might be expected to understand, and secondly, as a subtle invocation of the English text's French (but also highly metalinguistic) predecessor. As Mooney argues, 'Beckett's self-translations leak in prolegomena and supplements, so that his translations are haunted by their own half-acknowledged predecessors' ('A Roving Cancellation' 229).

Beckett's apparent attempts to compensate for untranslatable jokes lead both Cohn and Cockerham to explore the question of whether the French or the English texts can be considered to be funnier. Cohn argues that the French text of *En attendant Godot* 'remains the more authentically colloquial of the two versions, and thereby the more comic' (258), while Cockerham suggests that 'in translating his plays either way, Beckett takes great care to maintain the humour of the original whilst at the same time often varying its character' (150). The textual examples cited above show the potential for humour in Beckett's practice of self-translation, though Cohn's position in particular illustrates the difficulty of judging a quality as subjective and as culturally specific as humour from within the confines of one language or another, the 'more authentically colloquial' French of *En attendant Godot* might better be described as funnier to a different audience, or on a different level, to the (less colloquial, so more self-consciously artificial) English of *Waiting for Godot*. Oustinoff criticizes Cockerham's analysis, like that of later critics like Federman and John Fletcher, on the basis that their logic of 'gains' and 'losses' is especially problematic when dealing with a writer whose oeuvre displays a tendency towards increasing linguistic poverty (129–33). Similarly, it is important to bear in mind the possibility that the non-translation of a given joke or utterance, may in itself constitute a form of metajoke, or of self-conscious intertextual humour. Mooney notes that 'the fact that Beckett is his own translator [. . .] generates uneasiness about the slight but pointed slips and glitches between the French and English versions of the texts' ('A Roving Cancellation' 223); while the full effect of these differences is limited to the minority of readers familiar with both versions, they offer further evidence of a subtle play with the bilingual reception of his work. Comparing the French *Malone meurt* (1949) with the English *Malone Dies* (1956), Collinge notes that cuts to the English text far outnumber additions and that many of the additions present have the effect of closing off ambiguities present in the earlier French text ('Auto-traduction' 58–9). Collinge suggests that these changes can be understood at least in part in terms of a translator's desire to interpret and clarify, but also that the relatively restrained English of *Malone Dies* results from Beckett's return to the structuring authority of his native language after a period of writing primarily in French (61–2; developed at length in her monograph *Beckett traduit Beckett*). It also seems possible to read such differences in translation as a form of self-conscious, self-effacing commentary pointing forward to the increasingly sparse prose of Beckett's later career. Mooney explores how Beckett's use of increasingly inexact self-translations functions as a way 'to further his own writerly obsession with death and silence':

> That he was entirely capable of producing extraordinarily fluent and memorable versions of his own work and that of others is well-documented; that he increasingly chose to forgo this for consciously pale, threadbare or ill-fitting second versions of his own work becomes overwhelmingly evident in his late prose. ('Translation and the Discourse of Death' 166)

Beer has emphasized the role of self-translation in the genesis of Beckett's late trilogy of *Company/Compagnie* (1979/1980), *Mal vu mal dit/Ill Seen Ill Said* (1981/1982) and *Worstward Ho* (1983; published in Edith Fournier's translation as *Cap au pire* in 1991), a series of increasingly sparse texts that 'fused the conventions of drama, prose and poetry, as if seeking a way out of "literature"' ('Beckett's "Autography"' 774). But Beckett's propensity for 'threadbare' self-translations can be observed earlier, as in the transition from *Mercier et Camier* (completed 1946, published 1970) to *Mercier and Camier* (1974), in which a slapstick scene centring on Mercier's request for a 'massepain' ('marzipan cake'; 45–7) is deleted in favour of the narrator's dry comment that 'an altercation ensued, too foolish to be recorded, so foolish was it' (30). Commenting on this passage, Connor notes that such ellipses in Beckett's translation 'are rarely neutral; rather they convey the narrator's disapproval or disdain of the original, and therefore provide, not an elegant concealment of the ellipsis, but an elaborate allusion to it' (34). Especially in a self-translated work, the presence of such allusions offers fertile ground for humour, though it is worth remembering that, unless they are specifically recognized as translatorial incursions, their comic effect depends to a large extent on the reader's familiarity with both versions of the text. Translatorial or faux-translatorial commentary has featured as a plot device and as a source of humour in novels as far back as *Don Quixote*; however, in Beckett's case, the indirectly acknowledged connection between the different versions of his works suggests something more akin to a self-reflexive yet self-effacing metahumour.

Considered in terms of the trope of fidelity, self-translation raises the interesting problem of fidelity to an earlier, remembered and potentially mutable self. The problem of subjective instability preoccupies many of Beckett's narrators and protagonists, and Pascale Sardin-Damestoy concludes her genetic study of short self-translated Beckett texts with the argument that the 'économie paradoxale, elliptique et prolixe tout à la fois' ('paradoxical economy, simultaneously elliptical and prolix') of Beckett's self-translations resembles a 'structure schizomorphe, complexe et parfois incohérente' ('complex and sometimes incoherent schizomorphic structure') that allows the (Freudian) unconscious to express itself through the language of psychosis (218). Considered in terms of an alternative trope, that of commentary, self-translation can also be thought of as a type of reflexive metacommentary in which the self-translated work reflects on the prior version of the text, and by doing so foregrounds the workings of both source and target languages. In her recent study of the genesis of Beckett's bilingual oeuvre, Chiara Montini identifies Beckett's bilingualism as a basis for a type of writing she terms both 'fiction métalinguistique' and 'fiction métasubjective', in which both language and subject preside, paradoxically, over their own apparent disappearance (22). Bruno Clément's preface to Montini's work draws out the link between French/English (or English/French) and any number of other doublets or pseudocouples permeating Beckett's work, including that of discourse and metadiscourse (15). Sardin-Damestoy characterizes Beckett's self-translation as a work of rewriting, self-citation and often mis-citation, arguing that the primary evolutionary principle of his work is constituted in a 'langue aux accents étrangers, qui ne se soucie guère des contradictions, et affectionne jeux de mots et clichés' (217–18; language marked by foreign accents, which pays little heed to contradictions, and which has an affinity for puns and clichés). Sardin-Damestoy's evocation of puns (a form of humour dependent on linguistic reflexivity) and parody (defined by Genette as a specifically playful form of textual transformation; 27–68) also highlights the affinity between humour, metadiscourse and self-translation.[5] The relationship between humour and reflexivity is especially evident in the somewhat narrower French usage of the term *humour*, which differs from its English homonym in that it signifies less the general domain of the comic than a more specific capacity for self-derision as an alternative to despair that (in an appropriately Beckettian twist) tends to be regarded by French speakers as a stereotypically 'English' cultural trait.[6]

The possibility of interpreting self-translation as self-parody again highlights the danger of attempting to reconstruct a neat taxonomy of Beckettian originals and translations. Instead, the analysis offered here seeks to show that Beckett's writing is permeated by a sense of reflexive translatorial knowingness that can be identified both in comparisons between French and English pairs of texts and in single, nominally monolingual works, irrespective of the language of composition or of their place in the chronology of Beckett's oeuvre. Partly due to the focus on humour, most of the examples discussed in the later section of this chapter are drawn from the earlier, more linguistically exuberant part of his oeuvre ranging from the late 1930s to the early 1950s. This choice of texts draws on the chronology set out by Montini (23–8), divided into an early period of 'polyglot monolingualism' (1929–37) in the Joycean tradition covering his early works up to the English *Murphy*, a second period of 'Anglophone bilingualism' (1937–45) covering the French translation of *Murphy* and the composition of the English *Watt*, and a third period of 'Francophone bilingualism' beginning with the composition of his first French novel *Mercier et Camier* and covering his early 'Trilogy' of novels and his early plays. While space does not allow all these works to be covered in detail, these divisions in Beckett's oeuvre offer a useful way to explore the evolution of Beckett's relationship to both French and English prior to the more established and flexible bilingualism of his later career.

The earliest direct mention of translation in Beckett's published writing occurs in his 1931 monograph *Proust*, and includes a quotation from the earlier French writer amplified by Beckett's own parenthesis: 'The artist has acquired his text: the artisan translates it. "The duty and the task of a writer (not an artist, a writer) are those of the translator"' (84). This statement effectively separates the role of the writer from that of the Romantic artist in order to reclassify it as a form of translation, linguistic or otherwise, and scholars from Cohn (260) to Montini (40–1) have noted its potential to be read as an embryonic manifesto for Beckett's later career as a bilingual self-translator. However, translation to and from French is not the only possibility at work in Beckett's early writing. 'Dante and the Lobster', the first story in his 1934 collection of linked stories *More Pricks than Kicks*, contains an intriguing exchange between the protagonist Belacqua Shuah and his teacher Signora Ottolenghi on the problematics of translating a pun. The source language involved here is not French but Italian:

'In that connexion' he said 'I recall one superb pun anyway: "qui vive la pietà quando è ben morta . . ."'

She said nothing.

'Is it not a great phrase?' he gushed.

She said nothing.

'Now' he said like a fool 'I wonder how you could translate that?'

Still she said nothing. Then:

'Do you think' she murmured 'it is absolutely necessary to translate it?' (16–17)

This sequence is followed by a brief conversation with 'Mlle Glain, the French instructress' in which Belacqua is obliged to use the French for 'fish' due to his not knowing the word for 'lobster'. The exchange functions as a further marker of self-conscious engagement with language and translation although, again, French is not placed in an especially privileged position. Katz develops the potential pun on the name 'Ottolenghi' and its plausible, though morphologically incorrect, interpretation as signifying 'eight languages' in Italian, and goes on to suggest that Beckett's early engagement with multilingual play reflects formative experiences ranging from the collaborative translation of Joyce's *Work in Progress* to his work teaching translation studies to French university students (225–6).

Humour and linguistic instability both preoccupy the protagonist of Beckett's earliest published novel *Murphy*:

> Not the least remarkable of Murphy's innumerable classifications of experience was that into jokes that had once been good jokes and jokes that had never been good jokes. What but an imperfect sense of humour could have made such a mess of chaos. In the beginning was the pun. And so on. (65)

This passage demonstrates not only Murphy's interest in humour but also Beckett's interest in metahumour. Redfern emphasizes the tendency for Beckettian jokes to fall flat, effectively inviting the reader to laugh at the failure of an utterance that should have but did not generate laughter (162–3). In this context, 'imperfect sense of humour' can be read as referring (parodically, in either case) either to a divine or to an authorial creator, while the phrase 'make such a mess of chaos' can be interpreted either as a single action or as a double action, in which pre-existing chaos is fashioned (or translated) not into order but into an equivalently anarchic, though potentially more homely, 'mess'. The pun, in Beckett's linguistically reflexive universe, replaces the stability of the Word, and Murphy, the first in Beckett's line of increasingly unstable novelistic protagonists, is a connoisseur of the worst available.[7] A later joke offers a further case in point, this time playing on the names of alcoholic beverages and the confusion of grammatical categories:

> 'Why did the barmaid champagne?' he said. 'Do you give it up?'
>
> 'Yes', said Celia.
>
> 'Because the stout porter bitter', said Murphy. (139)

Redfern points out that this 'is a bad joke, since it contradicts itself unfruitfully': sham pain is presumably incompatible with being bitten, by a stout porter or otherwise (163). Yet this conceptual incongruity also offers its own potential for humorous effect, and the lengthy description of Murphy's reactions to the joke can also be read as a type of metajoke on the incongruity of literalizing a nonsensical metaphor:

> On the one hand the barmaid, fresh from the country, a horse's head on a cow's body [. . .] her eyes closed for the sweet pain, leaning out through the hatch of the bar parlour. On the other the stout porter, mounting the footrail, his canines gleaming behind a pad of frothy whisker. (140)

Murphy's joke depends in part on the need to pronounce 'champagne' in the standard English manner and on the homophony of this pronunciation with the phrase 'sham pain', and is too culturally and linguistically specific to be translatable. This passage and its long development are omitted from the French *Murphy* (completed in 1939 in collaboration with Alfred Péron, and first published in 1947) and replaced by the single brief sentence 'Il fit une plaisanterie de fort mauvais goût' ('He told a joke in very bad taste'; 103). As Fletcher suggests, this formulation represents a 'traduction d'autant plus curieuse que la plaisanterie n'est pas de mauvais goût du tout' ('translation [made] all the more curious, since the joke is not in bad taste at all'; 214). However, the French sentence can be read both as an intertextual reference to the English original of *Murphy* (establishing a pattern that is repeated with increasing frequency across Beckett's self-translated oeuvre), and as a metajoke about the interpretation of taste in jokes, and more generally on the difficulty of translating humour.

A final example from the English *Murphy*, consisting of a punning meta-play on bilingual puns, anticipates the use of Gallicisms characteristic of Beckett's postwar English texts:

> He found it hard to think, impossible to expand the sad pun (for he had excellent French): *Celia, s'il y a, Celia, s'il y a*, throbbing steadily behind his eyes. To be punning her name consoled him a little, a very little. (115)

This passage demands what could be described as a half-knowledge of French. The utterances '*Célia*' (in its usual French spelling, with an acute accent) and '*s'il y a*' are unlikely to be perceived as homophones by a native French speaker since the /e/ and /i/ sounds in the first syllable of each are distinct phonemes. The pun works considerably better if these ostensibly French words are pronounced with an English accent, giving approximately the same vowel quality to the syllables *Cel* and *s'il*. In this light, the speaker's 'excellent French' is called into question by a joke that requires, or at least calls for an appreciation of, the difference between standard and non-standard pronunciation, and the bilingual and translatorial implications of the passage can, again, be understood in terms of a form of metahumour.

Gallicisms are particularly evident in the early sections of *Watt*, composed in English largely while hiding from the Gestapo in France during the Second World War (see Knowlson 273–308). In an early dialogue, the initial protagonist Mr. Hackett apologizes for not rising, 'not having the force' (7). Part of the effectiveness of this joke lies in its subtlety: 'force' exists as an English word with the same root meaning as the French word of the same spelling, though its appearance in this context instead of the more natural 'strength' suggests a calque from the French.[8] A few pages later, Mr. Hackett appears not to understand a much more flagrant Gallicism committed by his interlocutor Goff:

> Not too osy with the sweet, I thought.
>
> Not too what? said Mr. Hackett.
>
> Osy, said Goff. You know, not too osy. (10–11)

'Osy' is an anglicized calque of the French 'osé', which can be translated approximately as 'daring'. The spelling confusingly suggests a pun on 'cosy', whose meaning is close to being the opposite to daring, and Mr. Hackett's request for a repetition affords an opportunity for this confusion to be emphasized. Mr. Hackett's apparent incomprehension and Goff's airy familiarity combine in a comic reflection on social pretension which, like the example of 'Que voulez-vous' in *Waiting for Godot*, plays on the transposition of colloquial French terms into cultivated English sentences. The passage receives a slightly different treatment in the 1968 French *Watt* (translated by Beckett in collaboration with Agnès and Ludovic Janvier),[9] which appeared in 1968:

> Pas trop gallois, me semblait-il, à l'heure de l'entremets.
>
> Pas trop quoi ? dit Monsieur Hackett.
>
> Gallois, dit Goff, vous savez, pas trop gallois. (14)

The French translation is essentially literal except for the use of 'gallois', which literally (and incongruously) means 'Welsh' but also suggests a pun on the lowbrow French tradition of ribald *gaulois* humour. In what amounts to both an intertextual and a metatextual reference, it also suggests a wink back at the Gallic*isms* of the original English text.

Beer has characterized *Watt* as being permeated by an 'extreme bilingual tension', reflecting its status as the last text Beckett composed originally in English before switching to French ('Beckett's "Autography"' 772). In a similar vein, *Mercier et Camier*, Beckett's first novel-length work in French, begins on a self-consciously ironic note of displacement:

> Le voyage de Mercier et Camier, je peux le raconter si je veux, car j'étais avec eux tout le temps.
>
> Ce fut un voyage matériellement assez facile, sans mers ni frontières à franchir, à travers des régions peu accidentées, quoique désertiques par endroits. Ils restèrent chez eux, Mercier et Camier, ils eurent cette chance inestimable. Ils n'eurent pas à affronter, avec plus ou moins de bonheur, des mœurs étrangères, une langue, un code, un climat et une cuisine bizarres, dans un décor n'ayant que peu de rapport, au point de vue de la ressemblance, avec celui auquel l'âge tendre d'abord, ensuite l'âge mûr, les avaient endurcis. (*Mercier et Camier* 7)
>
> The journey of Mercier and Camier is one I can tell, if I will, for I was with them all the time.
>
> Physically it was fairly easy going, without seas or frontiers to be crossed, through regions untormented on the whole, if desolate in parts. Mercier and Camier did not remove from home, they had that great fortune. They did not have to face, with greater or less success, outlandish ways, tongues, laws, skies, foods, in surroundings little resembling those to which boyhood, then manhood, had inured them. (*Mercier and Camier* 7)

The opening sentence establishes an ironic tension between the first-person narrator, the two protagonists and the implied reader, flagging the story that follows as being contingent on narratorial willingness, and claiming, as if to justify an omniscient perspective, to have been present for the entire action. The significance of 'being with them all the time' is complicated by the apparent nature of the journey undertaken, or rather not undertaken; as the mode of description shifts from space, to (not) leaving home, to unfamiliar 'ways, tongues, laws, skies, foods', both versions of the text hint, via a process of ironic negation, at a shift in linguistic and cultural context. It is especially tempting to read the French text as signifying a self-conscious shift from the 'Anglophone bilingualism' of the earlier *Watt* to the Francophone environment in which Beckett was to compose the first versions of his works for most of the next decade. This also allows a plausible interpretation of the (much later) English text as reflecting back on the now-foreign French version, following what had become by the 1970s the governing pattern of Beckett's oeuvre.

The irony of the narrator's claim to have situated Mercier and Camier in a monolingual and monocultural universe is confirmed by their own idiosyncratic use of language. Several pages into the story, a moment of silence is interrupted by a comic dialogue that turns not on the referential content at hand (whether or not to sit down) but on the alternative conjugations of a French verb in the imperfect tense:

Si on s'assoyait, cela m'a vidé.

Tu veux dire s'asseyait, dit Mercier.

Je veux dire s'assoyait, dit Camier.

Assoyons-nous, dit Mercier. (*Mercier et Camier* 15; my emphasis)

As elsewhere in Beckett's early French texts, this repetition of specific linguistic forms may well be funnier for readers who, while competent enough in French to appreciate the joke on alternative conjugations, have not internalized the idiosyncrasies of the language in the manner of a native speaker. In what can be read as a further joke on the process of self-translation, the equivalent passage in the English text appears to be self-consciously and literally translated from French:

Let us sit us down, I feel all sucked off.

You mean sit down, said Mercier.

I mean sit us down, said Camier.

Then let us sit us down, said Mercier. (*Mercier and Camier* 15)

As with the translation of 'osy' as 'gallois' in *Watt*, the odd syntax of this passage implies an intertextual reference back to the French text. The play between 'sit us down' and 'sit down' refers to the requirement for a reflexive pronoun in the formation of the French verb *s'asseoir* (to sit), rendered in English by the facetious repetition of 'us'. Back-translated into French as 'assoyons [*or* asseyons]-nous', the English phrase 'let us sit us down' highlights the difference between pronoun-verb constructions in French and English at the same time as it points back to the untranslatable pun on conjugations in the original French. Similarly, 'sucked off' for the more natural 'worn out' is a near, though not quite literal translation of the French 'vidé'; a closer English equivalent would be 'emptied', but Beckett's choice of words offers the further possibility of an obscene pun not present in the French original.

A deeper sense of linguistic uncertainty descends in the final pages of *Mercier et Camier*, when Watt, the protagonist of Beckett's preceding (English) novel, appears as a character within the French text. Beckettian figures often display a curious awareness of their intertextual predecessors, although Watt – an earlier character than his interlocutors in this scene – is apparently familiar with Mercier and Camier despite the sentiment not being reciprocated:

Je ne vous connais pas, monsieur, dit Camier.

Je suis Watt, dit Watt. Je suis méconnaissable, en effet.

Watt ? dit Camier. Ce nom ne me dit rien. (*Mercier et Camier* 193)

I don't think I recognize you, sir, said Camier.

I am Watt, said Watt. As you say, I'm unrecognizable.

Watt? said Camier. The name means nothing to me. (*Mercier and Camier* 111)

Leaving aside the question of intertextual relations between Beckett's characters – a theme that is taken to its fullest conclusion in *The Unnamable*, whose narrator appears both to negate and to incorporate his predecessors in Beckett's oeuvre – this passage raises the question of whether Watt can be considered as a 'real' character or a psychologically independent subject, a question that occupies much of the second half of his own eponymous novel. Here, his stated claim to be 'unrecognizable' implies a degree of self-consciousness about his status as a foreign entity within Mercier and Camier's textual and linguistic universe, and this is reinforced by the homophony between the name 'Watt' and the pronoun 'what'. Camier's interjection 'Watt?' punningly reduces the status of the character to that of an interrogative pronoun, and this effect gains a further level of linguistic ambiguity in the French text, as the utterance 'Watt' ['what'] stands in as a recognizable Anglicism for the French interrogative pronoun 'quoi'.

Mercier, Camier and Watt go on to discuss Beckett's earlier protagonist Murphy, who 'died ten years ago, in rather mysterious circumstances' (*Mercier and Camier* 111). The joke here is both intertextual and translatorial, possibly more so in the English than in the French text, since the gas explosion that ultimately leads to Murphy's 'mind, body and soul' being deposited as ashes on a bar-room floor (*Murphy* 275) is in a sense mediated through the French *Mercier et Camier*, the French *Murphy*, and the other intervening double, self-translated texts. Whereas the text of *Mercier et Camier* follows with an untranslatable joke on the use of second-person personal pronouns ('Retutoyez-vous, les enfants' 194), the English text has Watt respond to the news of Murphy's death with the simple phrase, 'My dream' (111), simultaneously holding up Murphy's disembodiment as an ideal, and invoking the title of Beckett's early novel *Dream of Fair to Middling Women*.

While it represents only one among many permutations of Beckett's bilingual humour, Watt's brief sentence encapsulates both the evolving sparsity and the reflexive intertextuality of his oeuvre. Its blackly humorous invocation of a disappearing subject suggests that the sequence of self-translation, self-reflection and self-derision could be completed by a final term of self-effacement. However, as the discussion of Beckett scholarship and subsequent textual analysis have sought to demonstrate, the supposedly negative potentialities of self-translation give rise, paradoxically, to a complex web of effects that runs across languages and texts. Writing on *Endgame*, Theodor Adorno positions Beckett's work as a marker of the 'barbarity' of poetry and the impossibility of affect in a world after Auschwitz (255–6), and scholars like Manfred Pfister have tended to emphasize the 'grim' aspects of Beckett's laughter as a reflection on the modern condition. Conversely, Vladimir Jankélévitch has sought to characterize humour (understood in its narrower, Francophone usage) as a form of second-degree discourse that can be distinguished from misanthropic irony by the presence of compassion or affect (171). This position can be aligned with Simon Critchley's analysis of Beckett's work as both a celebration and an exemplar of the human ability to laugh in the face of adversity (107–11). Enacting both the denial of Romantic creativity and the ludic potential of playing between languages, self-translation occupies a place in all of these interpretations. Both humour and self-translation have been discussed here as forms of reflexivity, and arguably the most elegant theory of reflexive humour to be elaborated can be found in a passage in Beckett's *Watt*, describing the movement 'from the lesser to the greater, from the lower to the higher, from the outer to the inner, from the gross to the fine, from the matter to the form', towards 'the laugh of laughs, the risus purus, the laugh laughing at the laugh, the beholding, the saluting of the highest joke, in a word the laugh that laughs – silence please – at that which is unhappy' (46–7).

Notes

1   On the bibliographical classification of Beckett's work, see Chamberlain (17–24). For reasons of scope, the present chapter will avoid the question of Beckett's Irish background and its effect on his English; for useful discussions see Beer ('Beckett's Bilingualism' 210–11) and Astbury (125–41).

2   As a personal case in point, this (native Anglophone) writer first came to appreciate Beckett's bilingual humour while studying his play *Fin de partie* during an undergraduate exchange semester at a French university. Attempts to explain my hilarity at the presence of English puns in the French text baffled my classmates and instructor alike, but sparked an interest in what eventually became a dissertation topic.

3   For early articulations of this problem in relation to Beckett's work, see Chamberlain (18–20) and Fitch (*Beckett and Babel* 21–3); for a classic and still influential Romantic position on translation, see Schleiermacher's 1819 essay 'On the Different Methods of Translating'.

4   Unless otherwise noted, translations from French in this chapter are my own, with the original quotation given in the text followed by a translation in parentheses. On Beckett's reported comments about his use of French, see Beer ('Beckett's Bilingualism' 215).

5   It is worth noting that Genette develops his account of parody as a 'transposition textuelle à fonction ludique' within the broader theory of hypertextuality set out in *Palimpsestes*. For a useful recent discussion comparing

Genette's highly formal approach to the relationship between parody, metafiction and postmodernity explored by scholars like Margaret Rose and Linda Hutcheon, see Sangsue (esp. 75–125).

6 See Escarpit for a useful, if slightly dated, account of the French conception of *humour*, including its relationship to the concepts of '*sense of humour*' and '*self-consciousness*' left untranslated in Escarpit's French text (21–32). The French perception of *humour* as an English cultural trait can be dated as far back as Voltaire, while the ongoing currency of the stereotype can be seen in the following remark by French comedian Pierre Desproges: 'L'humour anglais souligne avec amertume et déséspoir l'absurdité du monde. L'humour français rit de ma belle-mère' ('English humour highlights with bitterness and despair the absurdity of the world. French humour makes fun of my mother-in-law' 14). While the scope of this chapter does not permit an extended theoretical discussion of humour, it is also worth noting Freud's account of humour as the self-conscious play of the superego on the ego as set out in his 1927 essay 'On Humour'.

7 For a useful introduction to linguistic games and punning in *Murphy*, see Ackerley (15–22).

8 On this point, see Beer ('*Watt*, Knott' 53), who notes the presence of 'strength' instead of 'force' in Beckett's early drafts: 'The shift from the normal English phrase to the *faux ami* is thus a careful revision'.

9 For comments on the problems of translating *Watt*, including the difficulties of reconstituting Beckett's puns and culturally specific jokes, see Emmanuelle Klausner's interview with Beckett's co-translators Agnès and Ludovic Janvier (57–64).

Works cited

Ackerley, C. J. 'In the Beginning Was the Pun': Samuel Beckett's *Murphy*. *AUMLA* 55 (1981): 15–22. Print.

Adorno, Theodor W. 'Trying to Understand *Endgame*'. Trans. Shierry Weber Nicholsen. *Notes to Literature*. Ed. Rolf Tiedemann. New York: Columbia UP, 1991. 241–75. Print.

Astbury, Helen. 'Beckett et l'*Hiberno-English*: entre excès et toujours moins'. *Etudes Irlandaises* 31 (2006): 125–41. Print.

Beckett, Samuel. *En Attendant Godot*. Paris: Minuit, 1952. Print.

—. *Mercier and Camier*. New York: Grove, 1994. Print.

—. *Mercier Et Camier*. Paris: Minuit, 2006. Print.

—. *More Pricks Than Kicks*. London: Picador, 1974. Print.

—. *Murphy*. New York: Grove, 1957. Print.

—. *Murphy*. Paris: Minuit, 1965. Print.

—. *Proust*. London: Calder, 1970. Print.

—. *Waiting for Godot*. London: Faber and Faber, 1965. Print.

—. *Watt*. London: Calder, 1963. Print.

—. *Watt*. Paris: Minuit, 1968. Print.

Beer, Ann. 'Beckett's 'Autography' and the Company of Languages'. *Southern Review* 27.4 (1991): 771–91. Print.

—. 'Beckett's Bilingualism'. *The Cambridge Companion to Beckett*. Ed. John Pilling. Cambridge: Cambridge UP, 1994. 209–21. Print.

—. '*Watt*, Knott, and Beckett's Bilingualism'. *Journal of Beckett Studies* 10 (1985): 37–75. Print.

Casanova, Pascale. *Beckett l'abstracteur: Anatomie d'une révolution littéraire*. Paris: Seuil, 1997. Print.

Chamberlain, Lori. "The Same Old Stories': Beckett's Poetics of Translation'. *Beckett Translating / Translating Beckett*. Eds Alan Warren Friedman, Charles Rossman and Dina Sherzer. University Park: Pennsylvania State UP, 1987. 17–24. Print.

Cockerham, Harry. 'Bilingual Playwright'. *Beckett the Shape-Changer*. Ed. Katharine Worth. London and Boston: Routledge & Kegan Paul, 1975. 139–60. Print.

Cohn, Ruby. *Samuel Beckett: The Comic Gamut*. New Brunswick: Rutgers UP, 1962. Print.

Collinge, Linda. 'Auto-traduction et auto-censure dans *Malone meurt / Malone Dies*: Beckett traduit devant le tribunal de sa langue maternelle'. *Samuel Beckett Today / aujourd'hui* 7 (1998): 57–73. Print.

—. *Beckett traduit Beckett: de* Malone meurt *à* Malone Dies, *l'imaginaire en traduction*. Geneva: Droz, 2000. Print.

Connor, Steven. "Traduttore, traditore': Samuel Beckett's translation of *Mercier et Camier*'. *Journal of Beckett Studies* 11–12 (1989): 27–46. Print.

Critchley, Simon. *On Humour*. London: Routledge, 2002. Print.

Deleuze, Gilles. 'Bégaya-t-il . . .' *Critique et clinique*. Paris: Minuit, 1993. 135–43. Print.

Desproges, Pierre. *Les étrangers sont nuls*. Paris: Seuil, 1992. Print.

Escarpit, Robert. *L'humour*. Paris: PUF, 1960. Print.

Federman, Raymond. 'The Writer as Self-Translator'. *Beckett Translating / Translating Beckett*. Eds Alan Warren Friedman, Charles Rossman and Dina Sherzer. University Park: Pennsylvania State UP, 1987. 7–16. Print.

Fitch, Brian T. *Beckett and Babel: An Investigation into the Status of the Bilingual Work*. Toronto, Buffalo and London: U of Toronto P, 1988. Print.

—. 'La problématique de l'étude de l'œuvre bilingue de Beckett'. *Symposium: A Quarterly Journal in Modern Literatures* 38.2 (1984): 91–112. Print.

Fletcher, John. 'Ecrivain bilingue'. *Cahiers de l'Herne: Samuel Beckett*. Eds Tom Bishop and Raymond Federman. Paris: l'Herne, 1976. 212–18. Print.

Freud, Sigmund. 'On Humour'. Trans. James Strachey. *Art and Literature*. Ed. Albert Dickson. Vol. 14. The Pelican Freud Library. Harmondsworth: Penguin, 1985. 425–33. Print.

Genette, Gérard. *Palimpsestes: la littérature au second degré*. Paris: Seuil, 1982. Print.

Jankélévitch, Vladimir. *L'Ironie*. Paris: Flammarion, 1964. Print.

Katz, Daniel. 'Beckett et les huit langues'. *Samuel Beckett Today / aujourd'hui* 10 (2000): 223–9. Print.

Klausner, Emmanuelle. 'Traduire avec Beckett: *Watt*'. *Revue d'Esthétique* special issue: Samuel Beckett (1990): 57–64. Print.

Knowlson, James. *Damned to Fame: The Life of Samuel Beckett*. New York: Simon & Schuster, 1996. Print.

Montini, Chiara. '*La bataille du soliloque*': *Genèse de la poétique bilingue de Samuel Beckett (1929–1946)*. Amsterdam: Rodopi, 2007. Print.

Mooney, Sinéad. "An Atropos All in Black' or Ill Seen Worse Translated: Beckett, Self-Translation and the Discourse of Death'. *Samuel Beckett Today / Aujourd'hui* 12 (2002): 163–76. Print.

—. 'A Roving Cancellation: Beckett's (Self-)Translation as Poetics of Self-Divestiture'. *Journal of Beckett Studies* 10. 1–2 (2000): 222–34. Print.

Oustinoff, Michaël. *Bilinguisme d'écriture et auto-traduction: Julien Green, Samuel Beckett, Vladimir Nabokov*. Paris: L'Harmattan, 2001. Print.

Pfister, Manfred. 'Beckett, Barker and Other Grim Laughters'. *A History of English Laughter*. Ed. Manfred Pfister. Amsterdam: Rodopi, 2002. 175–89. Print.

Redfern, Walter. *French Laughter: Literary Humour from Diderot to Tournier*. Oxford: Oxford UP, 2008. Print.

Sangsue, Daniel. *La relation parodique*. Paris: Corti, 2007. Print.

Sardin-Damestoy, Pascale. *Samuel Beckett auto-traducteur ou l'art de l'"empêchement*': *lecture bilingue et génétique des textes courts auto-traduits (1946–1980)*. Arras: Artois PU, 2002. Print.

Schleiermacher, Friedrich. 'On the Different Methods of Translating'. *Translation Studies Reader*. Ed. Lawrence Venuti. New York: Routledge, 2004. 43–63. Print.

CHAPTER ELEVEN

Writing in translation: A new self in a second language

Elin-Maria Evangelista

Abstract: Questions of identity, loss and betrayal often arise when one chooses to write in a second language and subsequently engage in a process of self-translation. This article will look at some of these concerns and experiences of loss of self in a new language as well as the possibilities inherent in this choice. Bilingual writers engage in narratives shaped by the different perspectives and language-worlds they inhabit. Having access to more than one language, I believe, changes the way a writer approaches language creatively, often allowing for a sense of freedom and experiment, of being less restricted when writing from a distance – hopefully the fertile ground of which Salman Rushdie speaks. At times it might even enable a writer not just a unique approach to language, but also to subject matter, where what might have been too difficult to express, or forbidden, will find a voice in a second language. This article thus aims to show, without underestimating the challenges and issues raised by this choice, some of the potential gains when writing in a second language, a process where a new narrative, uniquely different to a first language narrative, is created.

In *After Babel*, George Steiner insists that 'inside or between languages, human communication equals translation' (49). This suggests that any form of communication entails a process of translation, in order to make this communication meaningful and understood. As Richard Kearney explains in his introduction to Paul Ricoeur's essays in *On Translation*:

> Translation [. . .] [i]n the specific sense [. . .] signals the work of translating the meanings of one particular language into another. In the more generic sense, it indicates the everyday act of speaking as a way not only of translating oneself to oneself (inner to outer, private to public, unconscious to conscious, etc) but also and more explicitly of translating oneself to others. (xiv–xv)

Writing in a second language would then be a process of both specific and generic translation, a translation process where the writer translates both language and self.

Self-translation is often used to define a bilingual text 'authored by a writer who can compose in different languages and who translates his or her texts from one language into another', as Jan Walsh Hokenson and Marcella Munson note in the introduction to *The Bilingual Text: History and Theory of Literary Translation* (1). In this article, however, I use the term to designate the translation process occurring when a bilingual writer chooses to write in a second or acquired language, translation thereby forming an integral part of the 'original' creative writing process. As Brian T. Fitch explains: 'The bilingual writer is not merely aware of the existence of a multiplicity of tongues but lives in the continual presence of this awareness during the very act of writing' (158). The consequences to language, identity and voice when a writer 'translates' him/herself by writing in a second language, in the presence of this sense of continuous duality, are my main concerns. I will look at bilingual writers writing in their 'stepmother tongue', as John Skinner so aptly calls it, as well as reflect upon my experiences as a Swedish writer composing in my second language, English.

Mary Besemeres' study of immigrant writers and the interconnection between language and selfhood in *Translating One's Self*, and especially one of the writers examined there, Eva Hoffman and her autobiography *Lost in Translation,* is a major focus of the first half of my chapter. The translation process is seen mainly as one of loss: loss of self, place and subsequently a betrayal of the first language. This is not a unique point of view. As Hokenson and Munson point out, referring to the genre of language memoirs, bilingualism 'is often introduced [by its editors] as a personal record of identity crisis, because they [. . .] subscribe to the tacit premise that bilinguality threatens identity and creativity' (208). This position is in contrast with that of Paul Ricoeur, who sees translation of self as a prerequisite for finding a true sense of self: 'The idealist romantic self, sovereign master of itself and all it surveys, is replaced by an engaged self which only finds itself after it has traversed the field of foreignness and returned to itself again, this time altered and enlarged, "othered"' (Kearney, xix).

First, I think it is important to note that many of the writers discussed by Besemeres were, in contrast to myself, 'forced to translate themselves' (278) and in that sense did not choose the challenges of a second language themselves. Immigrating as children and subsequently having to adjust to a new language in sometimes painful and disempowering circumstances, the language change was often a traumatic and abrupt experience.[1] On the other hand, I came to my second language mainly as an adult and by choice. My experience of a second language is therefore vitally different to many of the writers examined by Besemeres. I cannot compare my circumstances in this respect, but do acknowledge that the loss of self in translation Besemeres' points to might partly come from this initial experience of displacement.

Loss of self in translation

The greatest risk, Besemeres argues, for writers 'translating themselves' into a second language is the threat to their identity, an identity formed in the first language and thus reliant on this language for a true expression of self. By pointing to the interrelation between selfhood and language, Besemeres believes bilinguals live inside conflicting versions of selves and that a choice seems necessary between these two selves/languages.

The second language is seen by Besemeres as 'the upstart' with a desire to take over, 'to contest the first' (26), whereas one's native language is depicted as the true home of self, a home in need of protection. She quotes Alice Kaplan ('On Language Memoir' 63), 'that the "emotional consequences" of language change – "principally" "loss"– testify that language is a "home, as surely as a roof over one's head is a home" and that "to be without language or between languages, is as miserable [. . .] as to be without bread"'(208). This is a theme reiterated throughout Besemeres' study: translation as a dangerous threat to self. For an adolescent changing languages, it may even, she warns, 'threaten sanity; at least in the short term' (50), and at times, as the previous quote shows, translation equals starvation with the consequent death of the self. At least the death of one's 'true' self, according to Kaplan, who in her memoir finds that there is a sense of performance, a 'false' self expressing herself in a second language: 'There was a time when I even spoke in a different register in French – higher and excited, I was sliding up to those notes in some kind of hyped-up theatrical world of my own making' (*French Lessons* 216).

In *Translating One's Self* Besemeres draws heavily on Eva Hoffman's autobiography, *Lost in Translation,* giving prominence to Hoffman's expression of her deeply felt loss, even bereavement, in her new life and language. Besemeres thus emphasizes that 'having to "translate oneself" from one's mother tongue into a foreign language and losing part of oneself in the process shows how deeply self is bound up with natural language' (9).

Hoffman's moving account of immigrating to Canada from Poland as a 13-year-old child with her family is a depiction of a harrowing displacement, or exile, when she was 'pushed out of the happy, safe enclosures of Eden' (5). Where she was once connected not only with place and culture but also language, the new language which was forced upon her is an empty language, disconnected from her, a 'loss of living connection' (107). It would take Hoffman more than 20 years to connect and reconcile with this alien tongue. This sense of bereavement is echoed by Andrea Witcomb, whose sense of being: 'robbed of growing up in my first language' resulted in 'a feeling of being territorially lost' (94).

Hoffman's prolonged sense of loss might also be due to her belief that connecting with her second language would form an act of betrayal to her first language. Besemeres expresses the view that 'something is owed in translation to the self who was "wrought" [. . .] in a native language and cultural environment' (279). This debt to one's first language is conveyed very strongly by Hoffman in her autobiography, where the new language is not only a threat to Hoffman's first language but also to her almost sacred memories of Poland. And whereas the old, untranslated language holds a yearning full of significance and associations connected to her 'real' home and identity, for Hoffman the new language is empty of substance. This sense that the new language does not belong to you in the same way as your first language is also evoked by Irene Ulman, who writes that '[b]eing a migrant, a self-translator and a copycat has created a sense of suspension and self-conscious use of language [. . .] It's as if I am asking myself: "Is this expression mine to use?"'(52).

On the other hand, in *Foreign Dialogues* Hoffman explains to Mary Zournazi that the first language 'seems to be attached to identity with a kind of absoluteness [. . .] words seem to stand for the things they describe' (Zournazi 17). Thus, where the Polish word for river is for her 'a vital sound, energized with the essence of riverhood, of [. . .] being immersed in rivers, [r]iver in English is cold' (*Lost in Translation* 106), an empty sign devoid of associations and memories. Although Hoffman feels that she has to make a choice between the two languages, and in the end chooses English over Polish as a means of surviving in her new environment, she keeps her distance from the new language.

In conclusion, even though Besemeres acknowledges 'the value of a readiness to engage with a new language and, hence, with another way of "being in the world," the possible gains of choosing to write in a second language do not compare favourably to 'faithfulness to one's native language and culture' (279). There is, I believe, a lingering sense in both Besemeres' study as well as in Hoffman's autobiography that to translate one's 'original' self implies a devastating loss. The stakes and risks involved seem too high, and if there is a choice one would do better to stay at 'home' in one's language and not venture out, or risk losing one's true self forever.

Gaining a new, translated self

The past, however, might teach us, as described so poignantly by Ariel Dorfman in his moving account of coming to terms with two languages, *Heading South, Looking North: a Bilingual Journey*, that even though many have been forced to switch language as a way of survival throughout history, many also actively choose and subsequently find a new identity as a bilingual:

> [I]f you look more closely at those countless victims who were forced, in far more traumatic circumstances than mine, to learn the language of those who held power over them, you will remark how many of them decided to become bilingual.[. . .] They dared risk being double, the anxiety, the richness, the madness of being double. (42)

Thus, for each perceived loss, I believe there are equally a number of possible gains to be found for a bilingual writer, if one is willing to take the risk to write in one's second language. Like Salman Rushdie, I too 'cling, obstinately, to the notion that something can also be gained' (17) in the translation process.

Furthermore, in her previously mentioned memoir, Kaplan also writes about the 'privilege of living in translation' (140), which might even suggest that the loss in translation belongs to writers who never have had the 'privilege' of having to confront such different aspects of self. As Hokenson and Munson point out, in many language memoirs there is now also 'a parallel and perhaps growing sense of more positive aspects of enrichment and adventure in the experience of bilinguality, with writers stressing gain rather than loss' (209).[2]

In the foreword to *Translation and Creativity,* Theo Hermans highlights the editors' linking of the restrictive quality of writing in a second language with creativity: 'the emphasis must be on constraints *and* creativity, creativity *within* and *thanks* to constraints' (10). Paradoxically, the limiting factors might allow for a sense of being unrestricted and inventive when writing in a second language. As Besemeres rightly points out, there is often a refreshing sense of newness in the language by bilingual writers: 'A new sense of humour, particularly of irony, is often seen and also manifested in the writing as a gain in translation' (278). Even Hoffman's writing benefits, Besemeres concedes, 'show[ing] a certain detachment – both a playfulness and a cool speculative irony' (53).

This detachment found in a second language lends itself to a freedom to experiment. 'People like us find it difficult to write 'straight'; our attitude to language [. . .] must remain to a large extent provisional and jesting', Andrew Riemer (180) writes of bilingual writers in *Inside, Outside*. Having a distance to one's own writing creates flexibility and daring, as in Riemer's example of Georges Perec, who was born in Paris of first-generation immigrant Polish Jewish Parents. Growing up speaking Polish and French contributed, Riemer believes, to Perec's 'outrageous liberties' with French, where Riemer finds the detachment both a violation and celebration of this language (179–80).

And although Riemer believes a learnt language never becomes 'fully personal' (178) the way one's first language does, he also shows how bilingual writers' different experience of the acquired language are often exhilarating: 'We are attracted to the structures of that learnt language [. . .] infatuated with its suppleness, its capacity to be twisted into surprising and unexpected configurations' (181). Sometimes it is a musical sense of the new language, an experience of rhythm and beat, perhaps sometimes lost in one's first language. In describing Ania Walwicz's writing, 'fraught with suggestion and insinuation, texts which are closer to music than to "normal writing"', Riemer (179) alludes to this musicality sometimes heard and expressed in one's second language more clearly than in one's first.

This sense of playfulness and detachment gained from writing in a second language could also describe Chinese writer Xiaolu Guo's novel *A Concise Chinese-English Dictionary For Lovers*. Every chapter starts with an English word from the dictionary, which the Chinese narrator comments on as she learns its practical meaning. The language in the novel is written in deliberately 'wrong' grammar and syntax, which improves along with the narrator's proficiency in English as the narrative progresses.

Gou shows in her novel, that learning a new language does not necessarily mean a threat to one's old self; instead it can coexist with new aspects of self, developed and found in this new language. The new language does therefore not need to take away one's sense of identity, but is able to add to this identity. Gou's protagonist learning a new language/culture, mainly through a developing love story with a man from this new culture, even allows the narrator to deepen her understanding of her 'old' self and language.

In contrast to Hoffman, the protagonist finds this sense of a split self through two languages comforting. Her 'old' identity from China is guiding her in a new and challenging environment, just like her 'new' developing self emerging in the new language/culture enables her to make different decisions when she returns to China. She is even able to see this 'split personality' comically: 'Maybe I not feeling lonely, because I always can talk to other "me." Is like seeing my two pieces of lips speaking in two languages at same time. Yes, I not lonely, because I with another me. Like Austin Power with his Mini Me' (38–9). The new language therefore does not need to replace the old, it can instead contribute to the old, creatively, allowing the self to express a new identity with new dimensions.

Even though cultural differences between languages make self-translation at times both complicated and perplexing, there is also the previously mentioned double perspective to be gained from having access to two languages. Both these issues come across strongly in *Translating Lives: Living with Two Languages and Cultures,* in which all contributors have other language backgrounds before immigrating to Australia. In 'East Meets West, or Does it Really?' Jock Wong explains that '[c]ommon Anglo rules of politeness, which express respect for personal autonomy, simply did not exist' in Cantonese, and an expression like 'Thank You' was unusual and 'Sorry' 'unheard of' (74). In another chapter, Eva Sallis writes about how differently she expresses herself in her second language, Arabic. Although 'Arabic is part of [her]', it is a different part of her expressing herself, the differences being 'deeper and more organic than role-playing'. She adds: '[e]ven when my fiction has nothing overtly Arab, it is about ideas that are born from the perceptions bilinguality has given me' (152).

In *Translating Lives: Living with Two Languages and Cultures* Besemeres and Anna Wierzbicka develop an argument which contrasts with Besemeres' former position. Loss, instead of being felt by bilinguals living in 'exile', now belongs to monolingual persons (and cultures), who are subsequently 'lacking a comparative perspective'. Rather, 'There is a world of human experience closed to speakers of only one language' (xv), which leads them to call for 'intercultural and cross-linguistic language training' (xv–xvi) to make up for this loss in Australia, for instance. The unique double perspective by writers writing in a second language is thus an important asset in their view, just as being monolingual is a significant loss, not only for individuals, but for a society as a whole.

Apart from offering a double perspective on life, a second language might even allow a writer to speak about what is too difficult or impossible to express in one's old language. Anne Malena, in her comparison to Edwige Danticat and Hoffman's relationship to language and self, explores this viewpoint in her article 'Found in Translation or Edwige Danticat's Voyage of Recovery'. Malena argues that writing fiction in her second language of English gave Danticat the space to work through not just her own personal experiences in Haiti, but also the wider traumas experienced by Haitian society as a whole. In this way, Danticat is able to 'reassemble the cultural fragments she brought into exile [. . .] through the creation of characters who, travelling along the path of recovery and self-integration, end up finding themselves in translation' (216–17).

Not only writers, then, but also fictional characters start to behave more independently in a second language. Maybe they would not be able to speak otherwise of the secret, of the forbidden, of that which cannot be said? Might not one find fragments of memoires which would have remained hidden from view in the safety of one's first language? '[T]ranslation might then', as Malena notes, 'find the obscured past

[. . .] to bring it closer and make it more familiar although it remains far away and largely unknown' (211).

Danticat also incorporates her old language as a post-colonial tool of resisting her adopted language, and in contrast to Hoffman, as Malena points out, she 'feels no need to let go of her native French and Creole but uses them [. . .] to mark her language of adoption with their Caribbean accents' (199). The new language can then become a way of exploring and recovering the past, without forgetting or betraying it. Instead, it is a past given a new voice, while marked by the old language.

The distance – sometimes geographical – that a second language and subsequent translation creates, can also give life to new narratives. Writing from this distance, a writer might find that not only do perspectives and characters shift but also the ability to create narratives which might not otherwise have found an expression. Swedish writer Linda Olsson, in her novel *Let Me Sing You Gentle Songs*, which is mostly set in Sweden with Swedish characters, writes in the Author's Note that: 'the process of writing this book has taken me to the other side of the world [. . .] [b]ut this book could not have been written anywhere but here, in New Zealand. The distance was essential' (257). In my view, the benefits of this distance are expressed very clearly in Olsson's novel, where the depiction of Sweden and particularly a longing towards its landscape, would have been very difficult to encapsulate without this distance – both geographical and linguistic. Similarly, in his essay 'Imaginary Homelands', Rushdie also shows when discussing the Indian diaspora that for a writer this distance is a fertile ground to explore: 'If literature is in part the business of finding new angles at which to enter realty, then once again our distance, our long geographical perspective, may provide us with such angles. Or it may be that it is simply that we must think in order to do our work' (15–16).

Writing, as I am, a novel set within a Swedish cultural context with Swedish-speaking characters expressing themselves in English, it is this distance to language (and place) that I too find so appealing. It is as if the distance creates a new space, where the translation process enables a new kind of writing. I do not find words in English empty signs even if I do not fully comprehend them. Instead they have attached feelings that might be unexpected and beyond my first language experience. Listen! There is music to be found; unexpected rhythms, sounds, strange encounters and experiments, a new language is waiting to be heard, a struggle is taking place to find something I do not yet have the name for. In Swedish, I do not need to invite words, to look for them, to challenge or play with them. They are there, already arrived. Translation, then, as Joyce Marshall argues, enables me to 'take leave of a too-familiar language' (15).

In his collection of essays, *Translation as Discovery*, Sujit Mukherjee finds the translation process to carry the potential for a new writing. He refers to a quote by George Steiner, who believes that from the act of translation something new emerges, a new, 'third language': 'At its best, the peculiar synthesis of conflict and complicity between a poem and its translation into another poem creates the impression of a "third language", of a medium of communicative energy which somehow reconciles both languages in a tongue deeper, more comprehensive than either' (83).

I think it is this 'third language' I am looking for, a voice speaking from an in-between space, where one is allowed to go deeper, to find something new, something that is more, created from a distance, although with what feels like a much lighter language. This sense of lightness enabled me to write my first novel, *The Stone Baby,* and revisit a personal trauma and find a creative and imaginative expression for it, the distance of English offering me a sense of protection:

> I revisit that staircase in Darlinghurst and the shabby looking terrace in Chippendale with the distinct smell of the brewery drifting through the windows. I do not linger too long over the words of gurus or the fragrance of perfume consultants. Perhaps I remember an unusual bus trip and a delegation of debt collectors instead. There is music and fire, a Chinese messenger to consider.
>
> And friends, I do remember friends.
>
> Most of all a scar so deep it keeps coming undone. (6)

Thus, like Kaplan, I am grateful for my new language 'teaching me that there is more than one way to speak [. . .] for being the home I've made from my own will and imagination' (*French Lessons* 216). In this article, I have tried to point to some possible gains of writing in a second language, and how this does not have to mean loss of identity or betraying the 'original' self, but a further exploration of different aspects of self, where the distance created from a learnt language lends itself to experimentation and a certain sense of freedom, sometimes allowing one to speak about the past in a way otherwise not possible, although this past might have been lived in a different language. A past, which, Rushdie points out, 'is a country from which we all have emigrated' (12).

Notes

1 Andrew Riemer, for example, depicts in his autobiography *Inside, Outside,* how he was put into what was commonly referred to as the 'Idiots' class upon arriving in Australia after Second World War. It was believed that he must have low intellectual abilities due to his lack of English. He subsequently spent his first year in school knitting (93–5).

2 This new stress on gain, rather than loss, in translation, can be found in *Post colonial Translation: Theory and Practice,* where new ways of viewing the translation process are explored by some of its contributors, the editors

first pointing out, that '[s]tudents of translation almost all start out with the assumption that something will be lost in translation, that the text will be diminished and rendered inferior. They rarely consider there might also be a process of gain' (Bassnett and Trivedi 4). One of the contributors, Sherry Simon, argues in her chapter 'Translating and interlingual creation in the contact zone: Border writing in Quebec' that one of the narrators in writer Nicole Brossard's *Mouve Desert*, the translator, and in extension Brossard, 'refuses to participate in an economy of loss, in the pathos of dislocation, the loss of spontaneous contact with one's inner self . . . which is so often associated with translation' (67).

Works cited

Bassnett, Susan and Harish Trivedi, eds. *Post-colonial Translation: Theory and Practice.* London: Routledge, 1999. Print.

Besemeres, Mary. *Translating One's Self: Language and Selfhood in Cross-Cultural Autobiography.* Oxford: Peter Lang, 2002. Print.

Besemeres, Mary and Anna Wierzbicka, eds. *Translating Lives: Living with Two Languages and Cultures.* St. Lucia, Queensland: U of Queensland P, 2007. Print.

Danticat, Edwige. *The Farming of Bones.* New York: Grove, 2006. Print.

Dorfman, Ariel. *Heading South, Looking North: A Bilingual Journey.* New York: Farrar, Straus and Giroux, 1998. Print.

Evangelista, Elin-Maria. 'The Stone Baby'. MS, 2009. 'Oscar's Place'. BA (Hons) Diss. La Trobe U, 2006.

Fitch, Brian T. *Becket and Babel: An Investigation into the Status of the Bilingual work.* Toronto, Buffalo and London: U of Toronto P, 1988. Print.

Guo, Xiaolu. *A Concise Chinese-English Dictionary for Lovers.* London: Chatto & Windus, 2007. Print.

Hermans, Theo. Foreword. *Translation and Creativity: Perspectives on Creative Writing and Translation Studies.* Eds Manuela Perteghella and Eugenia Loffredo. London: Continuum, 2006. ix–x. Print.

Hoffman, Eva. *Lost in Translation: A Life in a New Language.* 1989. London: Vintage, 1998. Print.

Hokenson, Jan Walsh and Marcella Munson. *The Bilingual Text: History and Theory of Literary Self-Translation.* Manchester: St Jerome, 2007. Print.

Kaplan, Alice. *French Lessons: A Memoir.* Chicago: U of Chicago P, 1993. Print.

—. 'On Language Memoir'. *Displacements: Cultural Identities in Question.* Ed. Angelica Bammer. Bloomington: Indiana UP, 1994. 59–70. Print.

Kearney, Richard. 'Introduction'. Ricoeur. vii–xx.

Malena, Anne. 'Found in Translation or Edwige Danticat's Voyage of Discovery'. *TTR : traduction, terminologie, rédaction* 16.2 (2003). U of Alberta.Web. www.erudit.org/revue/ttr/2003/v16/n2/010721ar.html

Marshall, Joyce. 'The Writer as Translator / The Translator as Writer'. *Mapping Literature: The Arts and Politics of Translation.* Eds David Homel and Sherry Simon. Montréal: Véhicule, 1988. 15–28. Print.

Mukherjee, Sujit. *Translation as Discovery: And Other Essays on Indian Literature in English Translation*. 1981. 2nd edn. London: Sangham Books Ltd, 1994. Print.

Olsson, Linda. *Let Me Sing You Gentle Songs*. Auckland: Penguin Books, 2005. Print.

—. *Nu vill jag sjunga milda sånger*. Trans. Lisbet Holst. Stockholm: Albert Bonniers Bokförlag. 2006. Print. Trans. of *Let Me Sing You Gentle Songs*, Auckland: Penguin Books, 2005.

Perteghella, Manuela and Eugenia Loffredo, eds. *Translation and Creativity: Perspectives on Creative Writing and Translation Studies*. London: Continuum, 2006. Print.

Ricoeur, Paul. *On Translation*. Eds Simon Critchley and Richard Kearney. Trans. Eileen Brennan. London: Routledge, 2006. Print. Trans. of *Sur la traduction*. Paris: Bayard, 2004.

Riemer, Andrew. *Inside, Outside: Life between Two Worlds*. Sydney: Collins, Angus & Robertson, 1992. Print.

Rushdie, Salman. *Imaginary Homelands: Essays and Criticism 1981–1991*. London: Granta, 1991. Print.

Sallis, Eva. 'Foster mother tongue'. Mary Besemeres and Anna Wierzbicka. 150–9. Print.

Simon, Sherry. 'Translating and Interlingual Creation in the Contact Zone: Border Writing in Quebec'. Bassnett and Trivedi. 58–74. Print.

Skinner, John. *The Stepmother Tongue: An Introduction to New Anglophone Fiction*. London: MacMillan, 1998. Print.

Steiner, George. *After Babel: Aspects of Language and Translation*. 3rd edn. Oxford: Oxford UP, 1998. Print.

Ulman, Irene. 'Playgrounds and Battlegrounds: A Child's Experience of Migration'. Besemeres and Wierzbicka. 45–55. Print.

Walwicz, Ania. *Writing*. Melbourne: Rigmarole, 1982. Print.

—. *Red Roses*. St Lucia: U of Queensland P, 1992. Print.

Witcomb, Andrea. 'Growing Up Between Two Languages/Two Worlds: Learning to Live Without Belonging to a *Terra*'. Besemeres and Wierzbicka. 83–95. Print.

Wong, Jock. 'East meets West, or Does it Really?' Besemeres and Wierzbicka. 70–82. Print.

Zournazi, Mary. *Foreign Dialogues: Memories Translations and Conversations*. Sydney: Pluto, 1998. Print.

CHAPTER TWELVE

Self-translation as broken narrativity: Towards an understanding of the self's multilingual dialogue

Aurelia Klimkiewicz

Abstract: *This article examines self-translation as a multidirectional and multilingual dialogue with the self, creating a dense space of hidden passages, transfers and disconnections. Focusing on the uprooted and linguistically unsettled self, the author argues that self-translation is located in a traumatic experience of losing or breaking ties with the mother tongue. Two different categories are discussed: namely self-translation as a more or less simultaneous process, in the case of the expatriate Nancy Huston; and self-translation as an asynchronous transfer, as seen in the exiled writers, Nabokov and Kundera. These particular (re)writing strategies are embedded in the difficulty of locating and articulating the self; they manifest both its present and absent parts, making them visible and audible. At the same time, self-translation forges an effective channel for a multilingual dialogue with the self, one which will also assimilate unsuccessful or broken communication, as well as the incompatibility or untranslatability of experiences.*

Self-translation deconstructs the full range of Translation Studies' core concepts (author and translator, original and target text, equivalence, the target reader). Where they were once grounded in the movement between singular languages and cultural spaces, these concepts become increasingly dynamic, challenging a binary conceptualization of translation, inviting hybrid categories, such as, auctorial translation and the *texte croisé*, or hybrid text (Oustinoff 92, 248). Indeed, since self-translation typically confronts and plays with both conventional literary practices and translational norms it makes visible the translator and the translation process itself. This paper will thus focus on the hermeneutical constitution of the multilingual self during this process. The 'self' is understood here as a complex web of tensions produced by its multilingual dialogue with itself, and 'translation' as not only the relationship between the original and its self-translation, but the network of different readers of both versions of the text. Consequently, I will consider self-translation from a dynamic point of view, as not only a means of representing one's identity and particular way of thinking – seeing the self from the inside and outside, situated between others in different languages and spaces – but also as a particular writing activity in search of an effective channel of intercultural dialogue, one which can open a space for the enunciation of a diversity of voices, positions and sensibilities.

Literary self-translation

Literary self-translation implies the presence of at least two languages involved in the process of (re)writing, generating a dynamics of 'displacement', which can be studied from at least four perspectives: *text-oriented*, *author-oriented*, *reader-oriented* and *process-oriented*. From the text-oriented point of view, self-translation can be analyzed as the production of bilingual, parallel texts. Such texts may be created through synchronous self-translation (the simultaneous process of writing and self-translating, blurring the boundaries between original and self-translated text) or asynchronous self-translation (consecutive self-translation of the existing original). On the other hand, the author-oriented approach takes into account the author's identity and their experience of language according to such contexts as colonization, exile, diaspora, extensive travelling or, simply, relocation. A few linguistic scenarios are at stake here: interchangeability, in the case of perfect bilingualism; an opposition between the mother tongue and a foreign language, as experienced by many exiled writers; transnational linguistic mobility, for members of a diaspora; and, the successive acquisition of different languages throughout one's life. Powerful emotions, factors and decisions inform each author's personal language scenario – love or admiration, hatred or refusal, loss, oblivion or confrontation . . . Each can inform hierarchies in the author's relationship with their languages. As for the reader-oriented perspective, whose focus is on the addressee of the self-translated text, a parallel text explicitly invites bilingual participation because in this case the reader is left 'hovering, squinting verbally to try to make multiple signifiers coincide on the same referent' (Mooney 288). Here, normal reading practices are disrupted, since the reader's linguistic competence offers the possibility of moving or 'zigzagging' between linguistic spaces. Thus, the reception of the bilingual text is no longer situated in one specific literary tradition, language or institution, but rather a different concrete context, one which brings together the reader's own hierarchies and perceptions of their languages (minor and/ or/vs major) as a form of bias that affects the reception of the text. In what follows, I will discuss the mechanisms of self-translation from the process-oriented point of view. Central to this discussion are the problems of the multilingual self and its self-dialogue, as well as the constitution of the subjective space dominated by linguistic and spatial fragmentation.

The multilingual self

The problem of fragmentation, discontinuity and tension is particularly important in understanding the experience of someone who is fighting with the sense of losing the ground for their self.

> Were we to open ourselves utterly to the flux, the multiplicity, our own infinite capacity for reception, we should go mad. In order to preserve our sanity, we make ourselves short-sighted and amnesic. We strive to keep our experience within certain fixed limits.
>
> Every expatriate has the conviction–deeply rooted in her subconscious and regularly rejected as preposterous by her intellect–that a part of herself, or, rather, *another self*, has never stopped living *back there*. (Huston, *Losing North* 89, 91)

What is the motivation for writing or rewriting the same text via self-translation? Instead of composing directly in two or more languages, why do some multilingual authors make the decision to go back, sometimes obsessively, to the previous work, or write both the original and the translation simultaneously? Animated by a sort of inescapable desire to reshape a text that has already been written or is in the process of being created, why do they treat it as unfinished, imperfect, inadequate or complementary? Beyond the fact that the multilingual author is at ease with two or more languages, is there another, deeper or more 'serious' issue associated with the choice of self-translating, once it becomes a permanent strategy of writing?

   As a writing strategy, self-translation demonstrates the difficulty of locating and articulating the self, since two languages collide one with another and refuse to submit to each other, and consequently lead to a divided consciousness (Todorov 20). In this situation, self-translation becomes a two-directional circulation: first, from inner to external speech (from the self to the other); and then, from one language into another inside the divided consciousness (from the self to the self). According to Russian psychologist Lev Vygotskij, 'Compared with external speech, inner speech appears disconnected and incomplete' (qtd. in Matejka 172). Its articulation therefore remains problematic because:

> [. . .] the transition from inner to external speech is not a simple translation from one language into another. It cannot be achieved merely vocalising silent speech. It is a complex, dynamic process involving the transformation of the predicative idiomatic structure of inner speech into syntactically articulated speech intelligible to others. (cited in Matejka 172)

Thus, self-translation as a process of bilingual 'co-enunciation' makes the vocalization of silent speech even more complex, since the result is the 'twin work' produced in two different languages (Harel 153). This mental activity is located in a specific space where ties with the mother tongue are loosened or broken. Such a condition is very often provoked by exile, geographical and linguistic displacement; this was the case with Vladimir Nabokov and Milan Kundera, both of whom escaped the historical chaos in their respective countries. On the other hand, for Nancy Huston, the reason for her bilingual writing – even if she did move from her native Calgary to Paris – resides in the fact that she was abandoned by her mother in early childhood. Dispossessed of her 'maternal' tongue, she was unable to write directly into English.

> I suddenly see with crystal clarity that my vocation as a novelist dates back to my childhood – when, to reassure myself and perhaps even to survive, I had to learn to convincingly conjure up the love of the person who is usually the very symbol of proximity and presence – but who, in my case, was far away and permanently inaccessible. (*Losing North* 87)

Unlike monolingual writers who, as noted by Russian formalists, have to forge their literary language out of the distance away from the natural everyday idiom to discover the otherness of their mother tongue and its semiotic vitality, bilingual writers can create their own artistic originality by changing the medium of expression that provides them with a new or enlarged productive signifier. From translation to self-translation or recreation, the writer explores the zones of contact and transfer taking place in a multidirectional and multilingual dialogue, creating at the same time a dense space, a network of routes and passages that Emily Apter calls 'the translation zone', understood as 'zones of linguistic indeterminacy and interaction' (2).

On exile and (self)translation

From a purely aesthetic point of view, one might well consider self-translation to be a postmodern literary practice because of its potential to subvert origins and authority, offer texts which might be considered to be unfinished and whose meaning remains open-ended, the result of a cooperation between author and reader (here translator). However, from an existential rather than an artistic perspective, might not one consider the self-translator as an author who decides to occupy both spaces in order to maintain control over meaning in both languages? Is this always the case? Should we treat on the same level all writers who have written in a foreign language or played with more than one idiom (Kafka, Schulz, Conrad, Joyce, Ionesco, Beckett, Borges, Nabokov or Kundera)? The problem of geographical and linguistic exile is fundamental in understanding how language loss, the work of memory and trauma as the violent deformation of a constituted knowledge (Harel 154; Bohórques 89–90) play a fundamental role in the endless process of narration, whose main goal is the reconfiguring and repositioning of the self in a new language and in a different time and space.[1] The motif of the non-linear and anachronistic character of memory and the experience of exile is central to the literature of exile. The narrator of the Nabokov's novel *The Gift* expresses it in terms of 'the material metamorphoses which are taking place in us' (428), while Józef Wittlin, an exiled Polish writer, states that:

> In Spanish, there exists for describing an exile the word *desterro*, a man deprived of his land. I take the liberty to forge another term, *destiempo*, a man deprived of his time. The time of the exile is different. Or rather the exile lives in two different times simultaneously, in the present and in the past. This life in the past is sometimes more intense than his life in the present and tyrannises his entire psychology. (88)

However, being an exile does not always mean being stuck in the past; it can also mean a full investment in the present, the here and now. In this sense, self-translation appears to be a powerful means of inscribing the self in a new language and environment. The fragmentation of the spatial, temporal and linguistic unity fuels the imagination that not only makes possible the recuperation of the pieces of memory from the past in order to preserve a form of unity and coherence between then and now but also provides new strategies with which to inscribe the self in a new setting. What self-translation implies is not a celebration of difference and plurality, not a victorious claim of being or becoming *métisse* or a nomad; on the contrary, it tells the story of becoming the other as a painful, ongoing and fully resistant process. All forms of translation, self-translation included, tell us that this will never be an *affaire classée*, that there is no end to the process of narration once and for all. In fact, it is translation that helps the otherness of the self to come to the surface, because it makes the two parts of the self physically present, visible and audible. Moreover, I believe that translation and self-translation are powerful tools to resist assimilation, that which implies zero creativity, violence against the psyche and the severing of the twin, the other self which was grounded elsewhere. Becoming *as the other* means pretending to erase the past, the distance and differences inscribed in the exile's identity.

Self-translation – because it implies the existence of another version of the text – works finally as an anchor. The constitution of the self out of its broken unity in terms of language, identity, imagination and memory is the work of (self-)translation, because once the person becomes uprooted, once the 'centre' of the self is lost, the act of translation works as an anchor able to ground the self in the middle of instability. This does not imply a reconstituted totality or a reconquered centre, but rather the possibility of making sense of experience according to the precise living moment. Momentary grounding is perhaps achieved thanks to the foreign language which, compared to the mother tongue, will always remain more functional and less emotional, a tool of communication and exchange with others. Hence, self-translation also implies a transition from emotion to ratio that could help to tell the story behind exile, since the mother tongue recalls the bond, the intimate fusion and the comfort of being at home with others who are similar to us.

Self-translation: A matter of distance

The process of self-translation in Huston's case has evolved into something more or less simultaneous with creation, while conversely, for Nabokov and Kundera temporal distance plays an important role. Huston admits to having a double identity. Born in Calgary, she lives in Paris and is married to an exile with whom she communicates in French, a foreign language for both of them. She has written and talked extensively about her condition of expatriation, her bilingual and bicultural situation, although only a little about translation or self-translation. However, from the beginning of her career as a writer she practised self-translation as one of writing strategies, incorporating it variously into her writing, from self-translating her entire text in both directions to self-translating only some parts of the text.

Her English novel, *Plainsong*, and its French twin, *Cantiques des Plaines*, were published in 1993 in both languages. The story is situated in Alberta and recounts a granddaughter's desire to pursue her grandfather's philosophical work through the textual reconstitution of his unfinished and unreadable manuscript. The French text is regarded as a self-translation, but the process of producing both novels reveals that they were written simultaneously from the first draft of the original English version, which was used as a starting point. In other words, both texts were simultaneously written and self-translated, blurring the boundaries between original and translation, between writing and translating processes. According to the author, they are both originals. Her next novel, published in 1999 in French, *L'empreinte de l'ange*, was self-translated into English under the title, *The Mark of the Angel*. In that case, Huston declared that the translated version was not a simple self-translation but the pretext to rework the entire story. *L'Emprunte de l'ange* is actually a novel about a complicated language scenario. It tells the love story between Saffie, a German woman married to a monolingual Frenchman, and Andràs, who is a Hungarian Jew living in exile in France. Even though they both know German, they refuse to use it as a code of communication, preferring French, their adoptive language. The story is about translation, without which the protagonists cannot communicate and understand each other, especially in the contact between monolinguals and multilinguals. In her next novel, *Instruments de ténèbres*, Huston assimilates self-translation into the writing process as a textual strategy. She simultaneously tells two different but parallel stories. The first one is the journal of Nadia, a writer from New York, and the second is the novel Nadia is writing about a young servant from eighteenth-century France. The journal is written by Huston in English and then self-translated into French for the final version, but for the English publication of the novel, the author, instead of using the 'first' original which already exists in English, decides to translate this part of her novel from the derived French version.

Such narratives, centering on situations of linguistic confrontations, are emblematic of the fact that the bilingual work of Nancy Huston is an exploration of the linguistic and cultural distance that uncovers the coexistence of differences, the points of connections and disconnections, as well as moments of transformation and untranslatability. Her interlinguistic and intratextual strategies evoke her sense of the distances which separate individual selves, the instability of identity and the impossibility of being constantly equal to any sort of fixed idea of the self. Her bilingual texts are thus challenging for translators because they impose a very complex multilingual web of narration that has to be carefully analysed and understood before being transferred into the target language.

As an expatriate, Huston tries in her writing to explore how to live, think and communicate with different languages and how to maintain a provisional unity of identity, her uprooted self being always in transit (*Lettres parisiennes* 211). Her interrogation and literary creativity are articulated spatially; it is space that provides the adequate format used to discuss displacement. Instead of nostalgia, she rather talks about her condition, in *Lettres parisiennes*, in terms of friction (13), mutation (36), floating (77), intersection (154) and gap (169). For exiled writers, on the contrary, this problem is situated, I would posit, more in time than in space.

The reason is simple: while the expatriate keeps her passport, can freely travel from place to place and go safely back home any time she wants, the exile is condemned to live in the memory alone and can only go back home with an effort of imagination. The idea of having another life elsewhere is felt as a different chapter of life, a completely distinct period of time that will be forever impossible to recover.

In her writing, Huston's representation of space is expressed as a spatial decompression:

> The various strata of our lives coexist within our minds – and we somehow manage, at least until Alzheimer's sets in, not to mix them up. For me, the word *train* carries with it echoes of freight trains from my Alberta childhood, passenger trains in Germany, trains read about in novels or seen in films, the death camp trains exuding retrospective dread, and a train which I once heard in the gorges of the Allier River in Central France, its whistle filling me with a mysterious, piercing nostalgia as it faded into the blackness of the night. (*Losing North* 87)

On the other hand, Nabokov's imagination provokes a compression of space, a wild and poetic contraction which manifests in his novel *The Gift* when Fyodor is looking outside through the window of his apartment in Berlin: 'The night sky melts to peach beyond that gate. There water gleams, there Venice vaguely shows. Look at that street – it runs to China straight, and yonder star above the Volga glows!' (189).

The notions of loss, trauma or nostalgia imply that something is absent, broken or destroyed. Even if exile can be perceived as a positive experience in terms of a liberation and/or reinvention of the self, in the case of Nabokov and Kundera, exile is a traumatic experience where one's mental stability is lost in transit as the mother tongue becomes uprooted and is unable to provide meaning for the new reality. It is only with time that the mother tongue becomes, after many years of living abroad, more neutral and disconnected from its cultural and geographical contexts. In the absence of unity, fusion and proximity, self-translation works as a way of 'repairing' the broken tie and preventing the self from becoming dispersed, by finding the appropriate channel to produce an intelligible narration out of chaos. On the other hand, in order to articulate what is resisting representation, the use of a foreign idiom seems helpful as a form of mediation between the previous and the present self. According to Janine Altounian, writing in the language of the other is in fact a part of the healing process (125).

However, the healing process is not that simple for many exiles from Central and Eastern Europe. The impact of history, the lack of stability and the acceleration of events all through the second part of the twentieth century produces a highly complex relationship with the past. While the expatriate decides to leave her country and shape her own destiny abroad, the exile lives in constant confrontation of and torment about the events taking place in her native land. For Nabokov, the situation was clear: there was no possibility and no question of going back home; the only solution was to dwell obstinately and obsessively in his memory in order to save every detail from oblivion. Moreover, he remained faithful to himself till the end, using his freedom and imagination as an artist to create and recreate his own intimate universe 'by composing works in which interpretive meaning became available only between various intersecting genres, thus creating a perpetual delay in final and definitive signification', the process that 'mimics, both textually and linguistically, an expulsion, banishment or a movement of meaning out of the text, suggesting that language does not offer final signification (Tadevosyan-Ordukhanyan 176).

Alternatively, since the fall of the communist regime, Kundera can enjoy the freedom of going back home and being published and read directly in Czech. This impacts the status of the previous texts and the processes of rewriting and retranslating his existing texts. The following two quotes from Michelle Woods demonstrate the patterns which have developed in Kundera's self-translation technique.

[I]n the mid 1980s, Kundera revised all the French translations of the novels written in Czech and declared these, rather than the Czech versions, to be the definitive and authentic versions of the novels. The translations in other words became the originals. Later, to produce new Czech versions, he would use three 'originals': the Czech manuscript, the first published Czech versions (in Toronto, Canada) and the French definitive translations. (*Translating* ix)

After 1989, it seemed that translation would no longer be a necessity for achieving a wide readership; Kundera began to write novels in the language of his adopted homeland, French, and also regained his Czech audience. By the end of the 1990s, however, only three of his six novels written in the Czech language had appeared in print in the Czech Republic. Aggrieved readers prompted Kundera to explain the delay: he commented that no original Czech manuscript existed, and that, before they could be published, these novels had to be rendered 'definite'. ('Original' 200)

Nonetheless, the recent revelation about Kundera's past is somehow troubling. 'It is almost 19 years since the fall of communism, and most Czechs have sought to bury unpleasant memories of the period. [. . .] This case, however, shows that the country's totalitarian past is never very far from the surface' (Cameroun). According to Pavel Žáček, director of the Institute for the Study of Totalitarian Regime, Kundera 'had informed on a twenty-two-year-old student who spied for the West', indeed: 'The fact is [. . .] the student suffered more than the embarrassment Kundera endured for his youthful folly' (qtd. in Porter 131). However, my goal is not to plead his innocence or guilt, but to recall the difficulty in relating to the past once the situation back home has undergone a radical historical and political transformation. From a banned and exiled writer, who enjoyed the general sympathy of his fellow citizens for almost two decades from 1975 till the fall of communism, he became very quickly a 'vulgar' informant, a collaborator who was publicly denounced in his native country. Since this claim cannot be extensively developed in this paper, I only suggest that such a devaluation of one's social status and image might have a strong impact on the reevaluation of the 'self' and consequently on Kundera's eagerness to go back to his previous work, to rewriting, retranslating and generally reevaluating it according to each new situation and his actual reading audience. Interestingly, in 1985, after having published *The Unbearable Lightness of Being*, he declared in an interview that he wanted to become invisible and live anonymously (Wiznitzer 13).[2] However, as a writer sensitive to translations, he had become, according to Woods in *Translating Milan Kundera*, a 'ghost-translator' in the sense that he decided to intervene and control his translations in order to render them authentic and definitive (201).

The extensive practice of translation and self-translation by Nabokov, Kundera and Huston produces a very rich discourse on translation or, what Woods calls with more precision, the 'discourse of fidelity' that 'advocates the necessary fidelity of the translator to the author's style; the "absolute semantic exactitude" of the translation's relationship to the original' (Woods, 'Original' 201). Similarly, Nabokov's extensively commented translation of Pushkin reveals his own unique method of translation as well as the way he viewed his own literary work (Berberova 348). Multilingual writers often master many different genres (prose, poetry, drama, criticism . . .) and deploy various textual strategies (for instance, using abundant metalinguistic commentaries) (Klimkiewicz, 'Faire l'épreuve de soi'). Moreover, the practice of self-translation produces a rich multilingual discourse which tends not to be discussed in terms of success, clarity or accessibility, but rather in negative terms as a battle between 'competing linguistic identities' (Tadevosyan-Ordukhanyan 239) and untranslatability, since 'languages both deplore and cry out for in the way of their own incompletion' (Bontila 144–5).

Why study self-translation?

This chapter is an attempt to grasp the meaning of self-translation as a form of self-dialogue which takes place in more than one idiom. Self-translation, as a multilingual exchange with the self, can illuminate the shaping of a multilingual subjectivity and fragmented identity against a more fixed and rooted monolingual self. Examining self-translation as an existential and not an aesthetical phenomenon in the case of Nabokov and Kundera, both exiles, and Huston, the expatriate, I have tried to explain how it takes into account the intimate and unheard process of meaning-making across different languages, beyond the linguistically fragmented or even broken self. Since I consider self-translation as a strategy to overcome loss, trauma or nostalgia, I would argue that it also works as a call for trans-cultural explorations to find and forge new genres, new spaces of enunciation that allow one to articulate the experience of displacement.

In the meantime, exploring self-translation and the discourse of fidelity constructed out of author's notes, prefaces and other interventions (Woods, 'Original' 201) can help literary translators who are engaging with hybrid genres, innovative writing strategies and plurilingual texts precisely because in translating, they must also play, transgress and confront established traditions and genres.

Furthermore, self-translation increases the visibility of the translation process and challenges a binary logic of translation by introducing new hybrid and heterogeneous categories into Translation Studies and literary practice, playing with notions of author and translator, source text and target text, monolingual and multilingual reader. Its hybrid nature resists classification within literary systems, as well as in the professional field, where the subordination of the translator to the author, and the target text to the original, is not to be questioned. Self-translation might thus be studied together with other hybrid forms of writing and literary mystification, such as pseudo-translation, plagiarism, parody, adaptation, etc., because these forms also imply the existence of another text from which they are derived (see Jeandillou).

Finally, self-translation promotes new hermeneutics, because it challenges the reading and interpretation strategies that most readers acquire through the process of education and reading throughout life. Mastering more complex reading strategies could eventually develop the multilingual competence that in turn would create new words and concepts for a new public.

Notes

1 The reassessment of the experience of exile and its unachieved narration are directly linked to the dynamic and discontinuous process of exile. On this process and concepts of pre-exile, exile and post-exile, see Klimkiewicz, 'Les configurations chronotopiques'.

2 He says to the journalist: '*Mais rien ne me retient à Paris. Connaissez-vous un endroit à la montagne? J'ai toujours rêvé d'être invisible. Un coin perdu où je vivrais dans le parfait anonymat*'.

Works cited

Altounian, Janine. *L'intraduisible. Deuil, mémoire, transmission*. Paris: Dunod, 2005. Print.

Apter, Emily. 'Interview with Emily Apter'. *Arch Literary Journal* 1 (2008). Web.

Berberova, Nina. *C'est moi qui souligne*. Trans. Anne and René Misslin. Arles: Actes Sud, 1989. Print.

Bohórques, Paola. *Living Between Languages: Linguistic Exile and Self-Translation*. PhD Diss. York U, 2008. Print.

Bontila, Ruxanda. 'Vladimir Nabokov's 'Task of the Translator': Identity in Need of Editing'. *Translating Identity and the Identity of Translation*. Eds Madelena Gonzalez and Francine Tolron. Newcastle: Cambridge Scholars P, 2006. 142–51. Print.

Cameroun, Rob. 'Kundera Rejects Czech 'Informer' Tag'. *BBC News*. 13 Oct. 2008. Web.

Harel, Simon. Écriture de soi et traduction dans les œuvres 'jumelles' de Samuel Beckett et Wilfred R. Bion'. *TTR: Traduction, Terminologie, Rédaction* 11.2 (1998): 153–84. Print.

Huston, Nancy. *Cantique des pleines*. Arles: Actes Sud; Montreal: Leméac, 1993. Print.

—. *Instrument de ténèbres*. Arles: Actes Sud; Montreal: Leméac, 1996. Print.

—. *L'empreinte de l'ange*. Arles: Actes Sud; Montreal: Leméac, 1998. Print.

—. *Losing North: Musings on Land, Tongue and Self*. Toronto: McArthur & Company, 2002. Print.

—. *The Mark of the Angel*. Toronto: McArthur, 1999. Print.

—. *Plainsong*. Toronto: Harper Collins, 1993. Print.

Huston, Nancy and Leïla Sebbar. *Lettres parisiennes: Autopsie de l'exil*. Paris: J'ai lu, 1986. Print.

Jeandillou, Jean-François. *Esthétique de la mystification: Tactique et stratégie littéraires*. Paris: Minuit, 1994. Print.

Klimkiewicz, Aurelia. 'Faire l'épreuve de soi au travers de l'auto-dialogue multilingue. À propos du commentaire métalangagier dans la littérature migrante'. *La traduction dans les cultures plurilingues*. Eds Lieven D'hulst and Reine Meylaerts. Artois: Artois PU, 2011. 23–31. Print.

—. 'Les configurations chronotopiques de l'exil : de l'exil au post-exil'. *Temporalités de l'exil*. 15–17 Feb. 2007, Université de Montréal. *Poexil* 2008. Web.

Matejka, Ladislas. 'Appendix I. On the First Prolegomena to Russian Semiotics'. *Marxism and the Philosophy of Language*. Trans. Ladislas Matejka and I. R. Titunik. Harvard: Harvard UP, 1986. 161–74. Print.

Nabokov, Vladimir. *Le Don*. Trans. Raymond Girard. Paris: Gallimard, 1991. Print.

—. *The Gift*. Trans. Michael Scammell. New York: G. P. Putnam's Sons, 1963.

—. *Pnine*. Trans. Michel Chrestien. Paris: Gallimard, 1991. Print.

Oustinoff, Michaël. *Bilinguisme d'écriture et auto-traduction: Julien Green, Samuel Beckett, Vladimir Nabokov*. Paris: L'Harmattan, 2001. Print.

Porter, Anna. *The Ghosts of Europe*. Vancouver: Douglas & McIntyre, 2010. Print.

Shafiq, Muna. 'Linguistic Hybridity in Gloria Anzaldua's Borderlands, Antonia d'Alphonso's *Avril ou L'anti-passion*, and Hiromi Goto's *Chorus of Mushrooms*'. *Translating Identity and the Identity of Translation*. Eds Madelena Gonzalez and Francine Tolron. Newcastle: Cambridge Scholars P, 2006. 3–19. Print.

Tadevosyan-Ordukhanyan, Margarit. *Strangers in Stranger Tongues: Vladimir Nabokov and the Writing of Exile, with Reference to Joseph Conrad, Hakob Asadourian, and Roman Jakobson*. PhD Diss. Boston College, 2006. Print.

Todorov, Tzwetan. 'Bilinguisme, dialogisme et schizophrénie'. *Du bilinguisme*. Paris: Denoël, 1985. 11–26. Print.

Wittlin, Józef. 'Sorrow and Grandeur of Exile'. *Polish Review* 2 (1957): 99–111. Print.

Wiznitzer, Louis. 'Kundera rêve d'être invisible'. *La Presse* 21 Dec. 1985: 13. Print.

Woods, Michelle. 'Original and Translation in the Czech Fiction of Milan Kundera'. *Translation and Literature* 10.2 (2001): 200–21. Print.

—. *Translating Milan Kundera*. Clevedon: Multilingual Matters, 2006. Print.